This is
CUBA

This is

CUBA

An Outlaw
Culture Survives

Ben Corbett

Westview
PRESS

A Member of the Perseus Books Group

Library of Congress Cataloging-in-Publication Data
Corbett, Ben
This is Cuba : an outlaw culture survives / Ben Corbett.
    p. cm.
Includes bibliographical references.
ISBN 0–8133–3826–3
    1. Cuba—Social conditions—1959–.   2. Cuba—Economic conditions—1990–.
3. Cuba—Description and travel.   I. Title.

HN203.5.C67 2002
306'.097291—dc21

                                                                2002008515

Westview Press is a member of the Perseus Books Group.
Find us on the World Wide Web at http://www.westviewPress.com
Westview Press books are available at special discounts for bulk purchases in the U.S. by corporations, institutions, and other organizations. For more information, please contact the Special Markets Department at the Perseus Books Group, 11 Cambridge Center, Cambridge, MA 02142, or call (800) 255–1514 or (617) 252–5298, or e-mail j.mccrary@perseus-books.com.

Text design by Jeff Williams
Set in 11.5-point Dante MT by The Perseus Books Group

3 4 5 6 7 8 9 10—05 04 03

Me voy p'al pueblo, hoy es mi dia
Voy a alegrar todo el alma mia
Me voy p'al pueblo, hoy es mi dia
Voy a alegrar todo el alma mia
　　　　　—PIO LEYVA

CONTENTS

ACKNOWLEDGMENTS

Ask any author if they'd write another book on Cuba immediately after finishing a volume and the answer will likely be no. The pains of the labor are still too immediate. The intensity is too fresh. But time heals. We forget. We drift back and do it again. Cuba is addictive like that. And with Cuba comes this aching thirst to strip away the levels and get to the bottom of it. Anyone who has seriously pried open the island knows that as soon as one stone is lifted, ten more stones are quickly revealed. Just when you think you've got it all figured out, some new idea enters the mix and changes everything. There are so many important details, such a labyrinthine history, much opposing information. "Just two more months on the island," says the writer. "I'm only now piercing the flesh." And then later, "Just a couple more months, I've hooked into new material." Onward and onward this goes.

This book on Cuba devoured a total of four years on both sides of the gulf and involved hundreds of people. Instead of mentioning everyone in Cuba, I mainly want to express my gratitude to the central people herein—those who went to great lengths, often at personal risk, to help me discover their island. Those who comforted me when I became petrified with that same unforgiving paranoia that Cubans know so well. Those who patiently and selflessly showed me the steps because they cared. These people are family now, they know who they are, and in my deepest humility, I owe them everything. Besides them, special thanks to the IAS, ICAIC, Estudio Egrem, Casa de Tango, Casa de Comedia, Casa de la Trova in Santiago, my friends in Trinidad, Baracoa, Viñales, Varadero, Las Tunas, Holguín, Pinar del Rio, Havana. And to the customs agent at José Marti international airport who took my watch when I ran out of money and couldn't pay the $20 exit tax. *"¡Pero tiene la marca Timex! ¡Vale 40 dolares!"*

On this end, without a lot of good publishing chemistry, this book could never have been possible. A thousand thanks to everyone involved at Westview Press for seeing my initial vision and standing behind it through the end. How lucky I was to have had so much talent focused on this volume. Especially from my editor, Jill Rothenberg, who helped me knock off the slag, then file down the burrs, making this a good read. Also, my gratitude to all the magazine editors who gave me assignments, helping to keep me fed and in plane tickets. Dave Nichols and Frenchie Nilsen, Toni Brown, Lane Badger, Pete Miller, Malcolm MacKinnon, Aeve Baldwin, Richard Fleming, Joan Walsh, Tate Hausman, Jim Fortney, Mark Conley, and countless others. And many thanks to World Circuit Records, Higher Octave Music, and Michael Bloom for the permissions.

Lastly, thanks to my family. There is no measure to their unconditional love. To my sisters and nieces for their patience during my long absences and inability to be a better brother and uncle. To my parents for their ongoing support and belief in me, the rivers of coffee, the good debate, the shelter, and the enormous meals after returning from the island twenty pounds lighter. To my (few remaining) friends for their encouragement, criminal complicity, and standing by me. And, most important, to my Eliana, for her complete selflessness and inspiration. *¡Que mujer mas rica!* You're really something, baby. How fortunate I have been.

Saludos a todos.
Dale vamos.

BEN CORBETT

¡Patria O Muerte! An Introduction

*For we are alone—alone—here, on
this ocean of capitalism that surrounds us.*

FIDEL CASTRO

"*¡Rico maní! ¡Rosita rica!*" At the Payret theater on the corner of Prado Avenue and San José, an old woman drifts past, drawling out the tired vowels, her hand wrapped around a dozen *cucuruchos*, white paper cones of fresh roasted peanuts, as if she were clasping a bouquet of fragrant white mariposas. She's one of the Payret's permanent fixtures. As permanent as the "ay" burned out in the theater's neon marquee, or the cracked pane of glass in the box-office window, or the perpetual line of film-lovers catching the latest Hollywood hit, shown, for a lack of funds, a full two years after its U.S. release. The peanuts cost a nickel, the movie a dime. Eventually, these things will change, they say. "In the future, when the economy is better, we will have new movies and there will be food and wealth for everyone." It's always "the future," because in Cuba, there is no present.

"Mani, mani, rico mani," the old woman chimes as the pesos and centavos are palmed and counted. Each coin is quickly and carefully deposited in her apron pocket with one hand while the other continues waving the mariposas. After three hours, the last cone sold, she has accumulated about 15 pesos, half of which will go to the peanut roaster for another handful of cones tomorrow. The rest is hers to keep, equivalent to about U.S.$.38. Almost enough to buy four eggs. A little over 1.3 eggs per hour. This is how the majority of Cubans think. In decimals. Their world revolves around stretching the centavo. These figures cross the woman's mind. Her wrinkled face is a poem. Her eyes are like hungry mouths.

Most days, I would weave the streets, paying close attention to those mouths. Looking for contrast and irony. The poverty and the wealth held side by side, turned inside out, compared, digested, filed. Down Prado Avenue, the main artery dividing Old and Central Havana. Step after step of the marble island walkway; the wrought-iron lampposts; the Spanish laurel trees shading kids on their *cariolas*—makeshift scooters. The "Psst, pssts" of teenage prostitutes who ask for a light and giggle as they grab the crotches of passing foreigners. South past the Casa del Científico, Hotel Sevilla, Hotel Parque Central, Hotel Telégrafo, Hotel Inglaterra. Past the National Ballet and Central Park, then onward past the Payret theater and the Romanesque hulk of the historic Capitolio that housed Cuba's congress before the revolution.

This area is the best for contrast, where the Cuban and tourist realities overlap. Where the peso collides with the dollar. Where the '99 Mercedes Benz with tinted windows idles at the same traffic light as the beat-up '47 Ford sedan. Shadow and light. Like a film noir, where everything is in black and white, but the meaning lies in the melding of scenes. In the paradox. Here is the money, there is the poverty; between them is the unbridgeable chasm. And within this chasm lies the meaning of Cuba, as it has for five centuries.

Havana, the city of fragments. All that motion, turmoil, confusion. Trying to make collective sense of all the pieces is nearly impossible. You can inhale the entire picture and get an instinctual *feel* or impression, of what's going on, but there's always so much more. Small things. Important details. I learned during my trips to the island over the years that there's a real pulse to the fragments, and the key to Cuba is in finding this rhythm no matter how fleeting or chaotic it seems, and then operating in the beat. After observing the rhythm and learning the steps, I discovered a whole different side of Cuba. A very musical Cuba that operates in its own way, in its own time.

Like the night at a friend's dimly lit apartment watching *Fuerza del Deseo*, "Force of Desire," the triweekly Latin American telenovela that to miss in Cuba is sacrilege. Normally at this hour, the mother or grandmother of the household makes the *cafecitos*, the little *tazas* of sweet black Cuban espresso. But on this night, none was made. It was the coldest night in Cuba in twenty years and everybody was thinking steaming coffee. Finally, after waiting patiently, I went out to the kitchen and loaded up the little stovetop percolator, using the last of the fresh grounds in a small tin.

"Hey," somebody yelled from the living room. "We're out of coffee. If you make that, there will be none left for tomorrow morning."

"What? No fresh beans left in the big can?" I asked.

"No, that's the last of them."

With the grounds in the sieve and the water in the pot, I left the apparatus on the stovetop and returned to the living room.

"Sorry," I said. "I didn't finish it. Tomorrow morning you can just light the stove and it's all ready to go."

"No, you're right," the mother said. "It's freezing out. Let's make the coffee. We'll worry about finding more in the morning."

No sooner had I returned to the kitchen to light the stove than somebody from the street rapped on the window. This was ten o'clock at night, remember, a cold night of about thirty-eight degrees, midweek, during *Fuerza del Deseo*. Cubans are so sensitive to cold that when the mercury drops below forty-five, everyone heads for shelter, shuts tight the wooden louvered blinds, and lights a few stove burners. On such nights, Havana turns into a ghost town. Yet here was a lonely knock on the window, and everyone wondered who on earth it could be. Surely some friend or relative. The rap came from a young kid going door to door trying to unload a five-ounce package of black-market coffee for fifty cents. We all smiled, racing to see who could fish out a wrinkled ten-peso note first and buy the beans. And in the next breath, the mother said, "I guess we won't have to worry about finding coffee tomorrow."

These little miracles just seem to happen. They're part of that rhythm, part of the casual Cuban attitude of "be patient, everything will work out" around which daily Cuban survival seems to gravitate. And then there are the bigger miracles: The miracle, against all odds, of the Communist regime's survival after forty-three years. The miracle of the tourist boom that rescued Cuba's economy after the Soviet Union dissolved in 1991. The miracle that everyone has stayed fed and the people have retained their pride.

On certain nights, looking north from the Havana sea point, you can see the sky illuminated a faint violet from the lights of Miami, a little over a hundred miles, but worlds away. There is something calming about the warm breeze at the point, the ghostlike hulls of ocean freighters floating into the harbor, the lighthouse beacon, the rhythm of the foam splashing against the eroded mortar below. The point is a sanctuary, one of those sacred places to contemplate life. Marriages are proposed there, plots to flee the island are whispered, songs are written, the regime is debated, and the future is discussed. From the shadows, a flame bursts behind a cupped hand as a cigarette is lit. Down in the filthy coral baths, a *bruja* drifts along and kneels to the water, chanting her prayer to the gods, soon throwing a meager offering of aluminum centavos into the hungry waves. She finishes the ritual and climbs slowly up the crumbling steps, passing a few young people who are heading down below the wall, out of sight from the police, where they'll smoke a joint, have sex for lack of privacy at home, or, since there's nothing else to do, pass a bottle of rum and dream.

Through Havana's back alleys, a quiet melancholy hovers only blocks, but seemingly leagues away from the perpetual celebration of Havana's tourist sector. The amber streetlights cast a somber glow on the silence. A stray dog scampers past, nose to the gutter, routinely sniffing up a discarded chicken bone or forgotten crumb of food. A few men boisterously slap down dominos in a dimly lit apartment breezeway. Doorway after doorway, through the Parisian blinds, the screens of old televisions flash their blue phosphorescent hues across the pastel walls. The lights are kept off to conserve electricity because the fifteen-cent monthly bill is outrageously expensive for the average Cuban. Most of the televisions are sensitive, high-maintenance equipment that require a special tap here, a knob jiggled there, a certain wire touched in a precise way to keep them functioning through an entire program. A living room lit only by the television screen may suddenly black out mid-program, and a loud "*¡Aí, mi madre!*" will echo through the alleyway.

Sometimes it seems as if the entire island were rolling its eyes and sighing, "*¡Aí, mi madre!*" "*¡Aí, Cuba!*" The national sighs for the national curse. The people's surrender to the frustration, meaning "Not again . . ." or "What next?" or "When will it end?" Just when everything seems to be humming along fine, something inevitably breaks. It's plainly visible everywhere you look, from the household appliance to the entire nation. When something goes wrong with the economy, if there's a housing shortage, a natural disaster, a blackout of an entire municipality, the Castro regime gives the problem a few taps, wiggles a loose wire, prints a few more pesos, keeping Cuba operating until the next breakdown. Just trust in the beard. The beard will fix it. In the future. The beard always tells us everything will be better in the future.

I'll never forget my first encounter with Fidel Castro. It was during the 1980 Mariel boatlift, when some 120,000 Cubans fled the poverty and politics of Castro's regime for Miami in a mass exodus. On April 1, 1980, six Cubans hijacked a bus and crashed the gates of the Peruvian embassy in Havana. When Peru refused to hand over the asylum-seekers to authorities, an enraged Castro announced that anyone wishing to leave Cuba could also enter the embassy. Some 11,000 Cubans took up the offer. Three weeks later, when the United States offered to take in 3,500 of the refugees, Castro reacted by opening the port of Mariel to all Cubans wishing to leave; between April and September, 120,000 took to the sea. The emotions in Cuba ran high. The streets of Havana were in chaos as fights broke out between pro- and anti-Castroists on the island.

The first night of the exodus, my bedtime was 11:00 P.M., strictly enforced by my parents, but much too early for an eleven-year-old insomniac. Little did they know that almost every night after I had closed my bedroom door, I would quietly reopen it, tip-toe out to the top of the staircase and listen to the remainder of the news, catching the features, the sports, even the weather. The night of Mariel, a much younger Dan Rather was giving a dramatic account of how thousands of Cubans were setting sail in overloaded boats, fishing vessels, inner tubes, ferries, anything that floated. I couldn't see the screen, but throughout the program I imagined a sweltering desert beach, not a palm tree to be seen. Along the beach from horizon to horizon, a chain-link razor-wire fence stretched for miles. And there was Castro in his olive drab and beard, standing on the beach; with an assault rifle, shoving thousands of Cubans single-handedly into the ocean at gunpoint. "Why is he forcing them to leave?" I asked myself. "Who is this wicked man?"

Like most Americans, I came to know Cuba through the television portal, and Cuba became synonymous with the beard. And like most Americans, I came to regard Cuba as "the bad guys" and us as "the good guys." Here was the U.S. flag, and there was the beard that threatened it. They were the commies, the outlaws of the Western Hemisphere, and Castro was the devil. These were the Reagan years and, reminiscent of the 1960s, the word "Cuba" once again tasted foul on the tongue with its dark implications.

In the spring of 1998, when I announced that I was going to Cuba to write, I was met with a multitude of reactions, even hostility. "You're nuts. What if you wind up in one of Castro's jails? Are you Communist? Don't Cubans hate us Americans? Aren't you scared? You'd better be careful." And when I returned, "Were you ever physically threatened? Was it dangerous?"

When I explained that it wasn't dangerous, that I actually felt safer in the streets of Havana than in my own country's cities. That Cubans even adore Hollywood movies and listen to all kinds of American popular music—anything from the Back Street Boys to the Red Hot Chili Peppers, I was frequently met with a confused look. It just didn't jibe. It was contradictory to everything they'd heard about the rebel island.

After the media hoopla of the Elian González crisis in 2000, after the commercial success of the Cuban orchestra, the Buena Vista Social Club, and the Pope's 1998 visit when the world began training its cameras on the island, so many questions were still unanswered. Many of the cold war stigmas persisted, and new notions were formed. For many Americans, in the space of a decade Cuba had transformed from a mysterious, sinister island ruled by a Communist tyrant into an enchanting getaway of romance and adventure. We learned about the old cars, about the cigars, about the music of the golden years before Castro, about a so-called "land frozen in time," or "the last Communist stronghold in the Western Hemisphere," and other commercial versions of this misunderstood culture.

But there is another Cuba, often unseen and discussed even less. A Cuba that can't be summarized in thirty inches of space in the Sunday travel section. For me, it became a task of sifting through the contradictions and notions, comparing them with the true Cuban experience, and coming away with an idea of what was really going on. The alleyways, the little niches, the living rooms, the fringes of the Revolution are the doorways into this other Cuba, where the desperation for change continues to simmer. This is where the contradictions end and the endurance begins, the Cuban reality for the majority. The lines at the five-peso pizza stands. The piles of building rubble and dead furniture rotting for weeks on curbsides. The stench of dumpsters overflowing in the baking sun. Kids chasing chickens through the streets, pissing in the vacant lots. The *parqueos,* the bicycles, old people mulling around the stoops, the soiled glass of empty storefronts, threadbare clothes, holey shoes, pure poverty.

You could take a city map of Havana and draw definitive lines of where the two Cubas collide. There are the resorts. There are the slums.

And in between is the commercial gray area. It's like the visitor's concept of a very safe "third world" out there in tourist central, but the real third world, the real Cuba lies in here, just two blocks off Prado, where few foreigners stray. The sensation felt when crossing this border is very real. As if the glamour, the wealth, the dream is out there among the tourists with their crisp new khaki safari suits and guidebooks, while back here in the shadows it's a growing frustration, a tense daily grind of struggling for food.

Fraternity Park is one place where the two worlds clash with its massive ceiba tree, the tree of life that celebrates the brotherhood of the collective Americas. On one side of the tree is the historic Capitolio building with its steady stream of tourists scaling up and down the steps all day. On the other side is the mouth of Monte Avenue. . . . Cuba. Here the dollar shapeshifts into the peso. The tourist taxi into the people's peso taxi. The Viazul luxury coaches into mass transit *camello* buses. The Coca-Cola into sugar water. The steamed lobster into fried lard.

Enrique lives down there. Down on Monte Avenue. He's sixty years old. Eats fried lard. Rides in the people's taxis when he has some extra pesos. Takes the *camellos* around town. Drinks sugar water. Is one of the estimated 60 percent of Cubans who have no access to dollars in an economy where the peso is next to worthless. He's critical of himself and the government and, like all Cubans, loves to hash it out over the smallest of details. From the best market to buy *guayaba* to the flamboyant Cuban nightlife of the 1950s and the rectification of the mid-1980s when Castro completely revamped the Cuban economy and the Communist Party, his knowledge runs deep and wide on a range of subjects. Enrique has a mind for trivia; he can pull specific names and incidents from Cuban history, detailing their causes and effects, and give blow-by-blow accounts of what so-and-so did on such-and-such battlefield. When he reads or watches television, he pays close attention, analyzing, judging, memorizing, and, after much internal debate, throws out a comment.

"¡*Mierda!*" he'll say as he watches the evening news. "What shit! It's always the same. They never tell us anything. Who cares about the cleanup project in Varadero. That's not news. So what if they picked up a ton of garbage. What I want to know is what happened to Posada Carriles in Panama. Did you notice they're not talking about that anymore? Everyday it was in the papers and on the news. Everyday for weeks! And then suddenly, nothing. Something is going on there. They're hiding something."

I liked to watch the news with Enrique because he would always give me the straight dope. He didn't believe any of it. Enrique always treated me as a peer, someone who could engage in debate and really get to the bottom of things. Not as a *"yanqui"* or someone from a wealthy nation, not a symbol, but another human. Once I asked him what impressions he got about Americans from the Communist media; I explained how a lot of the conservative journalists in the United States had once made Cubans out to be devils, but that nowadays, people thought of Cuba romantically. My words surprised and impressed him, as he had no idea that Cuba was discussed so much in the United States.

"In the Cuban news," he said, "everything we do is right, and everything the rest of the world does is wrong. The only time they say something good about the United States is when one of your politicians speaks against the embargo. Besides this, they only point out your problems. They tell us about your homeless people, about the racism, that capitalism is inhumane. But look at our capitalism. Look at all the riches here and the new hotels. With Cuba's capitalism, it's okay, but for everybody else, it's inhumane."

For the most part, Enrique represents the majority of Cubans. They see all the contradictions surrounding them but have no means of acting or verbally expressing themselves to change the world they live in. There is no way to communicate their desires and needs. No complaint box to voice their frustrations. They sit back and watch the surface of the archipelago transform into a modern paradise to which they have no access.

Like Enrique, most Cubans spend their time worrying about the next meal. They are forced to break laws to eat, ironically sacrificing their personal dignity to preserve the dignity of the Revolutionary victory which is still slated to occur sometime in the nebulous future.

In the average age of its people, Cuba is a young country. Of the island's 11 million inhabitants, more than half were born after Castro and have known no other leader or way of life. These younger generations are desperately seeking new avenues of expression and opportunities to advance themselves after having sacrificed the entire decade of the 1990s to the poverty of Cuba's economic depression—the Special Period—and the survival of the Cuban Revolution. Still making the same sacrifices today, many are beginning to wonder when this future the regime has been promising for forty-three years will finally arrive, and like Enrique, many older Cubans are losing faith in the program they once supported.

For them and for younger Cubans, life is stagnant. They think Castro is an old man with outdated ideas. While they understand his political principles, those principles don't put food on the table, and they offer little opportunity for self-expression or financial independence. Many younger Cubans are now looking outside the system for economic advancement and solutions to their personal lives, new world solutions that the Revolution has failed to provide. To them, the anti–United States, pro-Cuba rhetoric is a broken record and the instability associated with it has become unbearable. They want new music, world fashion, video games, food. They want to compete with their global peers, not remain in a cultural isolation hinged on Castro's political ambitions. Many carry the torch of Cuba's non-Revolutionary parallel culture, which operates outside the restrictive government. The parallel culture started to emerge in 1968 when Castro first centralized Cuba after the Soviet Socialist model and began alienating the people, taking away their personal freedoms and a competitive private domestic market, forcing the entire population into complete dependence on a system that they're still at odds with.

More preoccupied with his position in the history books than with Cuba's everyday survival reality, Castro has become irrelevant today. He has lost the people and they are already playing with post-Castro, post-embargo ideas. Meanwhile, the regime ignores the reality that in order to eat, the majority of Cubans must break multitudes of laws, live in constant paranoia, steal, and hustle in the black market. For this, they are seen as outlaws by the central government for not starving like good Revolutionaries under impossible circumstances. While many Cubans have decided to leave these conditions behind and emigrate to other countries, those who remain on the island live in a mental exile, frustrated because they can't participate in the changing world and their own reality. Buying a pound of rice in the black market is seen by the Cuban government as social decay, yet the government refuses to provide the economic means to buy the rice legally. This is the problem.

Today this outlaw culture grows and evolves, often in opposition to the Revolution, as it continues its search for an identity, the *Cubanindad*, or "Cubanness" which Castro failed to deliver, and which, with the passing years, a desperation grows to lay claim, breathing that long sigh of redemption for its five-century-old colonial curse.

All colonized peoples face this curse, and perhaps Cuba, being the oldest colony in the West, faces it most. First came Columbus and the Spanish. Later, the United States transformed the island into a neo-colony. Then came Castro, who gave the people their first stab at true independence; this lasted about two years, until the Soviets moved in, creating a renewed illusion of pseudoindependence. Today, with the Soviet Union gone, many Cubans feel that they're being exploited and colonized by one of their own, in what some call a "prison," all for the sake of his regime's survival. This contradictory chasm between the people's survival and the Revolutionary ideal is in the same shade of gray as the tourist and Cuban realities. It is the next-level of gray in what has become a confused, island-sized paradox.

Consider, for instance, that about one-fifth of the island's income comes in the form of cash wires sent through Western Union from Cubans living abroad. Although the regime quietly calls these benefactors *gusanos* (maggots) for abandoning the Revolution, it couldn't survive without them. This is the true decay of the Cuban Socialist ideal: The central government profits and survives on those dollars, yet scolds the prostitutes and petty black marketers who are forced to break the law for such basic necessities as deodorant and cooking oil. The dignity of the people is sacrificed for the dignity of a Revolutionary ideal, and the Rev-olutionary ideal is hinged on *La Victoria,* the victory, set to occur some-time in the future when the U.S. economic embargo is lifted. Castro is almost desperate to realize *La Victoria* before his death so that he can enter the history books as Cuba's liberator.

A colonizing liberator? How about the Revolution is a broken bus? One day when I was taking a taxi across Havana, my driver and I saw fifty or sixty men heaving and panting as they pushed a *camello,* one of those rattley tractor-trailer mass transit buses, through an intersection. I was on my way back from *Ciudad Libertad,* the pre-1959 Camp Colum-bia military base, after celebrating the fortieth anniversary of Fidel Cas-tro's grand entrance into Havana on January 8, 1959.

"Only in Cuba," my driver said with a laugh as we swerved around the broken bus. "Only in Cuba."

Only in Cuba indeed. The irony of seeing fifty men pushing a bro-ken bus through an intersection on Castro's Revolutionary holiday made a serious impression on me. It would be the first of many. Ironies occur so regularly in Cuba that life itself has become a contradiction. And these contradictions, these ironies, all boil down to that rhythm, that pulse, those little miracles. This is the story of Cuba, the pulse of which is often hard to grasp, but one that I found was as fulfilling as it was exhausting. It is the story of a people dancing with survival, both personal and cul-tural, always confronted with a future that seems to slip farther away. Most of the people herein knew why I was writing this book, and they willingly and sincerely opened their lives to teach me that Cuban rhythm. They wanted to share their struggle with those who might listen.[1]

La Cola Cubana:
Waiting As a Way of Life

They wait.... And wait.... And wait.... And wait.... And wait.... They wait at the bus stops, the *bodegas,* the cinemas, the taxi pools, the *agromercados,* the *tiendas,* the hospitals, the currency exchange booths, the banks and schools, in the *panaderías, lecherías, carnerías, relojerías, cafeterías.* You see the disorganized files and columns everywhere, the bodies twisted in posture, arms leaning on blistering laminated counters, disgruntled looks, resignation, pants and sighs, groans and grumbling, small talk issuing from frustrated lips in the Cuban run-on sentence of fragments that winds and rambles and ambles on for years upon years through heaps of bureaucratic slips of paper and top-brass decisions yet to be made in the trail of time that Cubans have nothing but.

Patience is the Cuban way, and the word "convenience" has yet to find its place in the lexicon. One may wait fifteen minutes to buy a pound of rice, or thirty minutes for a bus that never shows. Another may wait four days in a provincial terminal for an airplane that's sitting in a hangar in some *other* province waiting for repairs from a mechanic who happens to be waiting in line at the doctor's office, but the doctor is late, still waiting for a permission slip from a government functionary who's behind schedule because she, too, had to wait in line all morning trying to reschedule her daughter for an eye exam that was delayed because the optometric lens was waiting to be repaired by the technician who was busy waiting at the train station for his relatives to arrive. But the train was late because the track was out somewhere between Camagüey and Santa Clara waiting to be repaired by the railroad crew, half of whom were late because they were waiting for a truck to pick them up that didn't come. The truck never showed because the driver, who works for the state and makes only 225 pesos in thirty days, had the opportunity to earn 200 pesos, or $10 *in one day*, laying tile for a cash-paying customer. So he called in sick and the truck sat in the garage.

This is Cuban efficiency, and the recurrent theme of the island is "What's the rush?" It's been the bane of the government to motivate a population that leans on the shovel. It isn't that Cubans are lazy. Far from it. When given the opportunity of tangible reward, they're perhaps the most industrious people in the Western Hemisphere. They have a natural drive to win. But the entire economy is set up so that no matter how hard a Cuban works, he or she can never make any more than anyone else.

The little slogans and reminders—hallmarks of Revolutionary commercialism—are tucked in every corner in bold print: "Socialism = Efficiency." "Efficiency Is the Future." "With Efficiency We Can Win." They're as prominent as the Budweiser billboards strung across the capitalist interstate, and they're ignored just the same. This is where the ideology and the reality always seem to clash in Cuba. The ideology beckons the people to work harder and make more sacrifices, but in reality it's impossible to live on 148 pesos, or U.S.$7.40 a month. Everyone must earn dollars to survive in Cuba—there is no way around it. The attitude is, "Hey, I'm making 185 pesos, 148 pesos, 325 pesos a month whether I lift a finger or not, so why sweat for it?"

The last thing on a state employee's mind is Socialist efficiency when the baby needs new clothes or the mother needs a special medicine, which are dollar commodities. It's as simple as that. So they spend their time on the clock worrying about how they'll scrape up those U.S. dollars (Cuba's dual currency) after punching out. They often leave early, even quit their jobs when the first opportunity of real money arrives. In these circumstances, the entire machine chokes and sputters, barely trundling along. I've seen crews of ten men take two months to remodel the floor of a small hotel that six men could accomplish in two weeks in a capitalist country. It's not that Cubans can't work faster but that building materials are constantly delivered late; not to mention the absenteeism—another byproduct of the interminable Cuban *cola*. For incentive, tourist hotel construction workers in Cuba receive a hoagie and a can of soda each day if they're on time, and a five-pound canned ham at the end of the month on top of their base salary of 185 to 235 pesos. When a demand arises in a certain industry, say in Cuba's historical archives or the computer industry, the state will also offer an extra stimulus of U.S.$50 (five months' salary) at year's end. However, if one day is missed or a person is late even once, the bonus incentive is forfeited.

Castro's government has been wrestling forever with the concept of workers' incentives, both material and moral. The problem began in 1961 when the Cuban economy began shifting into the Soviet Socialist model. At the time, Castro's right-hand man, the whip-cracking Argentinean insurrectionist Che Guevara, while not ruling them out completely, stood against material incentives as a weaker production stimulus. In Guevara's utopian design of the "New Man," if a person worked selflessly for the benefit of the whole, the people as a whole would rise above the bourgeois mentality and dedicate their souls to the Socialist cause. The milder, more moderate Castro has always been reluctant to give incentives, staying in line with Che's theories, but seeing things more realistically, even admitting in 1991 that Guevara's vision was ambitious and couldn't fit into Cuba's new Special Period circumstances. The new economic collapse required certain trade-offs in the Socialist ideal, and lower forms of incentive were needed to ignite the workforce.

The favored kinds of incentive had traditionally been "Best Employee" awards, which in the 1970s and 1980s were coupled with material incentives that enabled vanguard workers in all industries to receive loans for cars, appliances, and furniture. In Cuba, the *trabajadores*, workers, are one of the two fundamental keystones in the Revolutionary fortress; they are eclipsed only by the children, on whom the regime depends to carry the torch into the future. The incentives were need-based tools, awarded to the hardest-working Cubans with the highest Revolutionary morale and decided by a peer-vote annually in the factory and field. Winners would then be put on the waiting list for their loans and merchandise. The loan incentives did wonders in keeping the worker's nose to the Revolutionary grindstone; they also put a damper on whining, since complaints were seen as counterproductive, even counterrevolutionary. In a country where avenues of legal protest are nonexistent, one of the only ways many Cubans have found to fight the system and relieve their frustrations is in work absenteeism and the deliberate slowing of production. By creating a high demand for the limited supplies of appliances and cars, the incentive program was a means of keeping production high. However, in 1991, when there was barely enough money to keep Havana powered by electricity because Cuba's economy had taken the plunge after the Soviet collapse, these incentives were the first excess expenses to go.

Since the late 1980s, when the government began pushing desperately for foreign capitalist investment to re-stimulate its economy, the incentives and little perks have been dedication gifts of foreign investors who build hotels and operate tours in the service sector. The state has bent to the need of material incentives only slightly in its effort to halt rampant absenteeism; yearly cash or material bonuses are offered to a few selected technical fields where there is a high demand to maintain employment, such as in hotel building and the tourist trades. The bulk of bonuses come from foreign enterprises operating on the island, typically small cash gifts to ensure hard work. But most Cubans have no access to these fields; and for those who do, a ham at the end of the month, or $50 at year's end plainly isn't enough.

The ultimate result is the Cuban *cola*. And after four decades, the question ¿*El Ultimo?* "Who's last?" has been permanently grafted into the Cuban consciousness. The business being waited for never takes long. A few minutes maybe. But it's the waiting to get to the point of making the business that's the killer. Even if you're a tourist with loads of cash, there's no getting around the lines. Everyone waits, capitalist, communist, there is no distinction.

Time is money in Cuba, but the saying has an entirely different meaning. Cubans know the code, they live in a spendthrift rhythm, and they're shrewd consumers. With very little money and plenty of time, they'll walk twenty city blocks or wait for hours if necessary to save two or three pesos. Those who have dollars prefer to pay poorer Cubans a small sum to stand in line for them; other Cubans in the upper classes shop at the dollar stores and higher-priced private *agromercados,* the farmers' markets, where it costs a few pesos more, but the lines are short and fast. As a rule, poorer Cubans use the private *agromercados* only when the state produce stores and fixed-price cooperatives are sold out of the desired product, which is almost always. When the state window opens in the morning to sell rice at 3.5 pesos a pound, the line of shoppers is already stretched around the corner. And when those burlap sacks are scooped dry, the rest either pay 5 pesos a pound at the *agromercado* or go without.

For every transaction in Cuba, it seems there are always three or four little slips of paper to be filled out, signed, and filed. After waiting in line for an hour at any information desk, you ask Person A your question, and then you are sent to another line where you wait to talk to Person B, who finally tells you to go talk to the *jefe,* the boss, who after another wait informs you that you are at the wrong office and must go to this address on the other side of town. Once there, the process repeats itself. It's a vicious cycle and I've been caught in it so many times that I've often wondered how the society even begins to function. But this vicious cycle is part of the rhythm, and the rhythm always falls back on the little miracles.

I recall an especially funny scene at the Camagüey provincial bus station in central Cuba, about 250 miles from Havana. On my way back to

the capital from Oriente, I got stuck in Camagüey for eighteen hours
while I tried to find transportation. It was a nightmare. At the bus station, there was one seat left on the 7:00 P.M. Astrobus, the Cuban cross-
country coach system. It was 9:00 P.M., and the 7:00 P.M. bus was still in
the terminal being repaired. The price was 33 pesos, or $1.65 for Cubans,
and $33 for foreigners. As I was about to pay, the seller said, "Uh, that
ticket has been sold," and explained that seats were available on the luxury tourist Viazul coach at 11:00 P.M. for $38. I hated using tourist trans-
portation, preferring to ride in the rickety Hungarian buses with their
crying children and the luggage flying off the racks—to me a richer experience—but I had an appointment in Havana the next day, so reluctantly
I paid. As I left the ticket office, I had to run a gauntlet of twenty Cubans
who were huddled around a ticket sales booth and screaming down the
poor manager's throat.

"I'm sorry," the manager yelled above the voices of dissent, holding
up his hands. "We're doing everything we can. Please be patient."

"Look, there's a Viazul bus coming at eleven," one man yelled. "Why
don't you give up some of the empty seats on that bus?"

"Yeah, why not?" a woman spoke up.

"You know that's impossible, so why even ask?" said the manager.

I busied myself looking at a small photo gallery of Fidel Castro's personal inspection of the terminal some years ago. There were photos of
the comandante shaking hands with the managers, the comandante bent
over talking to a child, the comandante doing the white-glove test and
nodding his approval, the comandante looking up at the architecture of
the new vaulted ceilings. The photos were framed around a Cuban flag
that dangled stiffly from the wall with several newspaper clippings of the
event tacked in various locations. The irony in having a black-and-white
catalog of Castro proudly celebrating the new bus terminal on one side
of the depot and twenty Cubans screaming on the other about the broken bus is too delicious for words. The monument without the vehicle.
The ideal and the reality. As if to say, "We may have no buses, but we are
victorious with this terminal!"

The crowd of disgruntled Cubans grew more furious.

"These people have to get to Havana tonight," said one man. "My mother has an appointment with a specialist for her legs tomorrow!"

"Put her on the Viazul bus!" demanded another woman.

"Are we going to go through that again?" asked the manager.

"And why shouldn't we?" said the man. "We Cubans are human, too. When the buses break and we've paid, why shouldn't we get the next available bus? It's ridiculous! The tourists won't even use all the seats in the Viazul bus. And we must sit here all night and wait?"

"*¡De verdad!*" yelled the woman. "It's the truth!"

"*¡Es una injusticia!*" yelled the man.

"*Ai, Cuba. . . . ¿Que mas? ¡Que mas!?!*" The woman finished the thought, holding her palms to the ceiling.

I was surprised to hear these Cubans complaining so loudly in public. The manager was likely a Communist, and he kept looking at me nervously, almost apologetically, wondering whether I could understand Spanish. But my presence only seemed to amplify their ire. I was the audience. I was the foreigner who was going to board a new air-conditioned Viazul Mercedes-Benz dollars-only bus recently shipped in from Argentina while the mechanics toiled over their rickety Hungarian peso-coach now broken down in the terminal lot, and they wanted me to know their frustration.

With two hours to kill, I stepped outside. After rubbing the ears of a freckled hairless dog shivering in the corner, I struck up a conversation with the driver of the Hungarian bus, now loaded like a can of Argentinean sardines, most of the passengers passed out, leaning against windows and shoulders, sheets pulled over their faces, exhausted from waiting, again.

¡Turismo O Muerte!

Occasionally I would drift up to Central Park in the middle of Havana and hang around the *peña deportiva*, the sports club, to catch an earful of what's what in the Cuban street debate. Every day, there they'd be, a hundred or so men gathered loosely in the park to sound off in heated discussions about anything from the current sports figures to world politics, fingers jabbing the air, hands slapped against hips in disgust, arms thrown up in histrionic gesticulation, words flying from lips like fusillades of syllabic bullets in the gauntlet of one of Havana's most savored pastimes. It's never serious, nor does it come to blows. Somebody could be screaming down another guy's throat one second, and a millisecond later they're slapping each other's backs, booming with laughter. There is defeat and triumph, order and disarray, each person displaying his little quirks, the ball caps, the cigars, the home life, the little things that they all know about each other, the squeaky-sounding guy who hardly ever speaks up (but when he does get riled, watch out), the hunch-backed guy who carries a month-old wrinkled foreign sports page around and is considered a VIP because in Cuba, if you have a foreign sports page, you have something that nobody else can get his hands on, even if it is a month old.

In the night, these guys listen to all the Cuban, Mexican, Venezuelan and Miami sportscasts; then early the next morning, after reading the sports page in the morning edition of *Granma,* the Communist-controlled daily paper, they straggle in, armed with numbers and spreads, ready to go at it with anyone willing to take up the challenge of an argument. When it's slow, they sit along the granite benches from end-to-end of the park like crows on a wire, an antagonist or two chugging up and down the line trying to provoke a hot discussion. If things are really slow, someone will yell out something like, "Ah, what's all this hype about El Duque? Already he's an old man!" Suddenly everyone is on his feet surrounding this devil, and the debate begins, first to prove that El Duque, one of Cuba's whisper-level national prides, is one of the greatest things that ever happened to the Yankees, and then on to other more substantial subjects such as who's doing better this year, the Orioles or the Red Sox, or whether the Matánzas team will get their asses whipped this weekend in Pinar del Rio. All day, the *peña deportiva* winds up and down, up and down like this, from prelude to coda, small talk to crescendo, half-tones, quarter-tones, bars and measures, rests and clefs, movement to movement in *Parque Central's* daily orchestration.

The first time I entered the fray, my being a *Norteamericano* spoiled the candor I'd hoped for. Being an American in Cuba has its good and bad points. On the bad side, it changes the dynamic of conversations. As soon as someone finds out you're a *yanqui,* you're suddenly a hot commodity because Cubans want to know exactly how people from the United States think. In almost every first meeting with a new face, I became the symbolic representative of the entire United States, often vented on and flogged with complaints, or else felt out for opinions on everything from politics to what I thought of certain Hollywood film stars. Cubans generally don't hate Americans, as many believe, and during the time I lived in Cuba, I was met with hostility only a few times.

My always having to jump this initial hurdle of being the American symbol was sometimes tough; but for the discomfort, I consistently found myself a part of many sincere and thoughtful conversations. Obviously, every Cuban sees the connection between the U.S. economic embargo and his or her own poverty in a slightly different way. Some blame the embargo outright for the island's economic condition, others blame Castro. Since the embargo was enacted in August 1960, the regime has built the Cuban identity around it, so to be an American in Cuba is to be a source of clarification. "Why don't you lift the embargo? Why do you want to continue harming the Cuban people?" Because Cubans have been isolated from opposing information and points of view for over four decades, getting the other side of the story is important to them. And while Castro does shoulder some of the responsibility for his country's state of poverty, as a rallying point, he blames almost all of Cuba's woes on the United States. But Cubans are slowly becoming more critical of Castro's one-sided stance, and they spend a lot of time trying to pinpoint where the blame should be placed—on the United States? On Castro?—because they know that the stagnant rhetoric of the Communist-controlled media is biased. For this reason, every morsel of information they absorb weighs heavily into their constantly evolving worldview. The tourist explosion has created an even greater hunger for information from the outside world.

At the *peña deportiva,* as soon as it circulated that there was a Yanqui in the mix, everything changed. Who did I think would take this or that medal in the Olympics? Who did I think would match off in the World Series? The climate was getting chummy, so I decided to ask my own question: "What do Cubans think about the tourism?"

Instantly, it was as if the sun had ditched behind a cloud. About half of the group of forty or so boxed up their shoulders and packed it right off to another circle. They had come here to talk sports, not to hash it out over tourism, which can be a mighty painful topic in Cuba. Of the remaining men, one said, "*El turismo* is a good thing. Without it, Cuba could not survive."

"But we can't even sleep in our own hotels!" piped in another. "We used to be able to sleep in our hotels, and now, even if we have the money, it's for the tourists only."

Upon this remark, half the remaining men started looking around nervously to see who might be lurking, and they too moved off to join another debate. About ten people were left, and one of the men continued, "I think it's absolute shit that we can't enter our own hotels. Look at these tourists. They're treated better than we are, and they're not even from here! We can't rent the luxury cars they do, we have no money to use the *Panataxis*. This is supposed to be Socialism. What hotel are you staying at?"

"I'm in a private house," I said.

And in another turn, the rest of the group got jittery about surveillance and slid off to join the others in the *peña*, leaving me alone with the man who was talking and his best friend.

"We have to be very careful," he said, quieting down. "Notice how the police have moved closer to us so they can hear what we're saying? They always get suspicious when *los extranjeros*, the foreigners, come around here. But as I was saying, you may be in a private house, but most stay in the hotels. There's the Golden Tulip hotel, for example. They won't even let me through the door of that hotel, but it's supposedly my hotel according to Castro. Those taxis are mine. The airplanes are mine, but do you see me using them? It's a big lie."

"We would like to stay in the hotels," his friend interjected. "Before 1990, we would share the hotels with the foreigners. They would pay in dollars, and we would pay in pesos. There were never any problems. But now we can't even look in the windows without the *policia* giving us a hard time. We are tourists, too. We don't have the money to leave the country, but when we travel to another part of the island, shouldn't we be able to stay in the hotels as tourists?"

Until 1989, Cubans were permitted to stay in the same hotels as tourists and pay one peso to the tourist dollar. But the minute the government decided it was all or nothing for tourism, natives were barred from using the island's then-12,000 tourist-grade hotel rooms. A new policy of segregation followed, preventing tourists and Cubans from mingling in hopes of both isolating the people from new information while keeping thieves from robbing the tourists. The government framed the segregation in dollars, as Castro apologetically reminded citizens at the emergency 4th Party Congress held in 1991 after the grumbling in the streets had reached peak levels:

> The growth in income from tourism is considerable, and it's very important that everyone should understand how much Cuba needs tourism, even though it implies our making some sacrifices. We'd like to go to all of the hotels, but this is a matter of trying to save our homeland, the Revolution and Socialism, and we need those resources. . . . If only we had as much oil as Venezuela or Kuwait has, so we wouldn't have to think about international tourism and could build a thousand hotels! If only all of the hotels could be ours, but where would we get the capital? Who is going to lend it to us—the CMEA [the USSR's Council for Mutual Economic Assistance] or the socialist camp? So, we're resorting to foreign capital.[1]

It was the big hoedown, the 4th Party Congress held in 1991, when Fidel announced the bad news of the economy's broken back to his cadres and the populace. Before the speech, everybody held their breath, and to dampen the growing panic, everything had been hush-hush as Cubans whispered and complained about the cutbacks in rations and the oil shortages that doubled and tripled each week. Among other things, the Cuban people would lose the privilege of staying at the hotels, but this was nothing new; Cubans are used to having rights and privileges given by the regime, only to have them snapped away when the need arises. Before 1991, if a foreigner paid $40 a night at the Habana Libre, the upscale pre-Castro Havana Hilton, a Cuban visiting from another province would pay 40 pesos. This was back in the prosperous decade of the 1980s, when pesos rang in at five to the dollar. However, the 1991 Soviet collapse caused Cuba's economy to lose an immediate 80 percent of its imports. In a poor attempt to balance the catastrophe, the regime began printing money, causing rapid inflation of the Cuban peso, which peaked out at 140 to the dollar in 1994. Tourism and foreign investment became the only quick available and sustainable option for a bailout.

The conversion of Cuba back to a tourist destination wasn't difficult. After all, Cuba had been the crown jewel of tourism in the Caribbean of the 1920s and 1950s, long before any of the neighboring islands became competitive tourist traps. So Castro's controversial idea, after thirty years of allowing the industry to evaporate, was to provide the newest, cheapest vacation spot in the Caribbean for foreign sun seekers of all classes. Cuba succeeded, today following only the Dominican Republic by a nose as the least expensive destination in the Caribbean Basin.

What was once the pre-Revolutionary backyard playground for American sin seekers has now become an international center for every imaginable species of tourist. They swarm through the city, up and down Obispo, around the Capitolio, across the Spanish colonial avenues of Old Havana, down La Rampa, up Prado for a quick photo or two of the gnashing waves from the harbor point. Later a romantic stroll along the Malecón ocean seafront. And then back to the safety of the hotel. But how did it really happen? How did this controversial island go from having 7,400 visitors in 1974 to 1.8 million in only twenty-five years?

Having fallen into a comfortable stupor under Russian cut-rate trade credits, Cuba was anything but braced for the severe hardships that followed the Soviet dissolution. Losing some 80 percent of its annual umbilical cord by 1991, the island took a nosedive into what some still consider the worst economic depression in the Americas. While the government hit the ground running, there was really no substantial Plan B to turn to should an economic catastrophe like this occur. In 1990, when the Soviet Bloc was already falling short in shipments of oil, cereals, wood products, nearly everything, the big question was, "Now what?"

In a mad scramble, Castro ordered every specialist to brainstorm and every boss to begin cutting back all superfluous industrial expenses across the island. Tobacco, citrus, and rum were minor exports in Cuba's economy that could be modified only slightly for greater yields and gains. The only traditionally major export was sugar; but now, by being forced to compete in the cutthroat world market after enjoying decades of first U.S. and later Soviet preferential pricing, the commodity would prove fatal as an economic crutch. No Cuban wanted to launch into yet another *Zafra de diez millones,* the harvest of 10 million, necessary to pull the island out of the hole. It was an ambitious goal even in 1969 when Castro launched the national campaign, hoping to inspire all Cubans to get involved, doing whatever it took to harvest 10 million tons of raw cane. Year after year throughout the 1970s the harvest failed. The regime even went as far as placing tankers full of free rum in the cane brakes as a work incentive, yet the quota never broke 8 million tons.[2] In 1991, with the world crumbling to pieces, few wanted to bank on it again.

Permanently etched with the sugar mentality, the government held every alternative up side-by-side with the *zafra,* comparing the costs and gains. The reasoning was simple: "If we shoot for a harvest of 10 million tons, which on the world market is today fetching less than 10 cents per pound, we might bring in $2 billion per year. But if we shoot for building 200,000 hotel rooms and we take in $20,000 to $40,000 per room per year, we'll make two and a half to four times more than we ever could with sugar." With this equation, the sea, sun, and sand formula won hands down, and the regime began exploiting its virtually defunct tourist industry at full throttle. It would take some years to accomplish Cuba's goal of 200,000 rooms, but tourism was sustainable in the long run, whereas unpredictable sugar forces any nation into huge debt and an unstable dependency with buyers who virtually control them. A deadly thought for an island finally getting its first shot at true independence from superpower control.

Then the big task became how to siphon off a few liters of the world's 425 million annual vacationers from what at that time amounted to a $230 billion a year industry. Before the Special Period, Cuba's tourist industry was tiny, and the regime never seriously considered hinging its entire economy on this commodity. The years under Soviet dependency were hard times, especially in the 1970s, when the regime first began looking into other ways of supplementing the Soviet dole. In 1976, with Cuba's hotels going to shambles, the government created the National Institute of Tourism (INTUR) with the hopes of transforming tourism into one of Cuba's principal hard currency earners, since most of its Soviet income was mere trade credits. The problem with relying solely on the Soviet Union was the age-old curse of Cuban dependency. Castro knew that in order to transform Cuba into a utopian service economy like Japan, hard dollars were needed.[3] His idea since the beginning was to make Cuba an industrial empire, bursting with new science and technology, which would then generate even more cash profits, eventually pulling the island out of debt. These schemes are nothing new to Cuba. As early as 1965, the National Center for Scientific Investigations was founded for the purpose of discovering saleable technology so that Cuba could get away from sugar and Soviet trade. It was reasoned that, with effort, eventually Cuba could become economically independent. The economy changed so sluggishly, however, that in the mid-1970s, tourism was targeted as an undesirable but effective way to stimulate the economy. It was a trade-off in values, but by developing the Varadero Peninsula (two hours east of Havana on the north coast) as an exclusive resort, it would be easy to segregate the tourists from the rest of the island.

Jimmy Carter was U.S. president at the time, and *el dialogo*, the diplomatic backroom dialogue that triangulated between Havana, Washington, and Miami, was in full swing. The door began opening in 1973, when Castro signed an antihijacking agreement with the United States. In 1974, two U.S. senators visited Cuba to test the waters of negotiation. In 1975, the U.S. Congress passed a bill that allowed U.S. subsidiaries to sell products to Cuba. These diplomatic exchanges culminated in March 1977, when Carter lifted the travel ban that had been imposed on American citizens since the 1962 Missile Crisis, after which John F. Kennedy suspended direct flights between the countries. Cuba went forward with developing its tourist industry, banking on vacationers from the United States, the staple consumer of the pre-Revolutionary industry, who were essential to the plan. Tourism flourished immediately. In 1976, only 2,500 foreigners had visited the Varadero Peninsula, Cuba's chief tourist destination. For 1978, Varadero saw 18,000 visitors, and the numbers were increasing. But on April 19, 1982, President Ronald Reagan reinstated the travel ban with his "No More Cubas" campaign in the Western hemisphere. The reasoning went that money spent in Cuba fueled Castro's satellite wars in Nicaragua and Grenada. Since the late 1970s, Castro had been shipping arms and military advisors to the newly formed Sandinista government in Nicaragua, then warring with Ronald Reagan's newly formed Contra Freedom Fighters on all its borders. More, Castro had been sending workers to Grenada's Socialist prime minister, Maurice Bishop, to help build an airport, as well as furnishing arms for guerrilla groups in South Africa.

Reagan, out to halt Castro's abilities as an arms financier, quickly pulled the plug on his new tourist income. No doubt, political and electoral pressures from the Florida exiles' political powerhouse came into play. Castro's plan to achieve independence by developing tourism, advanced medicine and technology was well-known, which North American conservatives and the anti-Castro faction of the Cuban exile community wished to prevent. This travel ban on American tourism, only slightly modified, is still intact today. But in 1982, with Reagan's move, it was no dice for Cuba, and the tourist industry crashed on the Revolutionary agenda, not to gain momentum again until a few years later.

In 1986, the Communist government initiated the Cubanacán Corporation, its mission being to create an industry pocket for investors in foreign tourism who wished to form business alliances with Cuba. In 1988, *Grupo Gaviota*, the Seagull Group, was launched to handle specialized higher-end VIP tourism on the island. But these minor steps were meant only to supplement the Soviet economic lifeline, at best laying a framework for the whispered "What if?" scenario. The more aggressive development of Cuba's tourist industry wouldn't come until the Berlin Wall fell in 1989, just a few years too late to balance the devastating impact of Reagan's measures.

In 1991, with only 12,000 operable hotel rooms, most in poor condition, Cuba received only 340,000 visitors, who pumped approximately

$300 million into the dwindling economy. Yet between 1990 and 1999, Cuba's visitation rate grew at an impressive 19 percent annually, while its gross income flourished at a yearly increase of 26 percent. In 1998, 1.4 million people visited the island, bringing in a gross of $1.8 billion. In 1999, Cuba enjoyed 1.6 million tourists and an exchange of $1.9 billion. However, in 2000 and 2001, things began to unexpectedly taper off.[4] When Cuba desperately threw everything in for the industry at the beginning of the 1990s, the big goal for the turn of the millennium was 2 million visitors, but only 1.8 million had rolled in by the end of both years. Things were slow for the first half of 2000, the Ministry of Tourism attributing the vacant hotel rooms to the Elian González crisis. Because of all the media hoopla—the world saw millions of Cubans marching angrily through Havana and other provinces over the return of the boy from his relatives in Miami—many would-be tourists were understandably intimidated. For those who decided to go anyway, the Elian saga was just an inconvenience. These tourists came for the sun, not politics, and the big marches and demonstrations demanding the return of the boy only made it harder to get around town. In 2001, the global recession on top of the September 11 terrorist attacks were the most obvious factor in Cuba's declining tourist rate.

Cuba's ultimate target for tourism? According to the Ministry of Tourism, Cuba aspires to 7.5 million annual tourists by 2010, and 10 million by the year 2025.[5]

To average Cubans, these kinds of numbers mean only one thing: twenty-three more years of hardship and sacrifice without material reward; twenty-three more years of banishment from the hotels, of being penniless, of *la lucha*, the struggle to free the Revolution from the embargo's grip. When I mentioned this target of 10 million visitors to the two men in Central Park, the response was a high-volume sigh.

"*Es la nueva zafra de diez millones,*" said one, shaking his head in resignation. "It's the new harvest of 10 million."

Cuba's Stable Instability

Enrique, who lives at the bottom of Monte Avenue in Central Havana, has his own pet complaint when it comes to tourism. He explained how in the 1970s Cubans were once allowed to go family camping on the beaches.

"Every family had one of those surplus green military tents," he said. "You could pack the whole family in the car, or maybe a group of friends, and party on the beach for a week. I went to Playas del Este [just across Havana harbor] every year, and sometimes we would head out to the Varadero Peninsula if we had enough gas money saved."

Enrique explained that this was Cuba's national-style tourism, and everyone looked forward to getting away to live on the beach for that one week a year. Food, rum, grilled leg of *puerco seco* (white pork), music, dancing.

"And then at night we'd have a fire," he added. "This was until the government took away the camping privileges and invented the *campismo popular.*"

The *campismos populares,* or people's camps, were designed by the Cuban government in 1980 to clear the beaches of Cubans for the projected tourist boom after Carter lifted the U.S. travel ban. The new campgrounds were more like small barracks of twenty or twenty-five *cabañas,* each equipped with two double bunk beds, a sink, a private bathroom, or sometimes community showers. Every week, the newspapers run ads for interested parties to sign up for openings at the *campismo,* which is still the popular Cuban style of vacation. The use is free of charge, but the campers pay for transportation and food, which is reasonably priced.

"We once used the finest beaches in all of Cuba," Enrique went on, "but now they have moved us into swamplands full of mosquitoes, far away from anywhere there are tourists. Castro doesn't want Cubans near the tourists. He doesn't want the capitalists influencing the people. We get pushed aside, the capitalists get the best beaches all to themselves. I have some photos," he said, disappearing behind a curtain and returning with a plastic bag full of black-and-white snapshots from the 1960s and '70s. After digging through the bag, he drew out two or three.

"You see how it used to be?" he said, handing me the photos. "Those were the days. This is me with my pals in Playas del Este when we graduated from the military service. This is my old car, a 1953 Ford station wagon that my papa gave me. I ended up selling it in 1995 because we needed the money. And look at my tent. It was a nice one. I could fit six people in there. It was bigger than my living room. I sold it, too, because what purpose would I have in keeping it if I can't use it?"

Most Cubans I met feel like Enrique. They know that giving up the beaches and the hotels was one of the sacrifices made to fortify the Cuban economy, but it doesn't take away the discomfort of having one or two fewer freedoms in a land of constantly dwindling privilege. Currently, the island is developing its "culture tour" program, where visitors can meet Cubans and learn about Afro-Cuban traditions. These tours are Castro's answer to growing complaints about what many foreign scholars and human rights groups are calling Cuba's "tourist apartheid," the most controversial and distasteful side effect of the tourist boom. The culture tours are highly structured and controlled by the government, which is preoccupied with revealing only so much of the Cuban reality. Many feel the obsession with keeping tourists on the surface of Cuba, around the museums and on the Hemingway Trail where they can buy Che postcards, is a means of preventing Cubans from being empowered, while keeping the dollars flowing into the regime's coffers. Tourists aren't permitted to ride in the cheap peso taxis crammed full of Cubans, even if they'd like to. Rather, the dollar taxis must be used; these cost $5 for the same distance that a peso taxi would cover for $.50. Most tourists prefer to stay in the parallel dollar economy. But those that don't are discouraged from using pesos in a number of ways. Cuba's limited free enterprise system permits two types of licenses to operate a business, one for *divisa,* or dollars, and the other for pesos. Cubans who have a peso license can be fined or have their privilege revoked if they are caught taking dollars. A bicycle taxi with a peso license is not permitted to haul tourists. If selling peso pizzas, the Cuban is forbidden to accept dollars. Most will take the dollars and give pesos in change, but the mere illegality of these things curbs the behavior, and if the exchange is discovered, it's never the tourist who is penalized, but the Cuban. Tourists are permitted to use the peso economy in some areas, such as railways, national airlines, peso hotels, and the postal service, and pay in dollars. Sometimes, tourists can even use pesos, such as in city transit. But as Cuba grows its tourist industry, it looks for ways to eliminate the competition. Once, riding across Havana in a camello, a 20-centavo fare, I asked a friend what would happen if a tourist were injured or perhaps killed in an accident on a bus.

"That would be the end of it," he said. "Castro would get on the TV and say, 'From now on, foreigners cannot use the buses, and anyone who permits it will lose their job and be fined.' They're just waiting for this to happen so they'll have an excuse to make every tourist ride the state dollar taxis so they can get all of the dollars."

During the mid-1990s height of the Special Period, to stifle the increasing amount of pickpockets, purse snatchers, and burglars in general, the government turned the island into a repressive police state and dished out penalties to anyone harming tourists, damaging the island's prestige, or committing any kind of petty crime. As it was explained to me, the measures taken by the government were almost identical to Martial Law, yet without the declaration. As one man explained, "If there were five Cubans standing on a street corner talking, it was called 'illicit congregation,' and soon a truck would drive up and the police would arrest everybody. The trucks had nicknames. They were very loud, and you could hear them coming from the other side of Havana. We called it 'the snore.' 'The snore! The snore!' somebody would say, and any groups of people would run away."

These measures were done as a means to curb crime and prevent Cubans from organizing for fear of a possible overthrow in Cuba's darkest hour. The dual role was to provide safety for visitors, guaranteeing a better return rate, and to distance Cubans from the tourists. Between 1992 and 1997, Cubans seen with tourists in the street were harassed by police and often arrested. The profile was simple: A Cuban mingling with a tourist was either a hustler or a thief. This wasn't a written law, but a de facto stroke of repression, and all Cubans knew the limits; tourists were hands-off.

Then in the summer of 1997, the government did an about-face. Global human rights groups had been pummeling Cuba with accusations of tourist apartheid, and the fury was staining the island's image in the international media, which at the time had been following Cuba closely due to the Pope's upcoming January 1998 visit. Gradually, mingling with tourists was tolerated.

Today, Cuban-tourist associations are no longer punished, but they are still frowned upon. While arrests don't occur, detainment often does. If the police spot Cubans strolling down the streets with tourists, they check the *carné de identitad*, the personal identification card required by law that Cubans carry at all times. (Those who don't have their IDs when carded are arrested pending an investigation and can be legally detained for twenty-four hours and then fined.) Although the ID checks are more a hassle than a problem, it's the intimidation factor that sends the message home. I've stood and waited many times as my good friends—

mostly black Cubans—were run through the mill. As we walked away after they had been carded, there was always that awkward silence of embarrassment while we searched for words to soften up the unfairness of what had just passed. Not once when I walked with white friends did the police give them a hard time; this shows that the profiling of blacks in Cuba is a still a serious reality despite the government's rhetoric about the Revolution's having eliminated racial discrimination.

The police rarely check tourists' identification unless they have brown skin and are thought to be Cuban. These tourists experience the advantages and disadvantages of being able to blend in; they can ride the peso taxis anywhere in Havana, spend pesos where white tourists must use dollars, pay the "Cuban" price for drinks and meals. On the flip side, they get carded and bugged by the police. Other than this, only once did I see the cops bother a tourist, a white Vietnam veteran on a drinking binge in Havana. Each day he'd return under police escort to his hotel after spending the night in a jail cell. Apparently he would get sauced up in the bars and then accuse Cubans of stealing his money. One night he entered a Cuban home, three sheets to the wind, and began accusing a family who'd never even met him of robbery. The police arrived and hauled him off after these episodes, night after night for a week. The man was not deported, but tolerated, abuse after abuse.

Tourism is now the only tangible avenue towards making money, both for the government and for ordinary Cubans. While the regime reinvests its tourist earnings back into hotels and joint ventures, average Cubans thrive on the tourist industry. On the unlawful side, illegal chauffeuring, hustling, prostitution, and the illicit renting of apartments are the major means of obtaining dollars. Those who stay within the system ply the tourist trades as wait staff, room cleaners, security guards, desk clerks, pilots, flight attendants, tour organizers, guides, translators, hotel managers; they earn dollar tips, which the regime likes to control. One way in which the government taxes the tips is by obligating hotel workers to pay 50 percent of their earnings to certain state-controlled cancer studies and humanitarian funds. There is no accountability for these funds, so there's no way of knowing where the money goes. One man I know, a hotel porter, complained one day of having to pay his monthly $30. "In the high season, half of the year, I make $60 a month in tips. In the low season, I make $15 a month in tips. If you average this out, I get to keep nothing for myself." He was exaggerating, of course, but not by much.

Making up another group of those living off the tourism are the legally self-employed, dollar-based private *taxis particulares,* and the homeowners who rent rooms to foreigners in *casas particulares,* or private houses. In the summer of 1993, when the Cuban government legalized Cuban possession of the dollar and opened up a slough (by Cuban standards) of self-employment opportunities, many who were fortunate enough to have an extra bedroom became instant micro-entrepreneurs.

My friends Martina and Rolando Ibáñez were part of the wave of families who moved to Havana in 1994, the peak of the Special Period, when the government was cracking down on the flood of migration to the capital. But the Ibáñezes, like many migrants from the provinces, didn't want to come to Havana illegally. They wished to stay forever. In 1986, as part of the Communist regime's rectification period, the ownership and sales of private homes was banned to prevent people from profiting on their material possessions. Today, you can't legally buy and sell homes, but like everything else in Cuba, they are bought and sold illegally, and the title is kept in the former owner's name to skirt the law. Trading of houses is lawful, however, whether across town or with someone in another province, and often traders will give extra money on top for unequal exchanges. While foreigners are forbidden to purchase dwellings from anyone other than the state, I was offered the sale of several homes, ranging between $4,000 and $10,000 for a nice country ranch. The title would stay in the owner's name and, now wealthy, they would go live with relatives. But for the Ibáñezes, it was an even trade.

"I had a big beautiful house in Santa Clara," Martina told me. And Rolando added, "but we needed to make money and think about our children's futures. There isn't much tourism in Santa Clara."

"We had lots of windows," Martina said, "and a big yard with fruit trees. It was gorgeous. We moved to Havana to make a living, and the people that lived here wanted to get out of Havana because of the crime. They wanted to try the country living where there is more tranquility. So we traded."

"It wasn't an even trade," said Rolando. "Our house was three times the size of this apartment and in better condition. But since this apartment makes us money, that evens it up."

"We were able to put our girls through medical school," said Martina. "It's very expensive. Don't believe all that talk about a free education in Cuba. Someone has to pay for the books and the food. The students of medicine receive a stipend of only 30 pesos a month. That's $1.50. You can buy an apple and a loaf of bread with that."

Their move to Havana entailed many sacrifices, a big decision, but for them the only one. The Ibáñezes were both educated at the university and these sacrifices to ensure their daughters' educations made the family experience that much richer. But the time spent seeking the apartment and the move were only the beginning. Out of necessity, the daughters were forced to find fiancés they could live with so that the extra bedroom could be available to rent. Then came the inspections, the repairs to bring the quarters up to state standards, and the state licensing procedure.

"The whole thing took a year and a half to accomplish," Martina recalled. "And now the government is killing us."

They explained that if you have a two-bedroom house, by law, one bedroom must be used for the tenants, leaving only one to rent. If you have a three-bedroom house, only two bedrooms can be rented. The government charges a flat $5 per night licensing fee for each available bedroom, whether it's rented or vacant. Serving food in the *casa* costs an additional monthly $35 for the license, and hanging an advertising sign in the street costs $50 a month more.

"Then we must pay the income tax at the beginning of the year, depending on how much profit we made after the state expenses," Martina complained. "It's getting to the point that you can't even operate anymore. And now in January of 2001, they're going to raise the monthly license fee another $50. Fidel just announced it on TV this week. He said it's necessary to raise the fees because the distribution is too unequal and the government needs the money."

"But really," Rolando sighed with disgust, "they want to put the *casas particulares* out of business."

In 1993, when the *casa particular* phenomena was born, Cuba had a total of 34,000 hotel rooms, up from the 12,000 available when the tourism program was recast in 1991. By 1993, with tourism growing faster than the government had predicted, there were major room shortages at peak season. To deal with grumpy tourists wandering around looking for phantom hotel rooms, and to quash the growing cottage industry of illegal apartment rentals, the regime was forced to open private-home rentals in a manner that could be taxed heavily. Cubans who rented their apartments illegally were fined $1,000, and if they couldn't pay, their homes were repossessed by the state. These simple strokes gave the appearance of granting more independence to the people, quelled the rising frustrations, and kept money pouring into the government's pockets. But the Ibáñezes, like every *casa particular* owner I spoke to, have no illusions that the *casa particular* privilege won't last. The government still needs the *casas* because the current rate of hotel building can't keep up with the booming growth rate of visitors; but as soon as conditions change, the privilege will be snatched away. The Ibáñezes think that Castro's raising the licensing fees in January 2001 is part of an attrition program to force the struggling *casas* under.

"Drive out to Miramar and look at all the new hotels going up," Rolando grumbled, describing the new Spanish and Canadian hotels going up in Havana's poshest suburb. "There are also three new hotels under construction on Prado, and when those are done, the government will condemn another city block and build a few more. Soon they won't need us, and we'll be finished. Castro will shut us right down. Every time a new hotel goes up, these fees are increased, and more of us are squeezed out."

"But for now, we'll make as much as we can," Martina said with a laugh, as if the idea of losing her livelihood were just another of those government whimsies to which the people have grown so accustomed.

Gaining and losing privilege is nothing new. For forty years the Cubans have been jerked around as the regime experiments and makes mistakes, finally creating some stability only to throw it all into the shaker again. The tourist boom is the biggest shaker since the 1959 victory. Not to laugh would be suicide.

Rather than giving the people some of profits from tourism to curb hunger, the regime insists on dumping every last centavo into new hotels, even though the *casas particulares* are meeting the room demands of the industry. The big question is, why this neurotic obsession to force the *casas* under and maintain absolute control of Cuba's accommodations? Since the *casas* opened, the regime has had to compete with its own people in the rooming business. In many ways, the private homes give better service than the hotels, and many tourists prefer the royal treatment they receive in the *casas*. The incentive for those who run a *casa particular* is personal independence and a higher standard of living. They wait hand and foot on their guests and prepare extravagant meals, making sure that everything is perfect. *Casa* operators are so preoccupied with their guests' satisfaction that they lose sleep if they think the slightest thing is wrong. Clearly, the guests are the center of the *casa* operator's universe because the balance of life depends on them. All the *casa* operators I've met have quit their day jobs to dedicate every waking minute to the home and the guests.

This kind of attention cannot be found in the majority of state-operated hotels. Because the state wages of 180 pesos, or $9 per month, are so poor, hotel workers have no incentive to bathe guests in attention. After all, as has always been a problem with Socialism, and particularly now that Cuba is seeing more class stratification, you get your monthly $9 whether you go out of your way or not. A *casa particular* operator who has only one bedroom earns that same $9 in one day.

This has been the biggest quandary for the government, which continually wants to fall back on the old Socialist model of a small central government that runs the economy. Allowing a small sector of petty bourgeoisie to operate in Cuba doesn't jibe with Marxism-Leninism, and the regime sees this as ideological decay. While the Cuban government likes to make sweeping statements about "The People's Revolution," in reality, the people are very much at odds with the government after years of alienation from the Revolutionary process. The Ibáñezes, other *casa particular* owners, and Cubans in general gripe constantly about losing privileges.

Castro's address to the 5th Party Congress of October 1997 about the changing economy was probably the most incoherent of his speeches, mainly because he couldn't come up with a rationale to justify the growing domestic class structure. Regarding *casa particular* owners, he said, "Some people decide to live crowded together: some out in the garage, here or there. What we have to do is regulate that. If a number of citizens receive an income that way, on the basis of making a personal sacrifice or because they've got excess house space, that's not a tragedy for the Revolution. It's not going to suffer because someone has a certain income."[1]

That parents were booting out their sons and daughters to clear a bedroom for tourist rentals was one thing the regime wasn't prepared to embrace, not to mention the class gap of those fortunate enough to have available living space to rent, now able to survive in the parallel dollar economy. That isn't Marxism-Leninism, and although Castro made light of it, the hypocrisy is evident in the regime's obsession with striving to eradicate the *casas particulares* as soon as the opportunity arrives. The only other option available to the government in meeting the problem of tourist room shortages was to commandeer private homes and force people to rent for a state wage. I asked the Ibáñezes why Castro didn't attempt this. Rolando explained:

They tried that with the people's taxis in the '70s and it didn't work. Castro wanted to eradicate every kind of private business, so one day he said, "You will still drive your cars, but you will give all the money to the state, and we will pay you a salary." You can imagine what happened. The entire transportation system broke down. Why? Think about it. If you own your own car and your livelihood is based on that car, when you get a flat tire, you're going to run out and find a replacement immediately. If you get 200 pesos a month whether the car is running or not, why would you worry whether the car is running or not? Why not just sit at home and get your 200 pesos?

The 1968–1970 shift to strict central planning was the loftiest post-Guevara risk that Castro had undertaken since destroying the capitalist banana republic infrastructure upon seizing the island. But in the 1970s, after undergoing years of this failed experiment, after the failure of the harvest of 10 million, and after a complete fragmentation of society, the people's frustrations exploded into the 1980 Mariel boatlift. Shortly afterward, Castro was forced to launch his rectification program, which decentralized state control of the economy, opened up private enterprise a shade, redistributed decisionmaking power to local authority, and once again roped the people back into the struggle.

Personal independence and private enterprise is the best incentive for Cubans, who seem to have a natural entrepreneurial drive. This is a time-proven reality, but the regime, in its utopian fantasy, has always been slow to admit it. For the Ibáñezes, it was a huge sacrifice, a breaker of families, when survival in Cuba's dollar economy meant pushing their kids out the door to free up a bedroom. Although Castro said that some people "decide" to live crowded together, in reality there is no decision. If a sliver of opportunity arises to earn dollars, you jump on it. The Ibáñezes sacrificed years of their lives, moved away from the extended family, gave up their home and memories, sent their daughters packing with new fiancés out of necessity, and sacrificed their privacy so that a steady stream of strangers could occupy their living space, all for $20 a day, of which the regime takes $10, only to know this little niche will be short-lived.

On the government side, the slightest inkling of a free market doesn't fit into the Revolutionary Castroist-Socialist program, the primary goal of which is to create financial and living equality for Cuba's 11 million inhabitants. But to admit that these elements work, even under heavy regulation and taxation (which could easily be redistributed to the poor), is beyond Castro's ken. To him, the ideology takes a big hit when even the slightest elements of a free market exist, even under the constraints of the Socialist framework. They are seen as the seeds of capitalism, and if allowed to grow, mass corruption will follow and things will return to their pre-1959 state overnight. The alienation between the government and the people stems from this attitude because Castro doesn't trust the Cuban people to care for and maintain the Revolution's integrity. It's a "People's Revolution" that the people are considered too irresponsible to take part in.

5

Viva Buena Vista

"¡*Chico!*" said Ibrahim Ferrer, flicking his wrist above his head. "You wouldn't know! All day long they come. Writers for magazines and newspapers ... camera crews.... Five fans came already today. I don't know how they find me. Do you want a drink of water? A shot of rum?"

"I want to see your new place," I said.

"We just moved in," said Ibrahim. "The old place from the movie is down in Cerro. I want to stop there on the way to the studio so you can meet my sister."

Ibrahim Ferrer is always bouncing around, beaming with energy. Constantly on the go, he's the life of the party with his magnetic presence. It wasn't always this way, and merely emphasizing that his old apartment was in Cerro really says a lot. It's one of the poorest barrios of inner-city Havana and has the highest crime rate. During the Special Period, Ferrer suffered like everyone else, depressed and impoverished, enduring the twelve-hour rolling blackouts, scraping centavos for a few ounces of rice, hauling buckets of bath water up two flights of stairs.

"No, I never expected this success," he said, showing me a half-dozen gold and platinum records hanging from the freshly painted walls. "My life as a musician ended years before. The music had lost its popularity."

"In articles I've read about you," I said, "they always say you were 'forced' to shine shoes for a living. Is this true?"

"Ah," he said. "You know how it is. I did many, many different things. I moved furniture, whatever it took to put food on the table. I was struggling as a musician, and for a singer like me, there was little or no work."

Then one day in 1996 the phone rang. It was an invitation to audition for the Buena Vista Social Club. It changed his life forever. And now he was showing me around his new, freshly painted, spacious house in a quiet residential neighborhood of the Plaza district, which by the looks of it cost him at least $15,000. From nothing to everything in four years.

It was fun driving Ibrahim around Havana, getting the tour of his old neighborhood, spinning around the corner to see his old bodega, dropping in on his sister for a shot of coffee. And then onward to Egrem studios, where I'd been hanging out with the members of Buena Vista and the Afro-Cuban All Stars every day for a week as they rehearsed for their upcoming tours.

The excitement and electricity at these rehearsals is contagious. There are always a dozen fans hanging out in the dimly lit studio, cameras flashing, everyone joking and carrying on, thrilled about getting on the airplane and heading to Europe, Asia, North America, wherever. And the day before departure, there's always a big party at the Egrem bar next door. Omara Portuondo eats a sandwich under a shaded umbrella while she gives an interview to a Japanese journalist. Bassist Cachaíto Lopez lounges out over here. Timbalero Amadito Valdes signs autographs for two Venezuelan women. Ibrahim Ferrer cracks open a bottle of Havana Club rum, talking about the new Mercedes Benz he's thinking of ordering. Juan de Marcos drinks a beer and chats with some musicians visiting from Argentina. And Puntillita (who died in December 2000) always off by himself somewhere. Always observing everyone from a distance, having a quiet cigarette. The people in the street drift past, looking in to see the stir. Tomorrow is the plane out, and every country is a new frontier.

Performing before massive crowds, seeing those bodies swinging to the flavor of Cuba after being unheard for so many years is the most humbling experience for all these musicians. Once I interviewed Buena Vista guitarist Eliades Ochoa at his house in Santiago. Over a beer, I asked him, "What is the best part of traveling, of playing your music live for foreign audiences? What does it do for you?"

"I'll tell you," he said, looking me in the eye, running a finger down the side of his face. "It's not about what it does for me. It's what it does for them. When I make my music and they dance, that's one thing. When I see them laughing and celebrating, that's another. But when they cry, when I see the tears running down their cheeks, it's then that I know I've reached them. That's the thing that makes it worthwhile."

When Rhythm Barbarian Beny Moré died shortly after the missile crisis in 1962, his death served as an epitaph of the golden age before Castro. It was truly the end of an era. All of the music, the dance, the literature that had previously defined the culture were symbols of the old Cuba. A commercial Cuba whose national cocktail was the *Cuba Libre,* the rum and Coke, symbolizing Cuba's de facto U.S. statehood. A Cuba that, by 1959, some 60,000 American tourists streamed into each year to hit the strip clubs and casinos, and lap up rum and romance in Havana's year-long fiesta. No family vacation spot, Cuba was for denizens of the night, and at dusk, Beny Moré was god of the streets.

The New Revolutionary Cuba had no place for the kind of decadence that Beny Moré represented. The people were expected to become industrious workers, militiamen, cogs in the Revolutionary machine, and new music and culture was expected to continue oiling the gears of the victory. In 1960, the Revolution turned the volume down, and when Moré died in 1963, Castro turned the people's radio off. During the strife of the 1970s, the parallel culture turned the radio back on in the form of Los Van Van and Irakére, and only now are the streets finally twisting the volume back up to its pre-Revolutionary levels.

Today, almost 2 million tourists visit Cuba annually. According to the Ministry of Tourism, 200,000 of those are from the United States. And the 1997 birth of the Buena Vista Social Club is directly responsible, as

Buena Vista alumni Ibrahim Ferrer, Ruben González, and Omara Portuondo tour the globe and continue scoring Grammy nominations.
Cuban jazz pianist Chucho Váldez, one of the founders of Irakére, actually won Cuba's first Grammy in the mid-1970s, reflecting the almost
identical political patterns between that decade and the 1990s. Cuba got
noticed at the time, everyone pushed to lift the blockade, nothing happened, Reagan came in, froze everything, and the fever died off. Here we
are again.

During the 1920s, the traditional Cuban musical form of *son*
migrated from eastern Cuba to Havana and became the property of the
intellectuals. Before this time, *son,* originally born in nineteenth-century
Guantánamo from its parent musical form *changui,* an amalgamation of
Spanish, African, and French-Haitian folk influences, was considered a
vulgar peasant music. When Havana adopted *son,* adding a bass guitar to
the former set of the six-stringed *tres* guitar, bongos, maracas, and claves,
it became an instant commercial success; these variations resulted in a
split: *son oriental* and *son habanero. Son,* a formerly black music, and its rising popularity in middle-class Cuba, was timed almost perfectly with the
rising popularity of black jazz in the United States as the precursor to the
Harlem Renaissance.

In 1920, a Cuban composer named Moises Simons wrote a romantic love song called "El Manicero," "The Peanut Vendor," on a drink
napkin in Havana. He took his new material to New York, and this is
when America's love affair with Cuban music truly began. These were
the Roaring Twenties, the Machado years, when the Prohibition
spawned Cuba's first tourist boom as flocks of thirsty Americans fled
south where liquor was legal. The two cultures completely enmeshed
through this new musical bridge and triggered the southern drift of
North America's black jazz influence. In 1927, a year before Ernest
Hemingway made his first stop on the island, Cuban trumpet player
Lazaro Herrera formed Septeto Nacional de Ignacio Piñeira, adding
brass to the *son* mix, and the rest is history. Later came the chachacha,
the mambo, and the big brass orchestrations of the 1940s and 1950s,
immortalized by bandleaders Arsenio Rodríguez, Chappotín, and Beny

Moré, when *son* had reached its maturity. Later in the 1960s, a Cuban exile in New York, Celia Cruz, would become the mother of modern salsa, which has Cuban *son* at its roots. However, if Moises Simons's "El Manicero" spawned the marriage of Cuban *son* and American jazz in the 1920s, the Buena Vista Social Club represents the long-overdue consummation some seventy years later.

Today's global infatuation with Cuba is directly linked with the Buena Vista Social Club, which has become a musical bridge spanning the isolated island with the rest of the world. Because of the stringent U.S. laws, Cuban musicians can sign contracts only with foreign record companies, who then sell to the American audience through U.S. distributors. This process somewhat slowed the reception of the Cuban music revival in the United States. However, after its inception, the original album went multiplatinum in Europe, Asia, and, eventually the United States, selling a total of more than 8 million copies worldwide between the debut and all the spin-off solo projects.

Without Buena Vista, Cuba would likely be as isolated as it was in 1995, and tourism would probably have tapered off and hovered around a million annual tourists instead of soaring to the 1.8 million it enjoys today. Although a lot of fans attribute the group's commercial success to guitarist and Buena Vista producer Ry Cooder, in reality the credit belongs to the group Sierra Maestra, which dates back to the late 1970s and one of its founders, Juan de Marcos González.

"Well, you know, that's life man," Marcos told me with a chuckle in one of several interviews. "There was a Cuban doctor called Carlos J. Finlay who discovered the vector for *fiebre amarillo,* yellow fever. Yet an American doctor took all the credit. But it doesn't matter. That's not important. What's important is that Cuban music has reclaimed its place in the world."

Juan de Marcos is a humble guy. He usually runs around his house in flip-flops and a sun-bleached T-shirt, his graying forty-six-year-old braids poking out from a beret. Sierra Maestra was one of the top five most important bands that emerged in Cuba during the decentralizing reforms of the 1970s, after the economy had fallen flat. The group, essentially latter-day rockers, revived traditional Cuban *son*, rediscovering forgotten musicians from the 1940s and 1950s who had long since been swept under the Revolutionary rug.

"In the hard times, Sierra Maestra rediscovered the spirit of the Cuban music," Marcos explained. "We dressed as punks, and we were the first to bring out the maestros, the real maestros, people more well known than Ibrahim Ferrer or Ruben González. People like Tito Gómez and El Guayabero, all the top stars of their generation. We brought them to our concerts. But today, nobody talks about Sierra Maestra. Without Sierra Maestra, there would be no Buena Vista Social Club."

This rediscovery of the forgotten musicians was an important step in the late 1970s. It was the first time since the war that the street culture had tried to reconnect with their pre-Castro roots and search for parts of their history that had been erased. At the time, the economic conditions in Cuba were horrific, and the Revolutionary morale was at an all-time low. As the economy bottomed out, the people's faith in the Revolution waned, and the hunger grew.

In the 1970s, listening to North American pop music was still prohibited in Cuba as fascist deviancy, and younger Cuban musicians like González became infatuated with tuning into Miami radio stations clandestinely. They listened to everything from the Commodores and Stevie Wonder to Kansas and Santana, which helped lead to Sierra Maestra's rediscovery of traditional *son* and bring a newfound pride to the Cuban youth. Marcos elaborated:

Santana re-created the spirit of his Mexican roots in rock and roll. This was great for all Latinos, because we always thought America was better than us. Santana made us realize that we have a history, too. When I heard tunes like Santana's "Guajira" and "Oye Como Va," I changed completely. I said, "Well, I have a history," and I started studying traditional Cuban music. Sierra Maestra brought out this history. We were hippies with long hair and torn clothes, which was attractive for the younger generation, but we played traditional Cuban music. And we helped the people of the younger generation realize that we, as Cubans, are great.

Upon its formation in 1978, Sierra Maestra learned the forgotten *son* rhythms under the supervision of Lazaro Herrera and Septeto Nacional, the oldest *son* band still performing to this day. In 1994, when Marcos had been with Sierra Maestra for sixteen years, the band was in Britain recording their album ¡*Dundunbanza!* with World Circuit Records producer Nick Gold. The following year, Marcos ran the idea past Gold, a serious Cuban music lover, of putting together an all-star band of older Cuban musicians.

"I had the idea for years," said Marcos. "And when I went to the different record companies they said, 'Marcos, you're crazy! Why would you want to put together a bunch of old guys and make an album that will only sell two copies!?!' This is what they said. Until I met Nick. He and I both loved the music of the 1940s, and in December of 1995, he agreed to record the album."

First came the Afro-Cuban All Stars album, *A Toda Cuba le Gusta.* During the sessions, Gold brought in Ry Cooder to produce his own project. Cooder added ancient studio equipment to give the sound an older flavor, and the result was *Buena Vista Social Club,* band, album, and film, which featured the same veteran musicians hand-picked by Juan de Marcos, who also directed the sessions and wrote the arrangements. Released in 1997, what started out as a tribute to Cuban period music soon became one of the greatest world music commercial successes of the decade. And it's a delicious irony to think that the poverty of the 1970s and Castro's early restrictions on the people, which inspired Sierra Maestra, would eventually lead to Cuba's economic salvation in the 1990s with Buena Vista.

The only problem with Buena Vista is that it is commercial. It is period music. And it doesn't reflect today's Cuban culture, nor the past forty years of the people's parallel evolution as Sierra Maestra did. The impression Buena Vista fans get is that time stopped in 1960 and Cubans have since been living in a time warp. While he's happy that Buena Vista put Cuba on the map, Marcos resents this side effect of the group's success. Another problem is that in reality, younger black Cubans rediscovered the music in the 1970s and brought it to the world's ears some twenty years later when the time was ripe; yet many fans get the impression from the film and hype that Ry Cooder is a string-bending Columbus who rediscovered the Cuban rhythms and rescued a bunch of shoeshining musicians from poverty and squalor. I doubt that Ry Cooder, Nick Gold, or film director Wim Wenders intended these results, but they are very real.

"That's the subliminal message of it," said Marcos, who is currently working on Cuban rap and techno projects. "And that's a very attractive idea for people of the first world. It's a nice story. The Buena Vista Social Club was important because it caught the attention of the people of the world. But now it's important to show the world that a new generation of Cuban musicians exist and that the music didn't stop after Castro."

In reality, ordinary Cubans know less about the Buena Vista Social Club than visiting tourists. It wasn't until 1999 that rumors of this mysterious Buena Vista thing started trickling into the island, when more and more foreigners began flocking in, asking around in the streets about the group. I asked Ibrahim Ferrer one day why Cubans know nothing about Buena Vista. "Because the film only premiered for two nights at the Karl Marx theater," Ibrahim's wife explained. And Ibrahim added, "It's expensive to rent out the Karl Marx. It costs $5,000 a night to use the venue."

In fact, it wasn't until August 2001 that the film finally played in mainstream Havana, when the state scheduled it for a week at the Payret theater's video salon that holds about a hundred people. Other than that, Buena Vista is virtually nonexistent in Cuba, and few Cubans know exactly how important the phenomenon has been as a tourist lure. The older people know all the players, Compay Segundo, Pio Leyva, the late Puntillita Licea and Raul Planas, from their early fame. But the connection between Buena Vista and the 5,000 tourists buzzing in and out of Cuba's airports every day hasn't been made in the streets.

"This is news to me," said Armando, a friend who knows almost every detail of Cuba's musical history. "I remember seeing Pio sometimes wandering around the National Ballet with his hands in his pockets looking bored. I used to see Puntillita whenever I went to the farmers' market on that side of town. I had no idea they have become this famous again. We don't hear these things. How many millions of records did you say they've sold?"

These musicians defined Cuban music in the 1940s and 1950s. Today, they are essentially irrelevant on the island. The regime sometimes schedules Buena Vista–related shows at the Hotel Nacional for foreign audiences, and aside from an occasional Compay Segundo or Eliades Ochoa video aired on television, none of it has broken into the mainstream. The young people have no time for it, except to profit from bootleg compact discs sold to tourists. And older people, like Enrique, say, "Who is this Eliades Ochoa from Santiago singing 'Yiri Yiri Bon?' Nobody can do it better than Beny Moré!" When you ask around in the streets whether people know of Juan de Marco González, they'll typically reply, "Wasn't he the *tres* player for Sierra Maestra?" They have no idea that today he directs the important satellite touring band, the Afro-Cuban All Stars, nor that he was the initial fuel behind Buena Vista.

The only Cubans who really do understand the importance of Buena Vista are the musicians who go from table to table in the tourist restaurants and play requests. Rather than using the traditional arrangements, they now play Juan de Marcos's arrangements of the classic songs. And they play those arrangements because the tip-paying tourists expect to hear them. So a new phenomenon is occurring: Cuba is being defined by the tourists, who bring dollars, and who expect to see a certain "Cuba" when they step off the plane. Will Cuba, like Cancun and Nepal, transform into a commercially acceptable ghost of itself?

On my first trip to the island in 1998, I shot forty rolls of film and not once was I asked for money. On my last trip down, I shot another forty rolls and was asked for money five times. On one occasion, a subject posed for me knowing beforehand that I was a reporter. He understood there was no money involved and he didn't expect any, but twenty people nearby started cursing at me. "Give him a dollar!" they yelled. "Give him a dollar!" slapping the bottoms of their elbows, which means "cheap ass." I immediately got into a huge argument with half a block of Cubans. "Go talk to the boss," I yelled, pulling on my chin. "What do I look like, a wad of cash?" And the guy I had photographed wound up defending me, arguing on my behalf. Hilarious stuff.

One of my best friends, a Cuban artist named Ramon, dresses better than I, often expensively, and he's always mistaken for a tourist. On one occasion, we were walking under the overpass on San Lazaro when a little seven-year-old boy ran up. The only English the kid knew was "Chupa-Chup," which he repeated over and over, as if he expected all tourists to have a pocketful of lollipops. "Chupa-Chup," he kept saying. "Chupa-Chup," until Ramon finally stuck his thumb in front of the kid's mouth and said, "Here's your Chupa-Chup."

"I hate seeing this, the children begging." Ramon dipped his head sadly as we walked away. "Anything else in the world but this. The children have never begged in Cuba. Never!"

Ramon's pain demonstrates the anguish most Cubans feel about this growing problem. The children are the people's one point of pride, and keeping them fed and healthy has always been the first priority in the streets and in legislation. Nearly every speech Castro makes, he gloats a little bit about how well the children have been cared for. Every Cuban I met shared this mentality. Cubans also have a deep respect for animals, often saving up chicken bones for stray cats and dogs. But begging children is a new thing, and it's slowly gnawing away at an already aching pride; evidence that the government isn't providing enough so that parents might hand their own kids lollipops. The children, on the other hand, are also getting the message at a very young age that the world "out there" is better. Not that tourists should stop bringing token gifts; but there should be some responsibility on their part and on the part of the regime. It is unfortunate that the government fails to discuss the broader scope of these new social problems. And even more unfortunate is the idea that the government fosters the people's necessity to live on the good graces of foreigners.

I tried to avoid tourists as much as possible in my travels, but of those I did encounter, the majority came for the Buena Vista lure, the exoticism, the dance, the sensuality. But the problem Cuba faces at this time is a dwindling visitor return rate. Many European package and higher-end tourists grumbled about Cuba's being expensive. The experience didn't live up to their Buena Vista expectations. The deficient state accommodations—many hotel rooms without toilet seats, lack of hot water, poor quality of state-prepared food, car rental shortages, et alia (mostly due to Cuban socialist inefficiencies)—deter many would-be visitors from returning.

Another problem is that the sheen of the Buena Vista Social Club is beginning to lose its luster. There are only so many Buena Vista fans in the world, and Cuba desperately needs a new commercial draw to bring in new waves of fresh tourists. One way of contending with this dilemma has been to build more golf courses in hopes of transforming the island into the Caribbean's golf mecca. These, new theme park development, and culture tourism are the road of the future.

In 2000, about 1.8 million tourists streamed into Cuba. In 2001, Cuba only saw 1.8 million again. The numbers are obviously tapering off for an island that got comfortable with a 19 percent annual increase in tourists throughout the 1990s. To reach the goal of 7.5 million visitors by 2010—a number absolutely necessary to sustain the Cuban economy—the United States tourist market must be tapped. Certainly when the Ministry of Tourism planned on the big goal of 7.5 million, the U.S. market was factored in. Today, with the dwindling tourist numbers, it's apparent that Cuba has now reached that impasse. The situation is almost identical to the same problem Cuba faced in the mid-1970s. And Castro, with extreme debt looming overhead, is desperate to realize it.

The indicators of this desperation are obvious. Since 1999 when Clinton began negotiating with Cuba, Castro has made concession after concession, appealing to U.S. agricultural interests, holding a potential $5 billion a year market under its nose, in hopes of triggering American food conglomerates to pressure Congress. When this failed, in January 2002, Castro invited former president Jimmy Carter to visit the island.

What better way to get the travel ban lifted than invite the president who had lifted it before?

As Carter's motorcade left the José Martí airport and spun off for Havana, one of the first things he must have seen was the big billboard that says "Welcome" in three languages, superimposed over a massive photo of Cubans smiling and waving. When Carter left, he couldn't have missed the other big billboard on the opposite side of Boyeros that says "Come back soon" in the same three languages, superimposed over a photo of yet more smiling Cubans who are waving, giving peace signs, jabbing thumbs-ups toward the Havana skyline, and holding single fingers in the air, as if to say "Cuba, #1." The big joke in Havana right now is that the people on the billboard are gesturing with their hands of what size shoes to bring back. "You see, that guy wears a size five," they say. "And his daughter needs a size two." When you hear this for the first time from a laughing Cuban who doesn't have two centavos to rub together, it gives you a chill. But laughing is the best escape from the growling bellies, and the jokes are many. Once I asked a guy in the street where he got a T-shirt for WDVE, a Pittsburgh radio station. "It was a gift," he said with a laugh. "It was too small for a cousin in the United States. The shoes are from an Italian friend. The pants came from a tourist, and I saved a year to buy the socks. Everything in Cuba is a gift."

A week after Carter's May visit, to stem a possible wave of liberalism concerning Cuba, President Bush gave a stiff televised speech to the Miami exiles, promising to hold the travel ban and embargo intact, even threatening to veto anything that passed Congress. Bush's message was clear: no deals unless Castro and Communism are gone and a people's democracy with general elections was adopted.

A week later, the Cuban government announced a 10 to 30 percent price hike on everything in Cuba, from simple rice to Sony televisions. The hikes affected both the peso and dollar economies. Immediately there was a mad scramble as Cubans cleared the shelves, buying the goods en masse to beat the increases. On the government's part, the price hikes were purposefully orchestrated to get all the dollars that the people were saving up back into circulation. But these kinds of quick-fix mechanisms can only work once or twice to give any economy a boost. They aren't tangible and sustainable solutions to Cuba's continuing economic crisis.

A week after the price hikes, and in reaction to Bush's announcements, Castro held a nationwide poll to add a new permanent article to the Cuban Constitution, making Socialism "untouchable" into perpetuity. The government reported that 99 percent of Cuba's voters (age sixteen and up) cast affirmative ballots. The catch was that the voter was required to write their name and identity number on the ballot. So big brother could track both those who failed to vote and those who voted no. After spending a little time in Cuba, you soon learn that the second most spoken word in the streets is "control." The first are *no es facil,* "It isn't easy." With *control,* the message is, "We're watching. We know that you must commit crimes to survive. We can easily make your life miserable." Naturally, everyone is going to vote yes. For those who waver in Revolutionary faith, historically each time a U.S. administration locks horns with Castro, it foments the Revolutionary fever, and in spite of U.S. policy, the people rally behind Castro as new multitudes of paper flags strike the air.

For the millions that visit Cuba and will continue to visit Cuba each year, Buena Vista was the phenomenon that flung the door wide open, salvaging the island's flagging economy as a tourist lure while bringing the island out of its decades-old isolation. This is no small thing. Buena Vista was the doorway. Yet many fans fail to penetrate the island culture beyond this doorway, much to the joy of the regime, which prefers to obscure certain realities of the Cuban experience as it promotes a stylized commercial version of itself to the outside world.

Yet the short-sightedness of Cuba's central government rolling the dice and banking the entire economic future on tourism could prove deadly. The regime refuses to recognize that Buena Vista and its appeal was largely responsible for the new tourist influx, and without this recognition, other similar draws are unlikely. Rather, brilliant economic planning, a strong administration, wise leadership, are the elements that made Cuban tourism successful. Without alternatives to tourism, without considering the possibility of a world recession or low visitor return rate, the Revolution has created yet another monoculture crop like sugar to which it has now become an economic slave. This at the expense of the people, who have become a serving class to *los extranjeros,* the wealthy foreigners. By refusing to open up free domestic markets and allow Cubans to empower and sustain themselves, the Cuban Revolution is setting itself up for future catastrophe: an island, much like that of pre-Castro Cuba, where the people have nothing to sell but their flesh.

6

Jineterismo: A Dollar Commodity

T here's nothing more refreshing than seeing familiar faces in the streets of Havana after months of being away. They're like grounding beacons in a nebulous sea of thousands of small events. Off the plane, out of the taxi, into the street, and magically they begin to appear. A friendly wave from the counter girl at the state *cafetería* on the corner of Neptuno where they serve exceptional deep-fried *croquetas*. An *"¡Amigo!"* from the gay guy strolling down the other side of Galiano who still wants you to find an American wife for his next door neighbor. A quick high-five with the kids you see each morning at the newsstand, still playing marbles under the trees at the Iglesia del Cristo. A friendly smile from the woman who occasionally pours you shots of peso coffee from her thermos, forever trying to push you into buying one of her sugar-coated *guayaba* jelly pastries. The old dumpster diver with his telling stubble, chin held high, pulling his noisy cart through a back alley as he re-lights his cigar and reveals the treasures he's found today: a lid from a broken tackle box, seven plastic pop bottles, a burlap sack with only one hole. All this in only two hours.

These are your friends. The people you see every day. You talk to them, catch up on their families, let them know how long you'll be around, and then move on. They are many. They are versed in the streets. All of Havana is "the streets," a loose network of acquaintances and allies. And everyone is related whether through distant blood or the black market. It's a phenomenon of epic proportions, and there's a lot of that particular Cuban rhythm at constant play.

Inevitably I would run into my young buddy Juan, a twenty-two-year-old hustler, or *jinetero*. As soon as I stepped into Havana, I would think of him, and somehow we'd soon cross paths. There's no explanation for this. It's just one of those things.

"Mah frenn. Maybe you wanna see Havana," he gave me the line the first time we met during the Elian González debacle. "Maybe you looking for restaurant or girl? Yes, you look like the kind who looking for girl. Maybe I can help you. Yes, we can have one beer and discuss this business."

Some of the *jineteros* are merely beggars, amateurs explaining with grave detail how they desperately need a pint of milk because the baby sister has gone without today, even though the state provides a pint a day for children under seven. There is the possibility that the mother indeed sold the milk in the street for cash, and I've seen mothers do this. But my friends say it's rare. However, the chore of the *jineteros* is to zero in on that weak spot and push those buttons, whether it's a lie or not. After all, a dollar is a dollar, a commission is a commission, and if they can squeeze a beer or a sandwich out of you, it's all in a day's work. With some luck and properly placed persuasion, it might even turn into a weeklong source of entertainment.

For each tourist, the *jinetero* wears a different mask, and for each occasion there's a different routine. There is the "Mah frenn, you wanna buy cigar? Chica? Casa Particular?" routine for solo passersby. For the student types there is the "tour guide" gig. And then there are more detailed sketches for tougher customers: "Hey, don't you remember me from last week? We met at such-and-such disco on such-and-such night." Of course, this meeting never occurred, but this one always stops tourists in their tracks as they scan their memories to place the face. And by that time it's too late. The *jinetero* has his or her hook into them, and from there it's a matter of talent.

My friend Juan is different. He's the kind of guy who can run through the smooth phraseology of one of his routines, which are completely irrelevant, and yet he never misses. In his eyes you see a convincing human sincerity, and in this tool lies the prowess to win over the stodgiest of misers instantly. When I met him the first time, I liked him immediately.

"Look," I said. "I know the score. I don't want *chicas*. I'm not hungry. I have a house. But I'm impressed with your style, and I want to hear your story."

"Yes," he said, a little surprised, his smile revealing a sparkling gold crown on one of his incisors. "Yes, I think we can make this business."

It's always business with these guys. To insinuate it's a hustle would be unthinkable. It would injure the *jineteros*' pride. They are entrepreneurs, skilled guides, influential players of the street who have gone to serious lengths to master their skills. They learn their English through the painstaking study of subtitled Hollywood films. And the gold crown is an important detail. Many *jineteros* have them, and it means they paid $70 cash to have the tooth capped instead of having it pulled free of charge under Castro's socialist healthcare system. In Cuba, gold teeth are status symbols.

To elude the police, the *jineteros* work in groups of two to five, and they switch areas with other groups to stay a step ahead of the law. Although they look like street urchins, they are really part of a sophisticated web of small syndicates. They're true professionals. Juan explained to me on our first meeting that the groups practice their routines together in the evenings, arguing and hashing out the details, which strategies have worked better in the past, which new things to try. During the day they make a game plan and then fan themselves out over several blocks. When a tourist passes, one *jinetero* will try one tactic, and if that fails, after certain predetermined hand signals and whistles, the next *jinetero* down the line will try something else on the same tourist.

"Today we work on Obispo. Tomorrow we will work on Prado. Please, step back here," said Juan, pulling me under a storefront. "The police in this zone have warned me twice already. They know me very well here, and it sucks because it's harder to make my business."

Seeing him talking to me, thinking he'd scored, Juan's three partners, all in their early twenties, suddenly appeared from nowhere and surrounded us. They came for two reasons—first to help Juan chisel off some of my money and second, to make sure he wasn't embezzling any possible profits. Even if they are partners, none of the *jineteros* trust one another with a "client" in private, and they constantly police each other.

After the introductions, and when my intentions were made clear, the masks of the others dissolved and I was able to take a peek from their point of view. Tourist after tourist passed by, pointing, wobbling, snapping pictures, leafing through the guidebooks.

"Mira," said one of the *jineteros*, jerking his head toward a tourist in the street. "Look at this guy. Italiano."

"No," argued another. "Solid white shirt with tan shorts. Clearly French."

"Yes, French," agreed the third. "Italians always wear the striped shirts. Look at the hands, soft and white. Why bother?"

"The French spend nothing," Juan explained. "They are, how you say, *muy raro*. Very rare. But the Italians, they always looking for girls."

"Who are the biggest spenders?" I asked.

"Definitely the *Norteamericanos*," said one of the partners with a laugh. "They spend it like it grows on trees. One dollar to them is nothing."

There are unique differences between hustlers in Cuba and anywhere else in the world. For one, *jineteros* live a higher lifestyle than average Cubans because they trade in dollar commodities. Hustlers everywhere in the world are essentially middlemen who live on inflating the price of the thing sought. In Cuba, Castro's mission from the beginning was to eliminate the middlemen and the petty bourgeoisie, yet the majority of Cubans play middleman on every possible occasion. Indeed, the entire black market system, or *bolsa negra,* without which Cuba would rapidly fall apart, is based solely on the middleman. The *jineteros* are the most glaring example of this. They're the direct link where the *bolsa negra* bleeds over into the tourist sector. But the most important ingredient in Cuba's hustlers is the self-righteousness stemming from decades of living in Castro's bubble of superiority over the rest of the world. While it's a means of survival, the very act of *jineterismo* is one of unfounded pride. The *jineteros* really do see themselves as superior to the tourists, whom they consider a medium to some goal, no matter how petty.

Enrique, Rolando, everyone would always throw out little laughter nuggets such as, "In Cuba, we're all *jineteros.*" You hear these kinds of comments a lot in Cuba. Given the situation, many Cubans would jump at any opportunity to make a few dollars aiding a tourist.

"This is always the case," Enrique told me. "When Cubans meet foreigners, the first thing they think of is money, and then, afterwards, it's possible a friendship will develop. It is the same with women who meet foreign men here. The women want the marriage to escape Cuba. Maybe love will follow, maybe not. The first encounters are never sincere."

He admitted that when he met me, he thought I might provide a sandwich and some good conversation. That he might be able to learn a few new things about the outside world. But a lasting friendship had never occurred to him. Enrique went on:

> Most of the tourists just come around and stick their cameras in our faces. They just want a little memento of Cuba. I remember once this girl came up and asked me if she could take my picture. I don't know why she wanted my photo. I'm just an average Cuban. Look at my home. It's not some beautiful mansion worthy of a photo. But she wanted to have a picture of me standing in my doorway. I couldn't understand it, but I said, "Sure, why not?" We never talked or anything. She just took the picture and left. But it made

her happy, so I didn't mind. At least she asked. I like it when they ask. Sometimes this will lead into a good conversation and I can learn a few things. But normally, the tourists never ask. Many come here just to take.

Enrique and I got into a fairly heavy conversation about this psychological Cuban zoo phenomenon. About why tourists come here. What do they hope to achieve? Are they merely dipping into Cuba to see human oddities stirring in their island-sized third world cage?

These were ideas that Enrique and I talked about a lot, and we arrived at some strong conclusions. First, Cuba and its tourists share a symbiotic take-take relationship. Cubans take from the tourists, the tourists take from the Cubans. When tourists visit Cuba, they like to bring little trinkets and things to give as gifts to the poor helpless Cubans—toothbrushes, deodorant, aspirin—but in the act of giving, they're actually taking, empowering themselves as good Samaritans at the expense of the people they're trying to help. It stems from the worldwide Peace Corps mentality of trying to save everyone else in the world; but the truth is that the economic policies of the tourists' home countries are one of the root causes of third world poverty. Whether it's Cuba or somewhere else is incidental. But the bottom line is that if we keep Cuba poor, then we can always "help" Cuba, and it makes us feel good when we "help." So by helping, we only do more harm while serving our own psychological needs of being the good guy, the master and ruler. Castro, of course, has fed into this symbiotic relationship by pounding the "self-righteous victim" position into the Cuban mentality since the mid-1980s.

"The problem is, not everyone in Cuba thinks in these terms," Enrique told me. "A lot of Cubans, and especially young Cubans, aren't this sharp. They don't think about what the tourist wants or what sacrifice is being made. They just think about what they can get out of them. When they see a tourist, they see a dollar sign and nothing more."

This is not to say that real bonds are never forged between Cubans and foreigners. But the odds are stacked against it. The biggest problem is that Cuba's tourism program caters to package tourists there for a maximum two-week stay. Much to the regime's satisfaction, it's very difficult to build anything but superficial bridges in such a short time. To the Communist government, tourism is a necessary evil, and tourists are no more than dollar signs. Castro said as much in his speeches when tourism was launched. "It's out of necessity," he would say apologetically. "Tourism is a sacrifice we must make. There is no choice."

It's important to try to understand what kind of consequences such an attitude and approach to tourism must have had on Cubans, this fostering of the idea that tourists are merely dollars. If you couple this with the forty years of propaganda that made Cubans think they are superior to the rest of the world, which has been misled down the path of capitalistic ruin, you get this concoction of self-righteousness that results in *jineterismo*, the one thing that Castro is constantly at odds with. But he created his own monster. The last thing tourists want is to be harassed around every corner with offers of cigars and sex. And the last thing Castro wants are low tourist return rates as a consequence of this harassment. Oddly enough, a lot of Cubans are keen to the government's distaste for *jineterismo*, and in many ways, while they publicly despise *jineteros* as scoundrels, many also secretly praise them in the vein of Robin Hood or Bonnie and Clyde, heroes who take from the rich and live on the edge of the law. In Cuba, social deviancy is admired because it challenges the system, and *jineteros* give some Cubans a vicarious outlet for their frustrations.

The *jineteros* keep it light with the tourists. They don't care that this person may have recently had heart surgery, or perhaps has lost a child or been through three divorces. And the tourist never penetrates the *jinetero*'s life beyond the mask. They don't know that perhaps he had to sleep with a man once for some cash; that maybe there are problems at home, that his parents are pressuring him because they want him to be a doctor; that he's forced to steal to survive and feels guilty all the time. All these possibilities are hidden behind that mask. A lot of rich understanding is lost in the notions and the charade of the Cuban zoo, and the mask of the *jinetero* itself is a sign of desperation.

Take Juan, for instance. He lives with his mother and sister in a small second-floor apartment in Central Havana. They are extremely poor, and having no circuit into the dollar system, they live in pesos, they struggle, they get by. Juan's father was one of many that left Cuba during the 1994 Balsero Crisis, when 24,000 Cubans took flight to the United States. Castro had opened the floodgates by saying that any Cuban who wished to leave could do so. Like many of these rafters, Juan's father had left with big promises of returning for his family, but they never heard from him again. I heard the same story from many other single-mom families I met. No money sent, no word, no nothing. Gone forever. In fact, every time I see Juan, the first thing he asks is whether I remembered to stamp and mail the letters he wrote to his father and asked me to deliver.

"I got this address from my aunt in New York," he would say. "Send the letters there." And then on my return, "Did you send those letters to my father? I haven't heard anything from him. I thought maybe you never mailed them."

It always broke my heart to tell Juan that I did mail them, and I quickly scrambled for excuses. "Well, maybe that address you gave me was old. Maybe he's moved. Are you sure you gave me the right zip code?"

A little depressed, Juan would write more letters, giving me other addresses to try, in care of other relatives. Sometimes he'd ask me to scour the Internet to find him. Each time he would write his father's name and address very carefully on a shred of paper, cross-checking everything before handing it to me.

"I know this is correct," he'd say. "If you can find his phone number and tell him to call, this would be good. But make sure you tell him to call Marita's apartment one floor up, and then she'll yell down for me that I have a phone call, because you know we don't have a phone in our apartment. I hope that maybe he'll call or write me this time, because I miss him very much."

This is one of the many lifelines of hope that Juan thinks about each day. In Cuba, even if it is a fantasy, these small hopes get people through.

They are possibilities, and they are gold. Reconnecting with his dad would not only establish a sorely missed emotional need but also give Juan the opportunity to ask for a money wire. Which is probably why the guy never calls. But the determination to contact his lost father is symbolic of Juan's will to survive, even if he is fooling himself.

"Yes, I think this time he will write," Juan would say. "Most certainly this time."

At seventeen, Juan was thrown into the position of the family bread-winner. He dropped out of school, learned English, and began to work tourists as an amateur *jinetero*. It was the only way for his family to obtain dollars, and although his mother wished the circumstances were different, she knew there was no choice. On top of living in the youthful glamour of the *jinetero* streets, behind the scenes, Juan carries the water to the house and takes care of the day-to-day stuff. He's the black market bargainer for larger purchases. He's the one who keeps the family machine well oiled, and each night he puts a few dollars into his mother's palm for food and necessities.

"I never became a *jinetero* for myself. I always did it to provide for them," Juan reminisced one day. "My greatest satisfaction was the first time I bought mami a pair of shoes. Her old shoes were those cheap Chinese ones made of cotton. You could see her toes through the holes in the front. They were very old, and it was my desire to buy her a new pair. It didn't matter how I got them. I would have stole them if I had to. She deserved a thousand pairs of shoes, but if I could give her just one pair, I would be happy. The pair I bought her was leather. Not the handmade Cuban ones, but good ones imported from Europe. She cried when I gave them to her."

Season of the Night

At dusk, the tempo shifts on the dance floor of Havana. The eyes, the body language, the entire city seems to radiate with this strange narcotic luster, this hypnotic ambience. A '54 Chevy wheels around the corner from Prado onto Neptuno, bursting with a knot of tightly packed limbs and faces, horn singing out *"La Cucaracha."* The compact disc dangling from the rearview swings like a metronome over a sun-bleached plastic figurine of *La Virgen de la Caridad,* Cuba's patron saint. Hunched over the wheel, the driver's bare shoulders are twisted permanently forward. *"¡Oye!"* he yells out to an acquaintance in the street. His smooth baritone seems to emanate from the deepest part of his gut. It echoes between the curbs in a prolonged sustain and then fades away as the car rumbles into the distance. And silence.

"¿Puedo sentarme aqui contigo?" she asked when the din cleared. "Can I sit with you? Would you like some company?"

It's always the same. The routine questions followed by the routine, "*Estoy aburrida,* I'm bored," lips pursed with a pout, eyes robed with Havana's nightly drama. I always liked to entertain their passes, edging in as many questions as possible before they'd lose interest and wander off to another table, working the floor.

"*¿Si o no?*" she asked again.

"Sure, why not?" I said as she plopped down in the chair, leaning in with melodramatic interest, quickly firing off the same rehearsed questions, "Where are you from, what is your job, do you have a wife?"

Before long she began rubbing my leg, nibbling at my ear, her pitch smooth, rhythmic. Yet something set her apart from the regular cast of characters. She tried to play the party girl, but behind the veneer burned that unmistakable don't-take-no-shit wisdom of the streets that comes with the territory in Havana. You see this in the eyes of so many Cubans. A piercing shield of caution, of mistrust, of reading the environment and surviving in it. For me, that armor in the eyes was a compass point because I knew it was there to protect the heart. Maria wore that armor, but it softened a little when I told her that I wasn't interested in sex. If I paid her, I asked, would she take me through the routine and give me some honest answers? I wanted to hear about her life.

"We can go to my apartment," she agreed, "to spare you the extra $20 for the *casa particular.* I'll go first, and you walk behind me about ten meters and follow me into the building. Don't worry, it's not a trick. I'll meet you in the stairwell. I hope you understand. I never take men home. My landlady doesn't permit it, and if the neighbors see you they might inform her."

She gave my hand a squeeze and pulled me past a *peatón* cop at the corner, who scoured us up and down. I was more afraid for her than myself because I knew that tourists were never arrested for soliciting prostitutes; but the cop didn't seem to intimidate her in the slightest. Walking ahead, she looked back occasionally to ensure that I was still trailing. Then as she scooted through the final stretch to her home, man after man parked on various stoops in the barrio whistled and howled. From the doorway, she hastily dragged me up the flight of stairs and across the breezeway to her apartment.

Inside, an uncommon sight: All her furnishings were brand new. She had a new Sony color television, a new Panasonic VCR, a new stereo system, and new living room furniture. There was roughly $2,000 worth of goods bought at *La Epoca,* Central Havana's four-story shopping mall, where Cubans with dollars shop. A queen-sized bed sat in the middle of her bedroom, across from an antique wardrobe complete with full-length mirrors. One door was open; inside, the tiny shelves and hangers bent from years of use held her selection of expensive clothes, from skimpy lingerie and evening dresses to five pairs of expensive shoes and black lace leotards. The strap of a bra stuck out from the bottom of the other door. She quickly closed the closet when she noticed me taking an inventory.

"Usually I go to the bathroom and freshen up, but since you're different, I'll try to be more natural. Smell this scent," she said excitedly as she grabbed a tiny bottle of perfume from the vanity and sprayed a drop on her wrist, quickly holding it under my nose. "Isn't it enchanting? I got that from an American. And smell this one." She snatched up a different bottle, sprayed the other wrist. "That came from another American."

"How many men do you sleep with each day?" I asked.

"Are you joking? Never more than one," she said. "Never. The women like that wear themselves out. I prefer to stay fresh."

Like most of Havana's prostitutes, Maria is from another province. As the people suffered under the Special Period, and as the government fell back on tourism, single women from distant parts began traveling in droves to the capital, the destination of about half of Cuba's annual visitors. Most of the migrant prostitutes I met were from Manzanillo, Bayámo, Las Tunas, and other parts of Oriente, the easternmost part of Cuba. Maria, now twenty-four, moved to Havana from Holguín a few years ago. She wanted to score the much-needed funds unavailable at home because her city is on the back-burner in areas earmarked for tourism development. The money was so good in Havana that she ended up staying illegally.

"Holguín is a small town," said Maria, "much more charming than Havana. The people there are very cute and very innocent. And it's quiet. But Havana has the tourists, more culture, there's so much more to do. In comparison, Holguín was boring. Don't get me wrong, I love my family, and when I'm old, I'd like to buy a big house there. But for now, Havana is better for me. In the Special Period, it was such a struggle to live there. You can eat the fruit from the trees and rice is cheaper, but there is no money. I have eight . . . no, nine good friends who have moved to Havana."

"You must be friends with the police near the hotel," I said, "the way we passed that *peatón* on Prado. Do you ever get harassed by them?"

"There is an unspoken rule here in the streets," Maria explained. "As long as we aren't seen with more than one man per day, the police consider them *novios* [boyfriends] and not customers. There is a big difference between how the two are interpreted. If we keep a low profile and we're seen with only one man a day, the police leave us alone. The idea is to go get your man, and then not be seen around again until the next day. If a police inspector noticed them allowing us to work—for example, I'm standing in the same place for twenty minutes and the police ten meters away didn't arrest me—they would lose their jobs. We have to keep moving, not standing in the same spot for so long."

I recalled the time I sat with a Cuban friend in the breezeway of a dimly lit *solar* at 1:00 A.M. An eighteen-year-old prostitute I knew from Guantánamo walked in holding hands with a uniformed cop. They were on their way to a condemned apartment for a quickie. The cop was a regular in this barrio and I'd seen him daily over several weeks. As soon as they walked in, all four of us froze. It was a tense situation, and we all stared at each other in nervous pause. They didn't expect to see anyone in the *solar* this late, and we didn't expect to see a cop escorting a prostitute. You could see the white heat stinging the cop's nerves. Perhaps he thought I was Cuban intelligence. Maybe I would turn him in. Cops in Cuba are shouldered with the highest expectations of integrity and honor; if he were to be seen in uniform holding a prostitute's hand he would receive serious punishment. Fortunately, my friend knew the cop and shot him a wink, as if to say I was okay. He looked relieved as he led the girl into the dark; they stayed there for a half-hour before exiting again, grinning and jubilant.

"I know that prostitute works this barrio," I told my friend, amazed by the corruption I'd just witnessed. "I'm completely shocked by what I just saw."

"No, you're wrong," my friend said, correcting me. "I know that girl, and she likes sex with men in uniform. It's a fetish of hers. I've seen her with that officer before." But I didn't believe him, certain that he was try- ing to sugar-coat the incident. I asked Maria about it. Are bribery and favors common, and do the police abuse their authority and exploit the Cuban prostitutes?

"It's logical," Maria said. "Some police do get a commission from the girls. Sometimes they pay in sex. It is possible the girl you saw may have been forced into having sex. If a *policía* came up and said 'Amor, let's go have some fun,' are you going to say no? After all, you work or live on this block and you must pass him everyday. This is probably the case with this girl. But maybe she does like uniforms as your friend said. Some of us have a thing for men in uniforms."

In Cuba, Maria explained, more often than not, police turn the other cheek and let things slide, giving a patronizing look to show who's boss. A smaller group, she said, are strictly by the book. They're colder, more serious, dedicated Revolutionaries who believe that the long-term goal is more important than Cuba's everyday survival reality.

"But many are plain jerks," she continued. "It's just a matter of hav- ing confrontations with the good ones. Some are very friendly. You see them sometimes walking in the street with their wives and children, in uniform, which is rare. Most of them are caring family men. But even many of the strict police will ignore some things. For us, if we keep a low profile, and if we pay when necessary, we manage to stay out of trouble."

Although frowned upon by the government, prostitution has never officially been declared a crime in Cuba, and only residual crimes associ- ated with the trade, such as pimping and renting a *casa particular* for sex, have been enforced in crackdowns. But, as Maria put it, "they have a mil- lion ways to get you if they want to." Parts of the new penal code, or *Ley* No. 62, issued in 1992, deal solely with officials and employers who induce women into sexual favors, which in itself shows that there was a problem with corruption. But the penal code modification wasn't aimed at eliminating the trade, an essential lure for sex tourists and their dollars. The government's slow and somewhat measured reaction to the current rise in prostitution is partly due to the surprise of its rapid growth and partly because the regime simply hasn't been ready to admit that the marked increase in tourists is making prostitution an issue. Besides initiating the deviancy reconditioning roundups in the 1960s and imposing the small legislative shift in 1993 that limited Cubans' access to dollars, thus creating a surge in prostitution, the government had never been particularly concerned about the sale of sex. The authorities had seen prostitution more as a social disease, but one that wasn't too serious. During the 1990s, prostitution and delinquency suddenly became a rapidly growing problem. Due to the hardships of the Special Period, a flood of young people began plying the sex trade across the island. Life was so difficult that professionals were quitting their state jobs to join the force of the night in the tourist sector, where hard dollars were easily available. All this on top of Havana's housing shortage triggered by the domestic migration exodus, in which thousands of rural Cubans threw down their shovels and left the countryside for the cities and accessible dollars. Prostitution ran rampant during the tourist boom, growing exponentially and taking the regime by surprise. Naturally, the situation didn't jibe with the new siren of national prestige necessary to coax tourists.

In 1997 two laws were passed to deal directly with Cuba's prostitution problem. In April 1997, the first law put an end to the domestic migration issue by limiting Cubans to a month outside their home provinces for each journey. The stroke was two-fold; it kept rural Cubans working the fields and curbed the rampant *jineterismo*. This law, issued when the Havana housing shortage reached crisis levels, is still on the books today.

"In Cuba," Maria told me, "you're allowed to leave your province and go to Havana one month at a time. If the police stop you in the street and your *carné* address is from another province, they ask what you're doing in Havana. Naturally, you're visiting relatives, your aunt is sick, you're here to see a specialist. But if the police suspect you're lying, they hold you until they can reach the president of the CDR in your province, which sometimes takes all night."

The CDRs, the Committees of Revolutionary Defense, are essentially neighborhood watch groups that were formed by Castro in 1961 to become the backbone of Cuban Socialism. Every three hundred citizens are organized into a *barrio,* a neighborhood of the CDR, which is presided over by a volunteer president responsible for keeping tabs on everything that goes on in the lives of his or her three hundred neighbors. The president looks for anything suspicious, right down to the smallest details of what furniture is bought, who attends what marches, where everyone earns his money, and which neighbors are on leave to other parts. Some CDR presidents are tough and create a sensation of suspicion and paranoia throughout a neighborhood; others are relaxed and committed more to the individual care of the people rather than to state security. Neighbors often wake up a good CDR president in the middle of the night to discuss a personal problem. If a CDR president is a tyrant, the neighbors try to hide everything from him or her. Some CDRs run illegal businesses themselves. Others immediately report every illegal activity they see.

If the CDR president is okay, Maria explained, if you're in another province and get carded by the police, he or she will cover for you, saying you just left a couple days ago. But if the president is a stickler, or perhaps frightened, the truth may be told. Everything depends on what the president says. If he tells the police you left just last week, the information is written in a file; when you are carded again, the police have a record of how long you've been in Havana. But if the president of the CDR tells the investigator you've been gone more than a month, that's it, they send you home immediately; you're fined and put on travel suspension. Repeat offenders are sent to work in farms for punishment. In 1997, this legislative stroke worked like acid on the Havana sex industry because most of Havana's prostitutes were from distant provinces. At that time, the law was enforced. Today, because the migration problem has stabilized, the police usually won't even question the address on the *carné* unless there is a crackdown. Maria herself, who is carded occasionally, has been in Havana for three years without problems. I know of one man whose ID address is from Guané, but he's been living in the capital for twelve years.

The second law dealing with the periphery of prostitution came about on August 25 of the same year, when Article 302 of the *Ley* No. 62 was revamped with a new crime covering pimps or operators of brothels. A third party caught inducing a woman into prostitution or profiting from her carnal labors, or anyone operating a brothel, was given four to eight years in prison. There was also the *"confiscación de bienes"* clause, meaning that if a woman rents out her *casa* as a quick-stop motel she could be considered a "madame" and consequently lose her home. Putting the squeeze on homeowners who rent out to prostitutes put a slight damper on the trade, but it wasn't substantial. As with everything in Cuba, where there's a will, there's a way, and for a $10 tip, it's not difficult to coax a porter into sneaking a prostitute into a state-run hotel. Since Cuba's prostitutes are highly independent women, pimps, or *chulos,* have never been a real issue in Cuba, and only trace elements of classic Western pimping exist today. Because of this, Cuba's laws dealing with pimps seem more like a token gesture to give the appearance that the government is dealing with the problem rather than an act to wipe out prostitution wholesale.

But although prostitution is not a crime on the books, prostitutes are made to feel like criminals. Sex is a black market commodity, and prostitutes, like everyone else operating in this underground world, live in paranoia under the regime's omniscient pressure. Maria told me that Cuba's prostitution rehabilitation program is the same for hustlers or any other social deviant. If the police give you a verbal warning and you continue working an area, you will likely be arrested and sent to Cuba's deviancy program after being issued your first *amonestacion,* the citation for delinquency. Also lurking are the *jefes de los sectores,* the government sector bosses, undercover agents, one for every few quads, who watch specifically for delinquency and issue *Actos de Peligrosidad,* danger warnings, essentially red flags that point the police to delinquents. And, of course, the CDRs are cauldrons of gossip. After the third *amonestacion* for delinquency, a prostitute or *jinetero* is put on probation. A social worker is then assigned to help find the offender a job, set a curfew, call the new boss to check on attendance and progress, and pay surprise visits during the night to make sure the offender is at home. This could last six months or a year, depending on the "antisocial" behavior, or failure to abide by the rules. Misfits who can't adjust wind up in the work farm for six months under a plethora of crime codes, which range from the illicit enrichment law (which covers monetary gains through illegal means) to simple vagrancy.

"It happens," said Maria. "Some people cannot conform under the rules of probation. Others are very self-destructive. There is much tolerance for delinquency in Cuba. If you don't make waves, you can earn a living in prostitution without any problems. When they say move, you move and do not ask questions. It's that easy."

The first big crackdown on prostitution occurred in the winter of 1995, followed by another in the summer of 1996, when Castro ordered the national police to cleanse the streets of Havana and the Varadero peninsula. When the government became aware of the disintegration of Cuban society, the rise in prostitution, the petty drug consumption, and the overall increase in delinquency, the majority of dollar nightclubs in Havana were shut down. For two years, Cubans were barred from the few tourist *discotecas* that stayed open. Like busy spiders, the police rid the concrete web of Havana and the Varadero beach resort of prostitution. The official red flag for this initial sweep was the marked rise in STDs such as gonorrhea. But HIV-positive cases were particularly worrying; the number of new cases had more than doubled, from thirty-four in the first four months of 1995 to eighty during the same period of 1996.[1]

Maria, like a dozen other prostitutes I questioned about safe sex, uses condoms religiously. "A lot of the men don't want to use condoms," Maria told me, "but I don't want AIDS. I take every precaution, and I never let clients use their own."

As she talked, Maria showed me a strip of three heavy-duty Lifestyles condoms made in the United States, then broke out a new box hidden under a stack of panties in the wardrobe, a gift from a visiting

client. Condoms, as well as most prescription medicines, are hard to pro-
cure in Cuba. It's easy for prostitutes to purchase the cheap Chinese-
made multicolored models that reportedly break nine times out of ten.
In Cuba, a lot of parents blow them up as toy balloons for their children,
which is really all they're good for. The only place to purchase high-qual-
ity European condoms is in the hotel tourist pharmacies at a dollar a pop,
and they are always sold out.

Using the ripple in HIV cases as the official excuse, the government
initiated the 1995–1996 Havana/Varadero prostitution roundups. Hundreds of prostitutes were arrested in the first of a series of crackdowns
that contended with Cuba's sex-fever image then gaining momentum in
the world. The year 1996 was pivotal in the success of Cuba's tourist
industry, even more so after the United States signed the Helms-Burton
bill, which stiffened economic sanctions against Cuba, into law. It was
the worst possible time to begin losing potential tourists due to scandalous world media, and repressive measures were necessary to polish
Cuba's waning image.

Crackdowns in Cuba work like this: The order goes out, the sweep
comes down, and things stay subdued until the people meander back out
of their shells and learn the new limitations until eventually things return
to normal and get out of hand again. The second big crackdown came a
week before the Pope's January 1998 visit in a pavement-polishing
maneuver for the pontifical entourage—another step to raise national
prestige and sanitize the streets when thousands of the world's cameras
and journalists would be nosing around town. Of course, the official reason held that the Cuban government was taking steps to provide a more
"family-oriented" vacation spot in the Caribbean by stripping away the
deviant chaff from the bountiful harvest of the Revolution.

The latest crackdown occurred on January 5, 1999, the day President
Clinton announced his new measures "to step up contacts with the
Cuban people." In the shorthand language of *el dialogo,* Clinton was say-
ing, "We're ready to talk about normalizing relations." On the same day,
Castro ordered the island-wide sweep during the fortieth anniversary
commemoration address to the National Revolutionary Police (PNR).[2]

Things on the to-do list included destroying the seeds of the growing cottage industry in human trafficking as well as repressing domestic petty drug crimes, *narcotrafico,* and, last but not least, prostitution.

It wasn't pretty. I happened to be on the island during the January 1999 crackdown and it hit Cuba like a steamroller. Each night on television, the regime aired mock confessions of many of the arrested; they were made to repent to the camera so that the nation could see how their acts were counterrevolutionary. It felt like a trip back to the 1970s when these forced confessions were regularly scheduled programming. Just a week before, prostitutes had been dangling on every street corner in Havana like ripe grapes. The symphony of the night was "Psst-Psst," and the orchestra was in top form. After the crackdown, the avenues were desolate, quiet, reigned by fear and paranoia; it was as if the entire population had suddenly been jarred back to the 1994 repressive peak of the Special Period when simply standing on a corner would buy you a night in jail. Along the Malecón, at the corner of Agramónte and Obispo, across from Coppelia Park in Vedado, the white police minivans rolled up. Suspects were loaded, pouty lipped and teary eyed, wave after wave, leather purses, pumps, tight skirts, and off they went to lock-down. It was a tough week for the cops: in workload, in sacrificing what compassion they may have had for familiar faces, and in the quick cut in illicit pay they were making from the trade. Take any red light district police raid from Sunset Strip to New York's Times Square during an election year, multiply it by twenty, and imagine you're on the streets of impoverished Havana. It was surgical, effective, cold, unrealistic, and all about saving Revolutionary face, without any consideration for the destruction it caused for so many families on the island.

"It was crazy!" Maria tells me. "It was really, really bad. I was fortunate; I happened to be in Pinar del Rio with a boyfriend for the week. When we returned, I found out two of my friends had been arrested and were being sent back to their provinces. We were all so scared. You never knew if the knock on the door was the one, or if you'd be grabbed from the street. It was a very difficult time."

The main issue for prostitutes is that being self-employed, they and their families become dependent on a steady, and higher, income. When the crackdowns occur, suddenly they find themselves without a food source, forced back into instant poverty, or what Castro would consider "equality."

"No, I couldn't make any business," Maria continued. "It's hard to come up with $10 a day for rent when you can't work. It took a lot of effort to convince *la dueña* of my apartment to give me credit. She lives with her sister on San Lazaro. But she knows I'm good for it, and she likes the money. The funniest part was that she didn't hear from me for a few days, and she was afraid I'd been arrested. She was so scared. She was sure that in the interrogation I had pointed her out and that they were coming to confiscate her apartment. But I can understand her reasoning because it's happened to people I know."

Contradictions on top of contradictions. Within a year, prostitution was back in full swing. So the question becomes, if Castro rallies so hard against prostitution on television and in public forums, why is there more tolerance today? To contend with prostitution, or at least to maintain its current levels, the government is doing what it can up to a certain point. In an odd way, while prostitution is considered antisocial behavior, at the same time it is really a Revolutionary act because it brings in tourist money, and without money the island would crumble.

On another score, Cuba tends to be more expensive for travelers than most people expect, and many inevitably run out of cash. I have one Cuban friend in Havana who makes a few dollars on commission now and then by going to Western Union and withdrawing wires in his name for Americans who have traveled illegally to Cuba. These travelers don't want anyone to know they've visited Cuba for fear of fines upon their return to the United States. They ask my friend to receive the money for them, paying him $10 for a $300 wire. One day he said to me, "Benjamin, I think I have to stop getting wires for the Americans because I'll be interrogated. I've signed for more than $2,000 in the last two months. I'm very worried."

"But what you're doing is Revolutionary," I said. "Your government likes it when Americans come down here and disobey their own laws. Plus you're helping to bring in more dollars for them to spend. You're government profits from this. You're helping them to buy another hotel. You are helping to win Cuba its independence. You're a Revolutionary hero."

In a very real sense, the prostitutes should be considered heroes, not criminals, because they're a major attraction for the package tourist, Cuba's target consumer. The government could easily get tough with prostitutes and put the brakes on its carnal vehicle; but in the process, Cuba would lose perhaps a fifth of its annual visitors.

Even though Maria is a third-class citizen in a Revolutionary sense, she's a first-class citizen economically for being self-employed as a prostitute. Her earnings far exceed those of average Cubans. Younger girls now entering adolescence are getting the message that believing in the Revolutionary program is a dead-end street when you can make a small fortune in delinquency and sex. In Cuba, $30 or $40 is a small fortune. Most work three months to bring this in. Economics are the sole foundation of every individual Cuban's life. For the majority, the entire day, everyday, is spent thinking about the next meal.

"There is so much competition now," said Maria. "Even in the high tourist season it's difficult to pay the rent, plus send money to my mother, plus buy the things I need."

About *la lucha*, Castro's struggle for the future victory?

"That is a good question," said Maria, "I think Castro is a crazy old man. I think what he has accomplished is great, but I am not waiting around for the victory to live the good life. I like nice things, good clothes, good food, not the dog food they sell at the *bodega* or the cheap clothes on the street."

The media tends to focus on Cuba's professionals-turned-prostitutes—doctors and teachers who can't feed their families on their monthly earnings and quit their jobs or moonlight in the sex trades. While this is very real, it's not the whole picture. The majority of Cuban prostitutes that I met were neither professionals nor employed, and most had been taught simple trades in typical two-year high school programs.

"I studied bookkeeping," Maria explained. "I wanted to get into the *universitario* and study languages, but my grades weren't high enough, so I took what was for me the next best thing. There were lots of jobs for bookkeepers, but my best friend who left for Havana a month before told me how easy it was there to make $20 a day. It would have taken me three months to make that in bookkeeping. What would you do?"

"Will Castro ever improve the conditions?" I had to ask. "In the future, will women be able to make enough money at their jobs that they won't need to work in prostitution?"

"What future? There is no future here," she laughed. "Look, we've been here in my apartment for more than an hour. We really have to leave because the neighbors will talk. I'm going to make you a deal. Usually I can earn $40 in the time we talked. That's my rate. But if you give me $20 and buy me supper, we can continue. I'll do this special work just for you."

After she had thrown on some less fashionable garb, off we trudged through the marsh of Havana to an open-air restaurant in Chinatown five blocks away. It was peak season, and the table bands were in full swing, strumming romantic ballads and doing Buena Vista Social Club renditions of Cuba's classical love songs. The magicians betraying gravity with cheap card and cigarette tricks. Teenage kids drawing caricatures for tips. The guys with cameras taking portraits of exotic *amantes* seated in the dense red hues of one of the capital's finest tourist traps. And then the small groups of prostitutes, grabbing arms of passing single men like octopi feathering out their tentacles for lonely fish strayed from the school.

"Tell me about those girls," I pointed. "What's their story?"

"They're just little girls, *putas*," she said. "Bitches. They're not really professionals. The girls in my zone are in a different league. These ones are cheap. I don't know them, but you could have any of them for $20. Aha, look. She likes you!" Maria laughed, pushing my knee as the girl made kisses at me. "In my area, we give extra special work. We're very experienced. There are two kinds of prostitutes in Cuba, the kind with real style, and girls like these, who are just children, really. You see? Look how they make faces at the men like beggars. They're barely out of secondary school. Look how they giggle. They think it's all a big game. They're very innocent and I feel bad for them. But we all started out there."

Man after man passes by the young women, who look about eighteen or nineteen years old; their antennae are perked for wealthy foreigners, Polo tees, khaki shorts, slick Hawaiian print rayon unhitched at the sternum, Rayban sunglasses perched above receding hairlines, chaotic and contrasting for eyes accustomed to the drab. Rings, shiny hair, new crows feet grabbing at the corners of the eyes, personas dripping with cash. The girls make a game of it to avoid the sheer boredom of the Cuban nonfuture reality. This illusion of the moment is the only thing they can lay claim to, and they lay claim with a passion. But Chinatown, like Obispo, like La Rampa, like Plaza de Armas, is the tourist trap, the big mirage. The place where Compay Segundo's "Chan Chan" plays on the ears in a perpetual commercial wind. It is Cuba, the new Cuba, but not the real Cuba. It's the charade, the surface, and the girls are swimming in it because they've been thrown into it. Maria is more mature and self-aware. She understands the dynamics between Cuban reality and the big fantasy, and she has no illusions. She represents the thousand-faced prostitute that's been roaming the island of Cuba for four hundred years, first across the dirt paths of the Spanish colony, later across the cobblestone streets of the American neocolony, and today across the crumbling sidewalks, incidentally, of Castro's paradise.

8

The Cuban Survival Kit

C ubans never leave home without the standard issue survival kit: a
plastic grocery bag, the *jaba vinyl,* and a page or two torn from the
daily edition of *Granma,* an inexpensive alternative to toilet tissue. I
always carried mine wrinkled up in the hip pocket. There's nothing
worse than stumbling upon mangos, *guayabas,* or heads of cabbage
slashed for clearance at 2.5 pesos and hobbling across Havana with a
dozen cradled in your arms. Dollar-store cashiers and managers filch the
plastic bags by the boxful, later selling them in the black market at five
for a peso. In the countryside they're more valuable at three for a peso
and there's a higher demand because there are few dollar stores; when
habaneros, people from Havana, visit family in the country, they buy up
the bags in the city and take hundreds along to resell at a hefty profit. If
you're careful, a plastic bag can last you a month. The rule is this: If it's
sold in dollars, you get a plastic bag. If it's sold in pesos, you bring your
own. This is Cuba.

Everyone brings his own to the *Bodega La Sombrilla,* The Umbrella
Stock house, a typical Cuban ration store like the rest strung tip-to-tip

through Cuba's side alleys and rural roads from Maisí in the far east, 725 miles to La Bajada in the west. The average *bodega* serves between 1,400 and 2,000 Cubans for their basic monthly foodstuffs, and whether employed or unemployed, every Cuban has the right to receive the rations. How you pay for them is your own problem.

Bodega La Sombrilla is tucked into the corner of Galiano and Animas in Central Havana. Full-length plate glass windows smudged with children's fingerprints wrap the storefront, the panes smoked yellow from years of idling curbside motorists. Out front, two or three *bicitaxis* station themselves strategically on standby, waiting to pedal elders weighed down with their plastic bags full of rations for a one-peso fare. The July heat is just under stifling, one of those afternoons when the streets are teeming with activity. Everyone buzzing out and about, *Carnavál* in the air, the city engaged in that yearly social foreplay for the upcoming month-long ritual of rum and fiestas.

Inside the *bodega* stands a *cola* of ten souls, ten elbows leaning dreamily on the cracked Formica like the hundreds of thousands before them. The place is nearly empty of food, as it has been since 1991. Evaporated milk cartons stand in sad pyramids on time-worn simple shelves. Cigarettes here, cans of baby food there, aluminum tubes of bland state-issue toothpaste stacked in orderly rows. And it is odd, almost pathetic, to see so much space that was full during the Soviet occupation when times were good and the economy was at its peak.

Each customer has his or her plastic bags in one hand, with the four-by-six-inch baby-blue *libreta,* the Cuban ration booklet, loosely palmed in the other. Some of the *libretas* are worn around the edges, wrinkled and flimsy, but most are protected with clear plastic dust jackets, hand-sewn in some backroom by a self-employed artisan, the *libreta* dust jacket maker, who sells them on the street for three pesos apiece. Shoppers decorate their covers by adding the custom touches of a family photo, a picture of roses clipped from a dated color catalog from Spain or Italy, perhaps a shard of brightly colored wrapping paper from some long-past birthday party. Memories. Today, flower prints are in vogue. The Cuban *libreta* is the base symbol of Cuban Socialist power; it is also the hearth of the home, much like the checkbook log in most Western countries. The regime prides itself on the *libreta*, on this unequivocal right guaranteed to every person in the constitution of 1976 and three dozen affiliated laws passed by the Cuban National Assembly of People's Power. Every Cuban household has a *libreta*. Even Castro. Which has been the subject of many jokes.

On the front flap of the *libreta* is a little square box that's either stamped or blank. Those who are employed by the state have the stamp, which gives them preference in line. If you have the stamp, you can just shove your way to the front with a *"con permiso."* It is a way to ostracize the unemployed, to make them feel like social outcasts because they don't hold a state job and therefore aren't doing their part to advance the People's Revolution. After decades of being hammered with propaganda about social duty, social obligations, social responsibility, the shame associated with unemployment is deeply embedded in every Cuban's consciousness, and the *libreta* stamp is one of those small reminders. But except for an occasional Communist, few use the stamp trick. These 2,000 people are all neighbors in *la zona*, after all. They see each other everyday, and they don't play by the system's rules, which would have them rob the unemployed of their dignity. It is a means of resistance.

"Seis libras de arroz," calls out next in line, a feeble old woman.

"Seis arroz," repeats Luci, the *bodega* clerk.

"Seis," the woman nods.

Everyone knows Luci. Everyone knows everyone. It's like family. The barrio. *La zona.* The regulars. Luci's been at this *bodega* for one year, but her experience at rationing spans twenty-seven. She beams with a sort of resigned joy as she works. Tomorrow is her fifty-ninth birthday, she explains, but she doesn't look a day over forty-five. Dipping the cast-iron scoop into the rice bin, she mentally weighs out the six pounds; quickly and routinely she swings the works to the scale and shakes off a few kernels with a keen eye until the needle settles. All this in a matter of seconds. She ties the shopper's plastic bag at the top and plops it onto the counter. Meanwhile, the customer asks Roberto, the *bodega's* administrator, for two bars of laundry soap and a tube of toothpaste. Roberto obliges, skirting around Luci, who is now working on the customer's bean order. He grabs the shiny generic aluminum tube of toothpaste, straightens out the dents with a pat of the hands, and tosses it onto the counter; next he leans over for the pink-and-white marble bars of laundry soap that look like blocks of condensed hamburger, soon to be used with the cast-iron washboard in the backroom sink of the home—traditionally the woman's domain in Cuba.

The damages are tallied, 3 pesos, 30 centavos ($.17). The money is pulled with precision from the old woman's ragged coin purse. The brass plating of the tiny clasps is worn down, revealing the chrome underneath. To her, the sum is a small fortune, and her coin purse is a shrine. She's a senior citizen, and receives between 75 and 130 pesos a month in social security, or $43 to $72 annually. She is on the bottom strata of the officially nonexistent Cuban class structure. Her fingers rub and recount the change twice, eyes and mind calculating in a single reflex as Luci initials the sale in her *libreta*. The old woman grabs up her bags with a smile and walks into the sun, where the *bicitaxis* will pounce on her for a fare. Next. Next. Next. The *cola* slowly continues. Within fifteen minutes, the ten people who have been waiting are served and replaced by ten new familiar faces, continuing the daylong stream of leaning arms, plastic bags, and *libretas*.

At *Bodega La Sombrilla*, two people are standing in for wealthier families on commission. One, a woman with her hair bundled in tight cornrows, begins arguing with Luci. She wants an 8 oz. ration of *fideos*, soup noodles, rarely in stock, but the quad in her client's *libreta* for *fideos* has already been initialed for the month. They argue heatedly over this 8 oz. of noodles until Luci calls over Roberto, who scans the *libreta* and says, "This family's portion has already been issued." The woman shakes her head and storms out.

"Before the Special Period we had everything to ration," says Roberto. "Butter, rum, beer. We used to have a deep refrigerator full of stuff." He points to the empty wall where it used to sit. Through the cheap, opaque brown paint that was slapped on to cover the walls since then, the words "beer" and "rum" bleed through.

"We even had soft drinks," Luci throws in, "and margarine. At the *carnería* there was always chicken, 3 pesos a pound. You didn't need a *libreta* then to buy meat. Pork was only 6.5 pesos a pound. At the *bodega*, we had macaroni, spaghetti, a pound of butter per month."

"What about beef?" I ask.

"No, beef has always been controlled," she says. "But there was more of it." Beef is a rare luxury today. Canned beef is rationed at 8 oz. every six months per person.

"How often do you work each day?" I ask Luci, busy filling another order.

"Eight hours a day, everyday minus Sunday."

"And what's your salary?"

"One hundred forty-eight pesos," she says. "That's, what? $7.50 in your country?"

Which comes out to $90 a year. This is the typical Cuban salary for a forty-eight-hour workweek. If a Cuban buys every state-rationed item in the *libreta*, without special needs, the total sum in a month amounts to 23.45 pesos, or $1.20. A family of four earning 300 pesos monthly will pay out about 110 pesos a month, or roughly one third of their income, leaving around 190 pesos, or $9.50 a month for other necessities. Other necessities are fresh produce and meats, bought at the farmers' markets and food stands, which are peso commodities. A pound of chicken costs $1.25, a head of cabbage is $.10, plantains are 2 pesos apiece, extra rice is 3.5 pesos a pound, an apple costs 10 pesos, eggs are 2 pesos, a loaf of fresh bread costs 10 pesos. At minimum, the average Cuban family can spend no less than $5 of the leftover money for fresh produce, leaving around $4.50. Cubans must also pay for their utilities, in pesos; bus fares for a family of four cost perhaps $2 a month. With the balance of $2.50, Cubans must also purchase their regular necessities such as shampoo, toothbrushes, clothes, shoes, tampons, razors, diapers, dish detergent, condoms, deodorant, vitamins, pencils and paper for the children—what have you—all dollar commodities. The prices of basic dollar goods in Cuba match those of all first nations. For instance, generic shampoo in Cuba costs $2 a bottle. After a bottle of shampoo and an apple (which won't be bought, but as an example), there is nothing left. If the bicycle tire goes flat, if the house water pump—which costs $50 to replace—goes out, if an important letter needs to be mailed, if a special cream for some skin problem needs to be purchased, the Cubans simply walk, fetch their water in buckets, forget about the letter, and let the skin problem go unheeded. This is the mixed legacy of the Special Period, the U.S. embargo, and the flawed economic policies of the Castro regime.

9

The Cuban Diet: Hotels Over Rice and a Pinch of Control

In a Central Havana apartment, two women sit across from each other at an antique table with a small piece of cardboard tucked under one leg to prevent its wobbling. They are mother and daughter, seventy-four and fifty-six, and they are absorbed in the task at hand. A well-kept square of cheesecloth is spread out between them. And in the center of the cloth is a five-pound heap of sun-dried *chícharos,* peas, that will be roasted, ground, and blended with the coffee tomorrow. Since lights are never burned in the daytime, the room is dim. Both women are engulfed in their work, hands laboring through the peas, fingers spreading them out, sorting and sifting the good from the bad, eyes like pinpoints poring over the spoils. They don't talk. They concentrate on the chore.

Beside them sits a deep saucepan, the handles long gone, and into this pot goes the good *chícharos,* while the chaff gets pushed to the side of the linen. In the waste pile are the peas that have numerous lunar holes eaten into them by tiny black weevils, the *gorgojos,* a few of which are scrambling around the small mountain. The grandmother picks one out as it hobbles across the cloth and rubs its life away without a thought, as she continues to sift through the pile with her other hand, eyes meticulously searching for more waste. The daughter picks out another stray *judía blanca,* a navy bean, used for a Spanish *fabada* stew, which was carelessly mixed in during the drying process. She moves it to the waste pile while censoring the *chícharos* she sweeps into the saucepan with her right hand. Business as usual, the work continues for two hours. Tomorrow the coffee beans will be cleansed, and the next day, rice. But today it's the *chícharos.*

"*Buenos,*" I poke my nose through the grate of the door. "*Donde está Armando?*"

"He's getting water," Carmen tells me. "*Pasa. Pasa.*"

I walk in, exchange the *besitos,* the little kisses, sit down at the table, and help sort peas. Armando and Carmen have been in Havana for ten years, and Armando's mother, Vilma, is here on extended leave from the home province. Vilma's husband divorced her for a younger woman in Bayamo a few years back, and since neither Vilma nor her husband had money to move, they built a wall right through the middle of the house and out onto the porch, fifty-fifty. She lives on one side alone, he with his new wife on the other. Angry about being dumped after forty years of marriage, she packed her suitcase one day and took a bus to visit her son in Havana for a while.

I would stop by whenever I was in their barrio on San Lazaro in Central Havana. They always insisted that I stay for supper, and I would decline because I didn't want to eat what little they had. But they took it the wrong way, thinking I considered their food below standard, or that they couldn't cook, so I started eating there. I would bring along a few groceries to defray the extra expense, maybe some ham and a bottle of mustard to eat with the gritty *bodega* bread, or perhaps a stick of butter— real luxuries. On this morning I brought a one-pound bag of powdered milk, which at the dollar store costs $3, equivalent to ten days' state salary, enough milk to last three days. As soon as Armando walked through the door, without even putting down the two buckets of water, he said, "Where did you buy this? How much did you pay?" And when I told him, he replied, "You're crazy! I can buy that same pound of powdered milk on the street for only twenty pesos, and you pay sixty! You'll never learn, will you? What I could do with that extra forty pesos!"

He would always lay into me for wasting even a few pesos. Had it been him, he would have waited until some powdered milk came around in the black market, whether tomorrow, the next day, or next week. But using powdered milk would be excessive living for Armando and Carmen, and rarely having the 20 pesos to buy a pound, they would have simply gone without.

Preparing the milk and coffee, Carmen poured and strained, added sugar, poured again, and finally filled various cups with the steaming blend. I, too, had gone without milk in my coffee for well over a month. Raising our glasses to our lips, we all looked at each other, and as that warm mixture trickled down, our eyes sighed "Ahhhhhh."

"It's really a medicine," said Armando, taking another slow sip. "People need little things like this. Without these small luxuries now and then, the human spirit begins to atrophy and die. If only the government would give us some powdered milk for our coffee, we would all be content."

Before the Special Period, Cubans had always enjoyed *café con leche* for breakfast. They drank the little shots of stiffer, sweeter Cuban espresso throughout the day when socializing. But when the economy tanked in 1991, the monthly ration of condensed milk was one of the first items scratched from the Cuban diet.

"Historically, we've all hated the *libreta*," said Armando. "It's a form of control, of dependency."

"But why do you think they want to control the people like this?" I asked.

"Think about it this way. The average Cuban salary is about one hundred and eighty pesos per month. As you know, it's impossible to live on this wage, so all Cubans must spend all of their time in the *cola*, waiting for the bargains. This is how they prevent us from organizing."

"With the *libreta*," he went on, pulling out his two-year-old 1999 *libreta*, which he had saved, "we're only given a half pound of vegetable oil every other month. Look, here's February, a half pound each. Here's March. Nothing. Here's April, a half pound. May. Nothing."

His fingers flipped fluidly through the pages of the *libreta* as his eyes immediately focused on the target numbers.

"Look here, October, a half pound. November. Nothing. Aha!" he said, "Look here. December. Nothing! Three months in a row without oil! They blame the U.S. and tell all the people that the U.S. embargo is the reason there is no money. But look at all the new hotels being built. A lot of the money going into those hotels is Cuban money. But some months there is no oil. Other months there are no beans. It's always something, and there's never any explanation. The *bodega* administrator only says '*No hay*,' there is none."

At the sea point on the Malecón, just off the coast, freighters pull into the harbor all day. When the steamers are from Argentina, it means cheap food. When they drift in from the east, it's French grain or European merchandise for the hotels. When they're from Panama, it's dollar commodity merchandise from Asia, such as new televisions, stereo systems, and perfumes that will soon be doubled in price by the regime and sold in dollar stores to the few Cubans who have money.

About a hundred yards to the west of the point, small crowds of children dry themselves in the northerly sea breeze. They clamber up the crumbling steps from "the people's beach," where hundreds of poor Cubans wade everyday to cool off from the sweltering Caribbean heat. They call it "the people's beach" because the only people who swim there are those who don't have the 40 pesos for a round-trip taxi ride to the golden sands of Playa Santa Maria across the bay. Sure, there are cheap buses that go to Santa Maria, twenty kilometers away. But by bus, it would take four hours to get to and from downtown Havana, and nobody wants to spend four hours sweating rivers in a *camello* just to go swimming. At Playa Santa Maria across the harbor, where Cubans with dollars swim, there are colorful beach balls. The water is crystal blue and clear. There are boom boxes playing loud salsa. The teenagers dance. The sand is speckled with Miami Dolphin and Florida Marlin beach towels, family gifts from Cuban exiles now living in the United States. The foot police patrol the beach for thieves. The children laugh as they splash in the waves. Their parents drink good beer and soda bought at the state-run dollar concessions stand.

At the people's beach, there is no sand, only the sharp edges of coral, and sneakers must be worn to prevent cuts. Garbage lays about. Empty rum bottles. Fish scales. Scattered trash, which floats in with the waves. Coconuts and storm debris. Sometimes you'll see squids thrown onto the coral by a wave; the creatures quickly slink off to the nearest puddle where they wait for the tide or a storm and a path home. The water is murky and polluted with city sewage and spilled oil from the freighters. There are no beach balls. No Florida Marlins beach towels. No boom boxes. No nearby state-run concessions stand that sells beer and cola for a dollar a can. But the children, they laugh and splash and play just like their wealthy friends over at Santa Maria because it's a lot of fun. And they're too young to know the difference between the value of the peso and the dollar, or the difference between water that's polluted and water that's clean.

The classism only took a short nap between 1963 and 1993. And in the classism simmers the frustration because some have means and most don't. If a Cuban says, "I spent the day at Playa Santa Maria with my family," it is implied that they have dollars. Most get their dollars in *remesas,* or dollar remittances sent from Cuban exiles living in the United States. In 1995, the entire economic base of the island shifted to tourism, which earned the island just under $1 billion of the gross national product. It was the first time that tourist income surpassed sugar in GNP. Since only 20 percent of gross tourism dollars are actual profit, this translates into $200 million net profit for Cuba that year, which was immediately dumped back into more tourism development by the regime. Ironically, in that same year, the *remesas* amounted to $300 million, making dollars sent from "the enemy" one of Cuba's staple sources of income. Ten percent of Cubans receive some sort of family remittances from abroad, which places them in the higher class of the dollar economy.[1] By legalizing the dollar for Cuban possession in

1993, the government, in its weakest hour, was searching for any means to gain the island hard currency, even if it came from the very same exiled Cubans it considered *gusanos,* or maggots. This hard cash is obtained by inflating luxury items such as stereos and television sets in Cuba's dollar stores by over 100 percent. A nineteen-inch diagonal television that costs $150 in first nations costs $380 in Cuba. A bookshelf stereo system that costs $150 elsewhere is inflated to $350. A point-and-shoot camera costing $100 is valued at $300 in Cuba. Everything sold in dollars is merely doubled and tripled in price, and there is no competition and no state regulations on fairness in pricing.

No Cubans I met divide the peso economy into classes. Either you have dollars or you don't. Because the Cuban government likes to place emphasis on its peso salaries, it boasts that heart surgeons make the most at a monthly 575, while the highest officials and ministers earn 400 a month. Today, however, the peso system and the regime's incentives are meaningless because the dollar economy is thoroughly entrenched not only into the economy but into the Cuban consciousness. As a result, people of Armando's class are forced to look outside the state constructs for solutions.

"The people started losing faith in Castro in the late 1970s," said Armando. "It was an epoch very similar to the Special Period. There were shortages in everything, and Castro believed that we could harvest our way out of the situation with *la zafra.* When this failed, everyone believed he was incapable of running the economy."

Cuba's economic history can be broken down into four discernible sweeping changes that disrupted society on four occasions. The first change was the Revolutionary war victory, followed by the 1960–1961 Agrarian Reform which nationalized the majority of foreign holdings, a move that essentially isolated and alienated Cuba from the rest of the world.

The second sweeping change occurred in 1968. Every sector of the Cuban economy was centralized, which eradicated every form of free enterprise. Beginning this year, Castro started to enmesh the Cuban economy with that of the Soviet Union, joined the CMEA (Council for Mutual Economic Assistance), and let the Russian economists come in and show the government how to administrate the Revolution. It was Castro's biggest failure. Work absenteeism soared, production went into steep decline, and the people felt they were only being re-colonized by the Soviets.

Around 1975, when Cuba began to rethink its dependency on USSR subsidies, it searched for ways to sustain its own economy. The new plan was to transform Cuba into a Japan-like service island that exported goods and technology. Tourism was brought into the picture as a means of gaining the island hard currency. In 1977, Cuba went into another head-spin as the economy was slowly decentralized and sectors, such as the farmers' markets, were opened to free enterprise. In a broad sense, it could be said that the "Revolution" ended in 1959 and "Socialism" ended in 1977.

The next sweeping change began with the 1986 Rectification, when Castro decided to cleanse Cuba's bureaucracy and once again limit free enterprise. He felt the program had deviated too far from his vision of Cuban Socialism. The people were exploiting all the loopholes in the self-employment laws, and the Communist Party had deteriorated into a petty bureaucracy that thrived on favoritism and inefficiency.

Plainly visible patterns emerge as one observes Castro's reforms. When the economy bottoms out, he decentralizes, loosens the leash on the people, allows them to engage in free enterprise; the renewed activity, in turn, stimulates the economy. But once the economy is reinvigorated, he tightens the leash, recentralizes power, and creates new restrictions for the people. The 1980s were Cuba's best years under Castro. Because sugar was fetching an all-time high of $.25 per pound on the world market, Cuba was able to import greater volumes of subsidized Soviet crude and re-export it for even more profit.

To invigorate the economy even more, Cuba passed the 1986 Foreign Investment Act, which, in hopes of raising hard currency on the newly developed tourist sector, allowed international companies to enter into joint ventures with the island. Ironically, the first foreign investment came from a Spanish company that built a hotel at Varadero in 1988. Compared to the 1970s, things were shaping up. The Cuban peso rang in at 4–5 to the dollar, and the government was able to provide abundant food for the people.

The most catastrophic of Cuba's sweeping changes was, of course, the collapse of the Soviet Union and its domino effect on Cuba's economy. The shortages in Soviet shipments of oil, food, and materials began in 1989, but the government waited until 1991 to hold an emergency congress and declare the island's bankruptcy. Cuba's slow reaction to the Soviet collapse made the impact that much more devastating.

The magic year for Cuba was 1993, when Castro threw open the doors to a limited domestic free market. Before this time, U.S. dollars were called *"fulas"* because they were outlawed for Cuban possession. If a Cuban was caught with even one, he was sentenced to four years in prison. In 1993, the dollar was legalized and over 150 trades were opened for Cuban participation, mostly in peso enterprises, but some in the dollar exchange, such as the *casa particular* the Ibáñezes run. Due to the reluctance of foreign investors to commit capital in fifty-fifty partnerships with Cuba, the regime passed Foreign Investment Law 77, which opened the island for 100 percent capital ventures.

During the Special Period, Cuba dealt with its tanked economy by printing money until inflation devalued the peso to a low of between 135 and 175 to the dollar in 1994. In 2002, it stands at around 20 to the dollar, which is still less than 75 percent of its 1988 value. In 1988, the average income for Cubans was 180 pesos per month.[2] In 2002, it's around 250. Although this pay increase sounds healthy, in reality, Cubans in this bracket are consuming only a quarter of what they were before the Special Period.

"My portion of rice is six pounds per month," Armando said, showing me the rice page in his *libreta.* "I eat a lot of rice. About a half pound per day. After twelve days, my rice ration is gone. At the *cooperativa,* rice sells for three and a half pesos a pound. So I must come up with, I don't know . . . forty more pesos a month, just for my rice. They also ration me five ounces of coffee per month, which is gone in a less than a week. I must come up with twenty more pesos to buy a pound to last me the rest of the month."

The typical salary for most entry-level occupations is 148 pesos. The lowest salary on the island is 100 pesos for the street sweepers who clean tourist areas. Before the tourist boom, the regime liked to pride itself on paying Cuban doctors more than anyone else, and it held all other salaries lower than those of heart surgeons. Today, the highest paid state employees are the police officers patrolling the tourist area of Old Havana, who earn 800 pesos a month; the rest of the police force takes home 500 pesos. Retired elders on social security pensions bring in 75 ($3.75) if they live with family, and 130 ($6.50) if they live alone. However, if retirees have never worked for the state during Castro's tenure, they receive nothing. One of my best friend's mothers, a woman of eighty-five, worked in a U.S.-owned cigar factory for thirty years before Castro came to power. After the 1959 victory, her husband committed suicide and, out of circumstance, she was forced to raise her three children alone. Today she is unable to work, but the thirty years she put in before Castro doesn't count towards her pension. She lives alone, and her children are forced to support her. Despite its boasts that none go without, the government's inability to provide an adequate pension for the elderly has created a great strain on families and neighbors who can barely sustain themselves; yet, out of honor and familial responsibility, they take care of their own. It's another example of Cuba's parallel Socialism, which operates separately from Castro's Socialist Revolution, and it is indeed the very foundation on which the regime wobbles as it spends the island's capitalist income on building more hotels for the future economic victory.

When I asked Armando's son to recount his best memory of the Special Period, he laughed and said, "Every night on television they had a cooking program. You know, where a chef shows you how to prepare certain dishes. Imagine this, a cooking program during the Special Period! Well, one night, the program for the evening was how to prepare a rice dish using minced banana peels to add flavor. It was hilarious. But the best part was, there was no rice anywhere to buy. None. Even more hilarious was that half of Havana couldn't even watch the cooking program because they had no electricity."

"What about in the black market?" I asked. "Couldn't you get rice in the black market? I mean, there must have been some."

"Yes, there was some," said Armando, "but it cost fifty pesos a pound. Nobody had fifty pesos for a pound of rice."

"You couldn't even buy a bar of soap," added his son.

This was during 1992, they explained. The same year the Cuban government decided to invest $8 million to revamp the Varadero golf course. A bar of soap was a luxury, yet there was $8 million available to build a paradise golf course for tourists, priced in dollars without a peso equivalent for Cubans. I had spent some time at Varadero researching Cuba's new golf explosion, and the administrators, all Communists, boasted to me, "This course was built with one-hundred percent Cuban capital."

"*¡Que capitalismo!*" was Armando's response when I showed him the brochures. "What capitalism! I had no idea that this existed in Cuba."

Armando, like other Cubans I shared the brochures with, had never seen pictures of the golf resort. They had never even heard of it. None of them had been to Varadero in ten, and some twenty years, since it had been converted to a tourist vacation spot, a party they aren't invited to. Some just nodded their heads with a grunt of disgust when they saw the brochures. But in them all, you could see hunger, desire, want. Just watching the injured expression in their eyes revealed volumes in milliseconds, and the most obvious expression said, "I can't believe we have this in Cuba, I haven't eaten because of it, I've sacrificed the last ten years for it, and I'm not even allowed to use it if I wanted to."

"For a family of three," said Armando, "we need one pound of cooking oil each per month. In the dollar stores it costs two dollars and fifty cents a pound. For a pound in the street, we have to pay two dollars in *divisa*. Where are we supposed to get this money?"

10

La Bolsa Negra:
Stepping Into Cuba's Black Market

The blood of the Cuban life force is the nectar of mango. Sure, there are the pink Cuban *guayabas* that come to season in fall. There is the fluffy white pulp of the *guanabana*. There is *limón* and *naranja*, but these are all secondary fruits. The juice that pulsates through the Cuban heart is pure mango. And Cuban mangos have a distinctly different flavor from, say, the mangos of Venezuela or Colombia. Cuban mangos have a unique sweetness. When ripe, they seem juicier. The pits have more hair. The aftertaste is a little less pronounced. Without its mangos, Cuba would not be Cuba. No doubt, many Florida exiles must return after years of eating Costa Rican imports, and with that first bite of a genuine Cuban mango, must say, "Ahhhh. . . . I'm home." As any Cuban knows, the taste of a Cuban mango, and especially after going without it for a while, is an emotional experience. Eating a Cuban mango is like biting into the very roots of the island. It's like biting into Beny Moré's spine-tingling *"¡Como!"* which he chants with gusto before his songs. Eating a Cuban mango is like prayer.

Armando is a juice maker. He knows the finer implications of the Cuban mango. Unlike South Americans, Cubans never eat the mango skin. The fruit is always peeled, whether with a knife in the kitchen, or, if knocked from a tree by the wind and there's no knife handy, then with the teeth. When Armando peels a mango, he peels with such precision that the fruit itself remains perfectly untouched by the blade. When demonstrating to me the perfect peel, he would scold me when I carved even a tiny sliver of fruit away with the skin. "You have to be a Cuban to know how to peel the mango," he would say. "But maybe with enough practice you'll figure it out."

Armando never understood why I took such interest in his juice making, but he was glad of my curiosity, and it was always fascinating to watch him work. Every time I went to his house, there he'd be, slicing and straining mango, blending it with sugar, bottling it, careful to spill none, before stacking batches in his refrigerator. Armando's juice is the best in Havana, and I would always remind him of this as I paid him the two pesos for a twelve-ounce bottle.

"A lot of juice makers don't use enough sugar," he would say when I asked him his secret. "Others cheat by using too much water."

Armando's livelihood, like that of all Cubans, revolves around the *bolsa negra*. And like a lot of Cubans, he sells his wares discreetly and illegally, without state permission, which makes him an outlaw. There is a state license for selling juice, but Armando refuses to apply for it because, as he puts it, "If I got the license, it would be impossible to make a living."

This is a dilemma that all private business owners face in Cuba. The system works like this: If a Cuban wants to operate a small private enterprise in Cuba, he or she must apply to the state for a special license that costs between 1,000 and 1,500 pesos a month, depending on the market. First there is an inspection to see that the place of business, normally the home, meets the cleanliness codes set by the Ministry of Public Health. Then, after jumping through a bunch of other hoops and opening shop, forever onward there are periodic, random inspections to make sure that the business owner stays up to standard. Every receipt must be saved and logged for the inspector to prove that every item used in the business was purchased from state stores and not in the black market. If the business place falls below standard (which is solely and arbitrarily judged at the discrimination of the inspector), or if the operator fails to produce one receipt for any ingredient used in the business, the operator is written up and fined. If the operator can't afford to pay the fine, or if cited too often by the inspector, the business is forced to close. If this occurs, it is the operator's right under the Cuban Constitution to retain a lawyer and challenge the decision of the inspector in the courts. But most simply go back to work for the state because they are now living without a source of income to pay the 200-peso retainer for the lawyer, let alone living expenses. Some, after the heat clears, open up again and run their businesses illegally, outside the law, risking 1,500-peso fines and eventual loss of their homes on Cuba's three strikes system.

"I used to run a restaurant out of my home," Armando explained. "We made chicken and rice, pizza, pork sandwiches, everything. The whole family helped out. They never gave us inspections, and we were doing well. Then one day the state decided it was going to open its own sandwich stand just two doors down. Suddenly they were inspecting us everyday. Once they fined us because Carmen was cooking with her wedding ring on. Any tiny thing they found, even an ant walking across the floor, they would fine us. They inspected us right out of business."

"But couldn't you pay off the inspector?" I asked.

"Certain ones," he said, slapping his hands together as if wiping them clean. "I used to keep 20 pesos in my pocket that I could slip to the inspector. I'd pay, and there were no problems. But after the government decided to open its own sandwich stand, the bribes no longer worked. They didn't want us competing with them. They wanted us out. That's how they do it. They put you out of business, and then you're forced to work for their restaurant making the state wage of 200 pesos a month, right next door."

In Cuba, the state inspectors are public enemy number one. Every Cuban with a private business, either in pesos or dollars, is at their mercy, and they're hated and feared by most for their arbitrary power. Those who have illegal businesses are equally afraid, because an inspector could stumble across their operations by accident. The only ones who don't fear the inspectors are the Communists, unless they are also running some illegal operation. But the business owners and the inspectors are very clever, and the result is a big game of hide-and-seek. I've seen so many Cubans turn ghost-white when they hear that fatal rap at the door, many often not answering the knock because it was two raps rather than the specified three designated for family and friends. When there is a peep-hole, a Cuban might tiptoe over, lean his cheek on the door, and slowly edge the eye up to the scope from the side, then quickly retreat for fear the dreaded inspector will see the shadow. The occupants of an apartment building will quickly phone all the neighbors when an inspector or some other representative of big brother comes calling.

The Ibáñezes, like every *casa particular* owner, have a state-issued guest book. On each page are several quadrangles, and in each quadrangle the guest's name, passport number, and number of nights stayed must be recorded in a specific manner. The *casa* owners must visit the local immigration office everyday with the book and have the log of each guest stamped with an official seal. The immigration office then records each guest into a computer, and this is how the authorities track foreigners who prefer to use the *casa particular* system. The Ibáñezes rented two rooms, one legally, for the books, and the other illegally, which I used and they never recorded. I preferred this, since I didn't like the idea of the government's tracking my movements around the island. I would always offer the *casa* owners the option of not recording me in the ledger, and most would agree, only because they knew I understood Cuba and would do the right things if an inspector did show up. My cover was simple; I was a boyfriend of a daughter, a friend visiting the family, or my luggage was there because the *casa* owner had agreed to hold onto it for me because there wasn't enough room at the friend's house where I was staying. The *casa* owners loved me for giving them the option because it was money made that they didn't have to report and pay taxes on.

One evening, a French couple showed up to rent a room. The next morning, Rolando broke out the guest book to record their information and collect their money. As they signed the ledger, they explained that they were in Cuba because the music of the Buena Vista Social Club had lured them. They had been taking salsa lessons in Paris and now they wanted to dance the Cuban music on the island. Rolando, of course, wanted to show off his homemade red wine to the French tourists, people known to understand wine, so he poured everyone a *trago* and sat back to watch the French reaction. As they sipped, I could tell by the look in their eyes they were appalled by the vulgarity of the wine and its vinegary aftertaste, but at the same time were enamored by the Ibáñezes' Cuban charm.

In the excitement of the moment, Martina spilled a few drops of wine on the open guest book. The room instantly filled with tension. Even the French couple looked alarmed as they prepared to leave. They looked at me intently, thinking they'd done something wrong or acted inappropriately. And as soon as the door closed behind them, Rolando tore into Martina.

"How could you do this!?" he scolded her. "I have to go to immigration right now with the book."

"I know, I know," said Martina, running out to the kitchen to get a damp cloth. She sat down at the table and began daubing the three or four small wine droplets, which were already soaking into the page, with hectic urgency.

"Is it really that big of a deal?" I asked.

"You have no idea," said Martina. "If there is even one thing wrong with the way the book is filled out. If it looks like maybe we tried to erase something. Any little spot on the paper, they'll fine us and send an inspector."

That these two were frantic over a few drops of wine demonstrates the degree of fear under which Cubans live. What was at stake? An inspection for sure, possibly revealing that they rent out their extra room illegally, which could translate into a $1,000 fine, and even seizure of the home. This would be a complete catastrophe. What else? The

Ibáñezes, through the carelessness of these few drops of wine, could invite danger to the rest of the apartment building's inhabitants. They all operate in the black market in any number of petty crimes, from selling illegal beef to illegally taking in overflow guests when the Ibáñezes' *casa* is full. Not only this, but the Ibáñezes themselves are committing other crimes. For instance, it's impossible to run a *casa particular* in Cuba without a phone, so they paid a telephone company worker $200 to run an illegal line to their house. Since a phone line is useless without a phone number, and since there are too few numbers to go around, this worker then gave $100 of the money to someone at the main switchboard to set it up so that the Ibáñezes could permanently use the same number as their daughter, who lives across town. Now when someone calls, if it rings twice followed by silence, it's for the daughter. If it rings three times or more, it's for the Ibáñezes. Should an inspection occur because of those few drops of red wine, it's possible that the illegal phone would be discovered, which would result in another fine; in turn, the phone company workers who set it up would be discovered and sent to prison for stealing from the state. The apartment building might then also be targeted as a nest of deviants. Surely everyone would be inspected.

This is the Cuban black market reality. It is a web without proportion, and the entire population operates in it to different degrees, from the homeless man on the street, right up to highest officials of the Communist government. When most people hear the words "black market," they instantly think of guns, cocaine, caviar. But in Cuba, everything is the black market. It's not a matter of choice for Cubans, it's a matter of survival. If the Cuban government ever decided to crack down on every crime on the books, the entire Cuban population would serve prison time. As one friend put it to me, "In Cuba, everything is illegal. Everybody is committing one crime or another to survive. Not all the laws are enforced, but if the state wants to get you for something. If you ever talk badly about Castro too loudly in public. If you ever start thinking that you're better than them, it's just a matter of finding out which crime you're committing."

For Armando, his crime is selling juice without a license. Coffee is also a controlled substance in Cuba. Armando buys green coffee to roast and sell in the black market to supplement his juice income. The only coffee Cubans can legally buy is the ounce-and-a-half monthly ration in the *bodega*. When that's gone, usually after a few days, Cubans who have dollars can legally purchase coffee that is commercially packaged for the tourists or export. But so few Cubans have dollars that they're forced into the black market to buy from sellers who, like Armando, are willing to take the risk. The simple rule is this: If a commodity is valuable in dollars for tourist demand or export, it is tightly controlled. Average Cubans enjoy the benefits of these commodities and their labors in producing them only after they trickle through the decisive hand of the government. Armando, by purchasing and roasting coffee in the black market, is tapping into the government's profits. Even though it's only a couple of pounds of coffee a week, it is considered theft from the state. To the authorities, Armando is a parasite, a social disease.

I would always tease Armando about cutting his coffee with roasted peas. The state-rationed coffee at the *bodega* is cut with peas because the state wants to sell the pure coffee for dollars to tourists. It's another example of giving tourists Grade A goods while the Cubans get the cheap watered-down coffee, cut with peas to produce more bulk.

"Uh huh," I would say to Armando. "I see you're using about fifty percent peas these days. If only your customers knew you were cheating them so badly."

"No," Armando would strike back. "The state's coffee is fifty percent peas. My coffee is not like that garbage in the *bodegas*. My coffee is eighty percent pure. Never would I make a coffee with fifty percent peas!"

The interesting thing about these exchanges was the pride that Armando had in his business. That the watered-down juice sold at government food stands and the coffee sold in the government *bodegas* is cut for bulk doesn't escape Cubans, who prefer to buy higher-quality goods, like Armando's, in the black market. Armando prides himself on his ability to outdo the government in quality. But if he operated his business legally, with all the proper licenses, he, too, would have to produce low-quality goods similar to those of the state to keep his business alive. The state-run services are always low-grade, mainly because the workers are being paid 200 pesos a month whether they put care into the product or not.

"When I had my restaurant," Armando explained, "my pizzas were the best around. Everyone came to me for my pizzas. We always had a big line, all day. After we closed, a friend of mine bought a pizza at the new government food stand, and he found a maggot wiggling around in the crust. *A living maggot.* You would never find that in my pizzas. The people that work for the state just don't care."

One day Armando took me across town to meet his brother, Francisco, and watch a home video of the family. Armando's brother didn't have a VCR, but the neighbor a floor down did. They'd worked out a system whereby a cable was run outside the balcony to the upstairs apartment and into Armando's brother's new television, a nice nineteen-inch diagonal RCA. When I asked the brother why he kept the remote control wrapped inside a plastic baggie, he explained that he didn't want it to get marked up and the numbers and letters worn off from handling.

"I want it to retain its value. I saved two years to buy this television. *¡Ya, ya, ya!*" he yelled downstairs to the neighbor. "Start the movie already!"

Immediately the screen coughed to life, and Francisco left for the kitchen, returning with a broom handle from which hung twenty strings of *chorizo*, raw Cuban sausages. I followed him up to the roof where he kept his smoker, a fifty-five-gallon drum that once held industrial chemicals. After placing the broom handle full of sausage across the drum, he split some wood into kindling and started a small fire at the bottom of the barrel with some used motor oil. A large piece of corrugated scrap sheet metal towered above the barrel to prevent the wind from disturbing the smoking process. After the flames had ignited and the small fire was burning thoroughly, he covered the vent that had been chiseled on the bottom and placed a damp T-shirt across the mouth of the barrel to douse the flames and keep the smoke churning inside.

"In two hours, we'll have sausage," he said.

Francisco was doing well with his illegal *chorizo* business. Everyone in the barrio came to him for sausage and ham. The customers would stand down on the street three floors below and yell up, "Hey Daysi! Hey Francisco! Is there ham? Is there sausage?" Soon Daysi would lower a small plastic Easter basket tied to a string from the balcony with a "How much?" The customer would yell up the quantity. Daysi would then yell the amount to Francisco in the kitchen and he'd put it together. The basket would be raised hand-over-hand to the balcony, the pesos removed, and the ham or sausage, now nicely wrapped in newspaper, would be lowered to the street.

Armando's brother was a good connection for me. He isn't as pessimistic as most Cubans, and when he does complain about life in Cuba, he's not really complaining. He voices his frustrations with a half-cocked chuckle behind his words and eyes as if he understands that everything in Cuba is impermanent and he's completely comfortable with that. Plus he has a new television, a young wife and stepson, and he makes a comfortable living with his illegal sausage and ham business. And if I learned one thing from this small family, it's that Cubans are normal, regular people who face the normal things in life and have the same concerns that working-class people have all over the world. If you sat down and talked to these people face-to-face, all that "trading with the enemy" nonsense, all that cold war propaganda, all that Buena Vista romanticism, forty years of notions would be washed away in the space of two short hours.

The impressive thing about Daysi and Francisco was their commonsense, no-nonsense approach to everything. If something breaks, you simply fix it. You have these circumstances, this is what is available, there's no point in whining about it. Do what you have to do. This is Cuba, we're here to stay. Life could be better, but it isn't, oh well. Let's enjoy what we do have instead of dwelling on what we don't.

Later in the evening, we all converged in the living room, about ten of us. There was the American journalist, the family, and some neighbors from the building. Those who weren't familiar with me trusted Francisco enough to know that I wouldn't get them into trouble, and his outspokenness helped to loosen them up in my presence. It was one of those gatherings where virtually every aspect of Cuban life was discussed, from the economy to tourism, from life in other countries to Havana's poor housing conditions.

"Before I made sausages, I had a partner in another business," said Francisco. "We used to sell produce in the open market. On the third Sunday of every month, any farmer who had surplus food left over after the state sale was allowed to bring it to Havana and sell it directly to people in the street. However, the farmers didn't have the time to bring it to Havana themselves, so they were permitted to have a third-party agent sell it for them."

Francisco explained that he and two partners bought a big truck and drove it out to Oriente, where they bought surplus food from the farmers, then drove back to Havana. They earned as much as 1,500 pesos in three days' work, an enormous sum of money. Before the agriculture fair was legalized in Cuba, the state was the sole buyer of fresh produce and, with no outlet to sell surplus, farmers were forced to throw away their excess. The fairs were opened in the late 1970s along with other reforms when Castro began decentralizing Cuba. Then, during the Rectification, Castro again eliminated middlemen such as Francisco and his partners.

"I'll never forget that day," he said, with that same chuckle behind his eyes,

May 17, 1987. It was called *"Plan Maceta."* If there were more than three people in a business, it was considered an *empresa,* an enterprise, and they revoked your license. If you had two cars in your business, they confiscated them both. Castro didn't want anyone to make more than the doctors. Luckily, I had a friend in the Ministry of Agriculture who called and told me a week before what they were going to do, so my partners and I were able to sell the truck before they had a chance to confiscate it. Then I went into business making *chorizos.* I got the license and sold at the farmers' markets, but it was impossible to make a profit. So now I have a front man in the farmers' market who sells for me illegally. It's the only way, and we're both happy with the arrangement.

As Francisco spoke, the rest of the people in the room were paying close attention to my expressions as I took notes; when I looked up, they'd be smiling, punctuating Francisco's words with affirming nods. I sensed that this opportunity to share their frustrations with me satisfied them. I was someone who was sincerely interested in what they had to say, who wanted to understand their issues from their point of view. It wasn't that they thought anything would change by telling me their problems; but in a country where the means for venting is limited, it was rare to find someone who would actually listen and relay their daily reality to the outside world.

If the United States has its lawyer jokes, Cuba has its doctor jokes. During that evening, I asked around the room what everyone thought of Cuba's Socialist health care.

"One time I had an ear infection," a woman in the room said. "I went to the polyclinic to get it checked out, and you know what they told me? Come back in two weeks. So I went back two weeks later, and they said the doctor was out and to come back a week later. When I went back, I finally got to see the doctor, and he wrote me a prescription for an antibiotic, told me to drink lots of water and get plenty of rest. Then I went to every pharmacy, and none had this antibiotic. I waited three weeks to see this doctor, and they did nothing for me. I could have died in that three weeks."

"What about all these doctors Cuba is supposed to have?" I asked.

"Yes, yes, we in Cuba have one doctor for every two hundred inhabitants," someone said. "If you lift up a rug, thirty doctors pop out. You lift up your shoe, twenty more spring up. But as soon as you need one, you can never find them."

"They're all in Honduras and Africa and Haiti on internationalist missions," added a neighbor. "You see it every night on the news, where more and more doctors are sent to other countries who are having crises.

Every time a hurricane devastates Honduras, they send fifty over, acting like its done out of generosity."

"But you know that the state receives payment for sending these doctors over," someone added. "It's all for prestige. They send the best doctors out of the country for dollars and leave the worst ones for us."

"Another time," said Francisco, "a friend of mine went to see the doctor about a foot infection and it was the same thing, 'Come back in a week.' When she returned, this is what the doctor wrote on the prescription slip: 'Go talk to your *bruja* and have her say a prayer.' That was the prescription: 'Go talk to your *bruja* and have her say a prayer.' Can you believe it?"

If it's not a life-threatening illness, most Cubans don't even bother going to the doctor because it's a waste of time. On at least a dozen occasions when I entered tourist pharmacies to buy vitamins, I was asked by Cubans standing around outside with a handful of dollars to go in and purchase medicine for them. Special creams for blood circulation, anti-anxiety tablets, and once even heart medicine, because at the peso pharmacies it's always *"No hay,"* and even Cubans who have dollars aren't permitted to enter the international pharmacies.

"But anything you want is available in the black market if you have dollars," said Francisco. "Medicines, identity cards, beef. Everything is available."

"So explain the black market to me," I said. "How does something like rice make it into the street?"

"First," said Armando, "the rice is shipped in from China to the harbor. From there it is taken to provincial warehouses, and from the provincial warehouses it is distributed to the *bodegas*. Along the way, everyone steals a little bit."

"But isn't everything accounted for?" I asked.

"Sure," added Francisco. "Here's how it works. A truck pulls into the provincial warehouse to take two tons of rice in burlap sacks to the *bodega*. After the truck leaves, it stops somewhere along the road and drops off three hundred pounds of rice, which was thrown on the truck after weighing out. Later, this extra three hundred pounds is divided up between everyone involved. Maybe fifty pounds are given to the warehouse administrator for cheating the sheets, fifty are given to the weight man, perhaps fifty to the manager of the *bodega,* another fifty to the truck driver, on and on and on."

"Everyone is involved," one of the neighbors confirmed, slowly shaking her head, "from the cashier right up to the officials. In Cuba, everyone steals from the state. Even the state steals from itself."

"But of course no one steals in Cuba," someone added with a caustic laugh. "This isn't really happening. Not in Cuba. Here we are the victorious Cuban Revolutionaries waving our flags and fighting for justice. Haven't you seen us on television?"

Earlier in the day, when I would accompany Francisco up to the rooftop every half hour to learn the process of making *chorizos,* I asked him where he got the wood he used in the smoker, and he led me over to the edge of the roof.

"Look around," he said. "All of those open spots are where buildings once stood."

We peered over one side of the roof to an empty *parqueo* below. From another side, we scanned the cityscape of dozens of vacant lots from block to block all the way down Monte Avenue.

"With as many buildings that collapse in Havana," he said, "I never have a problem finding wood. It's important to use cedar. There's plenty of antique cedar furniture and bookshelves, and sometimes I can even get my hands on hickory. I don't go out myself to rummage through the collapsed buildings for wood, but I know several people who make a living doing this, and I pay them a good price to bring me specific kinds of wood."

"It looks as though your building is fairly strong," I said.

"Look again," he said as he touched a loose brick at the edge of his rooftop with the tip of his sneaker, sending it sailing down to the empty lot below. "Look again."

11

Paradise Crumbling

"*¡Derrumbe! ¡Derrumbe!*" The words spill out from the crowd in heightened whispers. "Collapse! Collapse!" The voice is dramatic. One of concern, despair. A thousand passersby huddle at the scene of the tragedy. "*Derrumbe. Derrumbe.*" Spoking outward from the scene, the chant works its way through the barrios, ear to mouth, mouth to ear, a muddy river of gossip slowly saturating the farthest reaches of the Centro municipality.

"*¡Derrumbe! ¡Derrumbe!*" North and south on Belascoain it meanders. To the far end of Avenida Carlos III. Down the hill to the bottom of Reina and up the other side. Another olive-drab ambulance pulls up to the scene as the police clear a hole in the crowd. The fire brigade and the volunteers heave rubble in lung-huffing pants. "*Uno, dos, tres, ¡Ya!*" another piece of wall is pitched onto the mountain of mortar, another plume of dust. Still nothing. Sweat pours, handkerchiefs mop brows, hearts race.

Walking back to Central Havana from the José Martí library, I heard the sirens and saw the speck of commotion at the other end of Avenida

Carlos III. In Cuba, the little daily accidents provide the much-needed fuel for *chismorreo,* the gossip at the heart of the know. It's the word-of-mouth circuit, the citizen band a *la Cubana,* an essential part of the street life. The slightest scrape of fenders, a minor bar brawl, a broken bus jamming up traffic, and fifty people gather around to see the stir. There follow careful calculations and big debates over whose fault it was, who ran the stop sign, who slandered whom to deserve the first blow. Havana is a cauldron of activity, but the stew is seldom fresh, and Cubans thrill over any hot new information to fire away at the dinner table. But when a building collapses, things are different. The mention is serious, uttered with gravity, talked about for years.

Shouldering my way through the crowd, I managed to squeeze to the front of the cordon. The building was four stories tall, about 50 feet deep and 120 feet in length, now a pile of cinders, dust, machines, and scrambling bodies. Foremen yelled orders, police whistles pierced the air, passing drivers rubber-necked and jammed the intersection. Avenida Carlos III, a four-lane street, had been barricaded, the mob pushed back to the grass divider. The entire two westbound lanes had been covered in rubble. When I arrived, the front-end loaders had already cleared the big stuff from the street and towed the crushed cars to a side alley. The city likes to sweep these things up and get past them as quickly as possible. The work is accomplished with speed and precision. The citizens' militia brigades have had much practice.

The group of now-homeless families and neighbors who lived in the building stood paralyzed under a nearby tree as the volunteers dug through the broken concrete and splintered wood in their search for the injured and dead. There were tears, faces covered with hands, sadness. These people, who already had next to nothing now lost the rest in the fate of erosion, the sun, the elements, when that last little bit of sand which had held those two essential bricks together finally blew away and the whole world came crumbling down.

I twisted the big 300mm lens on my camera and began snapping photos. After about five frames, I felt a tug at my arm.

"*Hombre,*" said Enrique. "Man, are you crazy? Put the camera away. If the police see you taking pictures of this they'll arrest you."

"Are you serious?" I asked.

"Yes, it's forbidden to take photos of these catastrophes. You must be careful," he said. "They'll think you want to make negative propaganda about Cuba in the foreign press."

"How many were killed here?" I asked.

"A young woman was killed. Twenty-two years old. That's her family over there under the tree. Seven people were injured, and two cars were crushed. You can see how far the debris scattered. It happens all the time. One minute you're standing next to a building, the next minute, Pum! Dust in the street. Last week, one collapsed over there on the next block. Three people died. And over there," he pointed to a vacant lot, "that one was last year. A big one. Fifteen people died."

"One collapsed across the street from my building," an old woman standing nearby added, her eyes simmering with concern. "It was four months ago. Fortunately no one was killed."

After we had talked about various *derrumbes* with the old woman, Enrique asked whether I'd like to see a few more recent collapses. We walked through the next block on Reina, where he pointed out three, explaining the peculiarities of each one, the number of injuries and fatalities, which cousins of certain friends had lived there or had relatives who were killed. One of the vacant lots had been converted into a government dollar food stand where people could buy soft drinks, beer, and candy. The other two were simply wrapped in corrugated sheet-metal with the words "*Peligro, Derrumbe,*" danger, collapse, splashed on all sides. You see these sheet-metal barriers everywhere in Havana; often a corner has been clandestinely bent back in the night for pedestrians to use as public bathrooms and garbage dumps. Kids like to employ them as improvised baseball fields, and adolescents as sanctuaries for midnight romance.

"Take a look around," said Enrique. "All of the parking lots you see everywhere in Havana are sites of *derrumbes*. The buildings collapse, the families are moved to the suburbs in Habana del Este and Guanabacoa, and now when they drive to work, they must pay a peso to park their bicycles and cars at the empty lot where their homes used to be. Havana is slowly becoming one big *parqueo.*"

In a study of building conditions in Havana, the City's Assembly of People's Power reported in 1995 that of the capital's 557,179 buildings housing 2.2 million people, some 52 percent were in good shape, 25 percent were marginal, and the remaining 23 percent were in bad condition. Bad meaning on the brink of collapse.[1] But there's no doubt, just by the appearance of things, that a little shake, say five on the Richter scale, would bring 75 percent of Havana down in seconds flat.

"When the hurricanes and heavy rains come," Enrique laughed, "those of us who live in the poorest buildings spend a lot of time praying. The saints receive little extras on those days."

During heavy rainfalls, I've sat with Cubans in buildings that should have been condemned long before. The air is always thick with this subconscious fear of impending danger. There is never much conversation during the storms. Everyone introverts into a jittery mute sigh. Talking about these fears falls in with that panoply of Cuban taboos that you simply don't toy with. These are sensitive subjects. The silence seems to say, "Why conjure up things that we're nervous about and trying not to remember?" As if the mere mention of the thing could invite disaster. But always there are those little reminders. The hunk of plaster that droops a little more each time it rains. The water leaking through the light fixture. The four buckets that must be placed in the bathroom under key drips. That 23rd percentile living in time-bombs for homes. And when the *derrumbes* occur like the big one at Carlos III, on a sunny day, all that suppressed fear suddenly rushes to the surface, the denial is shattered, and people start thinking hard about the condition of their own homes.

This is one of the myriad collective Cuban denials. Which are not bad things. Every culture and society has its own, usually adhered to more out of necessity and instinct than neglect. The Cuban government fosters these denials by sheltering the people and creating a buffer zone through its selective reporting. If Havana is the living room of the nation, the regime prays to its own saint, Vladimir Lenin, and introverts into that same jittery mute sigh during hurricanes. The Cuban national press, from fear of creating panic and showing signs of weakness, never reports on the *derrumbe* death and injury tolls, just as it never reports on victims of violence and capital crimes. There are never headlines about a murder, although I can rattle off a half dozen that I know occurred. "Of course not," a friend explained. "In Cuba there are no murders." The details are too specific. It's a big game of pretend. But the government is honest with the populace by way of statistics, which are always inclusive. When there's an ulterior motive, in the news you'll hear "We have this problem" or "We need to work on this a little harder" or "This many arrests have occurred for this crime last year, so let's work together and try to improve this or that." Instead of biting coverage, it's the moral spin, the press as social catalyst. But when there's no underlying agenda, it goes something like this, as it did in a December 2000 edition of *Juventud Rebelde:* "The provincial Civil Defense counted more than 200 dwellings with roofs partially or totally collapsed and another 1,000 inundated. Also, thirty *caballerías* [1,000 acres] of tobacco and six [200 acres] of potato were destroyed, and almost 2 million tomato seedlings were lost."

This, a clip after the Christmas weekend in which eight inches of rain fell in four days on the capital. The cloudburst had that sullen effect of hollowing out everyone's holiday spirit. It hadn't been raining much in Pinar del Rio, but on Christmas Eve, chugging back to Havana along the *autopista,* Cuba's cross-country interstate, I could see the storm hovering and gnashing its menacing teeth over the city. On the approach, my driver rubbed the dash of his '56 Pontiac and with a smile said, "It's a good thing we have a Pontiac and not a Lada. You can't drive them through two inches of water and they stall." No matter that the windshield wipers didn't work. That his faithful Pontiac could plow through a severe Caribbean storm like a Mack truck gave him complete and unshakable satisfaction. Pulling from the ramp onto Boyeros, the drops began slamming down like 10-centavo coins.

The government could rename the capital "Lake Havana" during storms like this. But the real miracle is how Cubans manage to drive so skillfully in zero visibility without windshield wipers, half of which don't work. In car after car, the wife handles the rag, wiping the steam from the windows when it gets too hard to see, while the husband leans within inches from the windshield, squinting for distance. One of those hilarious survival peculiarities in the Cuban jungle of circumstance.

I had the driver drop me at Enrique's, where I stayed for the next few days, occasionally hopping over to other friends' homes when the rain subsided long enough to escape. His sister Teresa was in for the holidays from Matanzas, an hour east of Havana, and we all spent a lot of time loafing in the chilly breezeway of his *solar*, his tenement, staring out the front window at the interminable rain. Bicyclists getting drenched. Pedestrians rushing around with plastic bags over their heads. Cars sloshing through the gutter ponds, stalling out. Occasionally a wave of water would splash onto a jumble of loose wires hanging from an archaic street lamp and create a powerful and explosive arc of electricity. The city was miserable. Cubans are sun people and the grayer it gets, the further the mood swings.

Finally, the day after Christmas, the rain stopped. I ran out and grabbed the morning paper, which had the stats for the *derrumbes*. There was no mention of the storm's two fatalities. If you want to know what's really going on in Cuba, the Cuban press is the last place to turn, and a well-placed call to the United States informed me of the deaths. However, of those who lived in the 1,200 buildings suffering total or partial collapses in Havana, *Granma* reported that 391 people who had been evacuated were returned home, while another 392 were sent to *alburgues*, the shelters.

In Cuba there are a dozen varieties of shelters for the victims of collapsed buildings. Some are emergency shelters such as schools and gymnasiums for short-term sanctuary. When the damage is a complete loss, the people are moved into the standard *alburgues*, semipermanent settlements where victims live communally until a house or apartment is located. When a Cuban dies or migrates to another country, the home is

repossessed by the government and redistributed to a family on the waiting list for a permanent residence. Often, though, many people stay with
friends and relatives while they wait for a living space to open up.

"But they end up staying forever," Enrique's sister Teresa explained.
"No one wants to stay at the government *albergues*, because they tell you
you'll be there a year, and ten years later, you're still there."

"Twenty years," Enrique threw in. "Twenty years. I've seen it.
There's one in Guanabacoa, Habana del Este, there's one on Boyeros
that I know of, another in Alamár. They're everywhere. The Harris
Brothers store in Old Havana was once an *albergue*, but the foreign company made an investment and they converted it into a dollar mall."

"Suburbs" is a foul word in Cuba. It's where the poorest dwell, but
living in the Havana metro, even penniless in a building barely holding
together, is considered a higher lifestyle of grandeur and access. The
albergues, in every sense of the word, are Cuba's third-world cousin to
North American projects. Essentially multifamily barracks, most have
bunk-beds and community showers, although some have private bathrooms and kitchens, but they all have one thing in common: Once you
get in them, there's no getting out.

I liked to tease Enrique, who lives in one of the marginal-to-bad ten-
ements, about his new dream home in Habana del Este.

"Enrique," I would say. "With this big tourist boom, soon Castro will
move all you *habaneros* out to the suburbs and the foreign population will
slowly replace the Cubans. They'll doze all of these old buildings, and
someday there will be a big hotel where you now live. And then Uncle
Sam will lift the travel ban and Havana will be all *yanquis*."

"That's a good one," he said. "Spoken like a true capitalist, but probably you don't know how much this is already happening. For example,
that dollar restaurant at Monte and Someruelos; that was once a *derrumbe. Que mas*. . . . Yes, and the Golden Tulip; that was a condemned
building converted into a hotel. . . . The Photo Service on Prado; the
government moved the families out of that building, saying it was too
dangerous to live in, and then a year later they refurbished it and opened
a photo service store for the tourists. How can the Photo Service build-

ing be too dangerous for Cubans to live in one year, and safe for tourists the next?"

He said it more as a statement than a question, as if punctuating the point of his cynicism toward the regime, which seems to build and churn when you get him onto a sensitive subject. A lot of Cubans are Socratic like that. They talk around things and slowly form an impression of a given topic, then allow the listener to come to his own conclusions about the accuracy of the impression. After making the argument, a Cuban will look at you almost with urgency, as if waiting for that nod to validate the claim.

"But doesn't the government provide maintenance for the buildings?"

"The government does nothing for the people," Enrique explained. "Never."

"But this is a Socialist . . . "

"Cuba is not Socialist," he stopped me cold. "Cuba is centralist."

"But what about all this talk of . . . "

"That's exactly what it is," he stopped me again, "it's all talk."

12

The Revolution Is the Culture

"At the beginning of the Special Period," Enrique told me, "we all thought it would last only two or three years. When they permitted us to have dollars in 1993 and reopened the farmers' markets, we thought surely it couldn't last more than another two. When 1996 came, there were a few more things on the *libreta* and the blackouts disappeared. *Poco a poco*, little by little, it got better. But now it is five years later and nothing more has changed. Nothing."

If you ask any Cuban what he or she thinks is Cuba's biggest social problem, the answer will come back, without exception, "The economy." "If the economy were strong," they say, "everything would be fine." As a partial answer to quell the discontent following Cuba's hyperinflation spawned by the Soviet collapse, which devalued the Cuban peso to a low of 140 to the dollar between 1994 and 1995, the government opened up more than 130 legally licensed trades for popular participation. Aside from the farmers' markets, which had been opened and shut down several times over the past four decades, it was the government's first real step into market Socialism. But was it real? By July 1995, more than 190,000 Cubans had received permits to operate legal businesses. This number peaked at 208,000 self-employed in January 1996, representing only 2 percent of the population operating legal businesses in the new nonstate sector.

When the state hiked self-employment taxes that same year, the number of self-employed Cubans plummeted to around 160,000 by 1998—a little over 1 percent of the population—where it still hovers in 2002.[1] The heavy taxation, the costs of permits, and the inspections and fines forced many legally licensed operators—Armando and Francisco among them—either out of business or into the black market, and discouraged newcomers from even trying. For average Cubans, scraping together the 1,500 pesos to purchase an operator's license is next to impossible. Those who do manage to put together the fees often find the state so competitive and the taxes so defeating that they'll be forced to shut down two months after opening, in the process losing the 1,500 pesos and anything else invested.

While it may seem wise of the government to make the transition into free market socialism a slow one rather than using the "Shock Therapy" model that devastated the Soviet economy, it's now obvious that Castro doesn't wish to revert to market socialism at all. If he did, there would be newer tax incentives for the self-employed, not hurdles. The reforms of the mid-1990s were Castro's own, yet today he refuses to see them through; he's waiting until the tourism income strengthens the regime to the point that he can revert everything back to central control. Because of his refusal to follow through on his own reforms, Castro is creating a funeral for the Revolution.

I've met only a few Cubans who are completely consumed by bitterness, usually those who hate Castro and his regime and are desperate to leave the island. They have nothing good to say about Cuba, and they spend all their time seeking avenues of escape. Most people seem resigned to the frustration, and they find small ways to avoid its sting. For instance Armando, who gets through by quietly bickering about the long line at the mango stand. Or Rolando Ibáñez, who, at fifty, will listen to an entire forty seconds of a Castro speech before turning off the television with a pant of disgust and a "What shit!" And then moments later, he'll throw a cassette of the latest salsa into his stereo, grab his wife by the hips, and dance her around the living room.

One day, my artist friend, Ramon, and I were sitting on a balcony overlooking the Malecón and the people's beach. It was a beautiful day with a big sky and a stiff northerly breeze throwing small waves up over the sea wall and onto the street below. Suddenly, a little curly-haired dog caught our attention when it wandered out into the four-lane street and just stood there in the coming traffic. Dozens of drivers swerved around the dog, some blowing their horns, others cursing. Yet the dog just stood there in the center of the lane. After several minutes, a guy on a motorcycle finally stopped right in the middle of the road, parked his bike, gingerly scooped the animal into his arms, and carried it to the sidewalk.

As Ramon watched all this unfold, I could tell he was moved by the scene; and when the motorcycle pulled away and the dog wandered back into the alley, he simply said, *"No es facil."*

No es facil is a phrase you'll hear spoken several times a day in Cuba. *No es facil,* "It isn't easy." It's like a national anthem, the people's slogan, uttered when a conversation about the contradictions spins into a stalemate and there is no answer.

"The dog was trying to commit suicide," he added tenderly after a long pause. "He has lost the will to survive."

It was sort of an epiphany for Ramon, who has dealt with his own depression after contemplating suicide on several occasions. During the height of the Special Period when crime was rampant, Ramon was a police captain on the Havana foot patrol. He explained to me in great detail the desperation of those times. The lootings and burglaries, the purse-snatching, then an hourly occurrence. Looking at Cuba in 2002, it seems hard to believe this was happening only eight years ago. Ramon enjoyed telling these exciting stories; sometimes he looked at the photo showing him in full uniform, which he still keeps in his wallet. He likes to reminisce about those days when he fully identified with the Revolution.

In Cuba, you'll often see cops with empty pistol holsters because the police must purchase their own side arms. Ramon was fortunate; he was able to put together the $200 to buy his. One day, though, the stress of the Special Period made him snap. He shoved his pistol into his mouth, threatening to blow his brains out right in the middle of the busy police headquarters. He simply couldn't take it anymore. The desperation was too intense, and he lost control.

It took a long time for Ramon to tell me these details about his life. Now in his late thirties, he's part of the generation who can remember the good life before the Special Period, the days when there was food on the table and when the people still believed in Castro's vision. And then came the economic catastrophe and the contradictions, which seemed to plunge Ramon's generation into a cultural limbo of wanting and needing to believe, yet finding fewer and fewer reasons to hold onto.

Later in the day, we walked up to the protest plaza. Castro built it in December 1999 (incidentally, the month Armando's cooking oil ration was cut) next to the former U.S. embassy for the purpose of staging demonstrations against the embargo and for the return of Elian González.

"This plaza cost the Cuban people $2 million," Ramon said. "That's one dollar for everyone in Havana. Why are we wasting money on building plazas? Who cares about Elian González? Give me that dollar. My mother needs medicine for her legs, which are stricken with poor circulation."

Two months later, while sipping a coffee in a peso café, I told Ramon that I really believed in Castro's Socialist vision, but that in this world of globalization and growing capitalism, it seemed more and more futile. That it was unfair to force the Cuban people to steal for food, pretending it's not happening, making them sacrifice their personal dignity for a collective Revolutionary dignity that, as the weeks and months rolled by, began revealing more and more holes.

"It is not futile," said Ramon defiantly. "We will be remembered in history as the model society of a fair and just world of the future."

As he told me this, I recalled a day not long before when he had pulled a negative from his wallet and said, "Benjamin, look what I've got. It's a photo of Castro passed out drunk." As I held the image up to the light, he continued, "Look at the bottle of rum knocked over. Look at him, he's wasted. I'll bet you can sell this in the United States to some newspaper for $1,000."

Where he got the negative is another story. But just posing the idea that he could make money by selling this photo to a newspaper in the United States would have landed him in jail for seven years as a counter-revolutionary. Yet he thrilled over the guilty pleasure of possessing this contraband. It was a means of resistance. And the oddest part about it was that he was resisting the very thing he defended. His own contradictions in questioning the regime's methods while defending the Revolution shows the conflict raging in the hearts of many Cubans. They still adhere to Castro's vision, but have lost faith in Castro to see it through in today's world.

The state of the Cuban Revolution closely resembles many of its crumbling old buildings, patched and held together at the hands of fate, slowly eroding as the world applies pressure for renewal. In actuality, the "revolution" ended with the January 1, 1959, victory when Castro and his rebel army defeated the Cuban military. The "Revolution" with a capital "R" then began, which was and continues to be no more than an unsuccessful, splintered social experiment. Whether it will succeed has yet to be determined, and the reasons for its failures are many. José Martí, Cuba's father of independence, whose doctrines are the thrust behind the Cuban Revolutionary ideology, called the primary reason "geographic fatalism." By this, he meant that any country which fell within the backyard of the United States would inevitably be held under its theater of control. The U.S. embargo, which has strangled Cuba's economy since 1961, was part of the reason for the Revolution's continuing failure, on top of a multitude of the regime's own economic errors throughout the past four decades. But perhaps the most important factor was Castro's refusal to concede power to the people. He has simply stayed around too long, and in the process of trying to control everything, has ended up disenfranchising the critical mass of support.

Castro's idea in the beginning was to create a new Cuba, a country that operated free from U.S. domination, a land in which the people operated as their own free agents in the world. What Cuba has transmogrified into, however, is a centralist groupthink bureaucracy in which a 5 percentile ruling class dictates and administrates the lives of the people; it's much like any other country in the world, but with different control mechanisms.

The decade of the 1960s was the decade of definition, when the island underwent its most sweeping changes in creating the new "Revolutionary Culture." By 1961, aside from a few lingering diplomatic accommodations, the majority of foreign enterprises in Cuba had been nationalized, and those who disagreed with the new program, or whose own idea of Cuba's new reforms didn't mesh with Castro's vision, were invited to leave. Many, and especially the poor, stayed because they had nothing to lose.

Between 1953, when Castro began organizing, until the victory in 1959, the poorest 40 percent of Cubans received only 6.5 percent of the island's income.[2] Forty percent of the sugar production was U.S.-owned, as well as 90 percent of the telephone and electric utilities.[3] Under the grip of foreign latifundismo, 1.5 percent of the farms controlled 47 percent of the land, and only 36 percent of Cuba's agricultural workers owned the land they tilled.[4] In 1959, the new Revolutionary society and Castro's Agrarian Reform promised to change all this. There was no reason for the poor to leave.

Some of the more privileged stayed because Cuba was home, and the changing of power, of dictators, of governments, had always created domestic instability. Castro was nothing new. Ride it out and see what happens. Some cheered, some grumbled, and others remained indifferent as the government took control of every sector of society and Revolutionized it. The culture, the music, arts, and literature, everything and everyone was expected to adjust to the Revolutionary ideal, and most did so willingly in the beginning. Everything was framed in the black and white of being either for the Revolution or against the Revolution, and to go against it was to go against the people and the newly won victory. To be "Cuban" was to be "Revolutionary," and there was no tolerance for deviation.

It was as if the culture that existed before 1959 had vaporized into thin air. Television musicals and romance films that had been highly popular were suddenly replaced with Revolutionary war documentaries. Advertisements in the newspapers were slowly replaced with Revolutionary propaganda. The ballet, the poetry, the fiction, the theater, the media, everything that defines a people, began reflecting the military victory, the defeat of Batista, the futuristic vision, and those who questioned it were deported or jailed as counterrevolutionaries. Today, if you bring the island prestige and money, you're a Revolutionary. If you don't, you can either conform or leave the island; or you can go to jail.

Juan the *jinetero,* out of familial responsibility, chose to conform. On my last trip down to Cuba, as always, I bumped into him almost immediately after hitting the street. It was an awkward encounter. Usually when I see him, he cracks a big carefree smile as he struts around in some new Tommy Hilfiger outfit, another one of those status symbols on which younger Cubans with dollars pride themselves. On this occasion, though, he wasn't smiling, and he wore a plaid button-down summer shirt, the kind seen on older, more conservative Cubans.

"*Hombre,* what happened to you?" I asked.

"Everything has changed. I'm different now," he explained. "I don't work in the streets any longer. I've decided to become a mason. Right now I'm in my apprenticeship, and I'm saving everything I earn so I can buy the tools. A trowel costs $3, so I think in a few months I can get one, and then maybe in a year I can buy a level. I've left the street behind. That no longer interests me." As he spoke, his words and newfound passion seemed stifled and artificial, as if by trying to convince me he was also trying to reassure himself. Here was a guy who a few months earlier was cracking jokes about Fidel Castro and Che Guevara, and now he sounded like Revolutionary spokesperson. He could tell I didn't believe him.

"Why the sudden change?" I asked. "You loved working in the streets. What happened to the old Juan?"

"Well," he said hesitantly. "I received my third arrest from the police for *jineterismo.*"

He explained that he was on house arrest for six months and that his caseworker had found him a job working with a mason. Every day Juan now had to wake up at 5:00 A.M. and be at work by six, when the caseworker called to make sure he had arrived. When work ended at 5:00 P.M., he had an hour to get home before the caseworker dropped in again to check up on him. One more altercation with the cops, and he'd be sentenced to six months on a state work farm without salary.

"If this would happen, my mother would never make it. The family relies on me. But it's okay, because I think in two years I'll be able to make a better amount of money with the masonry."

"Yes," I said. "And then you can go to work building the big hotels."

"This is what I hope for," he said with a smile. "But first I must save and buy the tools and learn the trade. I have to go now, I have only fifteen minutes to get home before she comes. Stop by the apartment before you leave again. I have some letters that I want you to mail to my father."

It was strange to see this new Juan. The Revolution had broken his spirit and forced him to conform. As Juan walked away, I recalled the day that Enrique had said, "Come with me. I have something to show you." Whenever he said, "I have something to show you," I knew it was going to be good. He always shrouded these events in mystery, and would never tell me what he was going to reveal. He'd just take me somewhere and let me figure out what was happening.

After walking about seven blocks up Monte, we crossed Prado to a work site where a foreign firm was building a new hotel. Each of these building sites is wrapped with corrugated tin to keep out thieves, teenagers, and drunks. And at each site there is a security entrance with a twenty-four-hour guard on duty. It was noon, a very hot day, and Enrique led me straight up to the security station.

"Give me two dollars," he said.

At the rickety security shack, a short line was moving quickly along. Enrique told the security guard "two," and was handed two sandwiches and two colas. We then made our way to a nearby park and sat down to eat.

"Here's a cheap lunch," he said, peeling off the plastic shrink wrap with his teeth, squirting a bag of included ketchup over the contents, a slice of bologna, a slice of ham, and gooey white American cheese, all wrapped in a dried-out eight-inch hoagie roll.

"This is the *estimulo* the hotel construction workers receive everyday."

"And they sell them," I said.

"Of course. They must to feed their families. How much do they pay workers like this in your country?"

"About $15 an hour," I said.

"Here they make 200 pesos a month. But the foreign company building the hotel pays the government, I don't know, maybe $8 or $10 per man hour for their labor. Do you understand? The government keeps almost everything and pays the Cuban worker nothing. It's exploitation. The government is exploiting the people."

Juan is a black guy. His new goal amounts to this: After his two-year apprenticeship, he'll be qualified to work ten hours a day, six days a week, building new hotels for white tourists. The foreign company financing the hotel will pay the government, not Juan, approximately $1,500 for a month of his labor, of which he'll receive about 200 pesos, or $10, plus a bologna sandwich and a can of pop each day, if he's on time, on top of the monthly canned ham if he's never late and never misses a day. Juan won't eat his bologna sandwich and drink his pop for lunch. Like the rest of the workers, he'll sell the combo everyday for $1 in the street to a Cuban who has money so that he can take home an extra $30 a month on top of his base peso salary. Why? Because it's the only way to survive. This is reality. What is Juan doing? Devoting two years of his life to learn masonry so that he can sell his lunch because it's the only way to get dollars within a system that he was forced back into.

He no longer exists in the parallel culture. He is a Revolutionary now, and the only hurdle was that of convincing himself of this truth. Deep down he doesn't like it. He's an intelligent businessman, not a slave laborer. *Jineterismo* just happened to be the only viable business option at the time. And now those options are gone. His new choices? Conform or go to jail. Out of familial responsibility, he conformed.

"Ex-plo-ta-*ción,*" Enrique repeated, putting a pessimistic emphasis on the last syllable before taking another bite of the sandwich.

This is where the regime and its new double standard gets sticky. Castro's intent from the beginning was to end the "exploitation of one man's labor for another man's profit." This is the foundation of Cuban Socialism, and the entire philosophy of the Cuban Revolution was built upon it. Castro fought the war in the 1950s and kicked out the United States to end the foreign exploitation of the Cuban people. So how can it be acceptable today that the same regime exploits its own, or allows foreign enterprises to exploit the people, any more than the regime's exploiting of prostitutes is acceptable as a means of luring in the necessary sex tourists?

Of course the regime, with its selective idealism, would never see it as exploitation, and for those administrators who do, the end always justifies the means. Everyone works for the cause. For *la lucha.* For the Revolutionary survival. And the administrators decide where the money is to be spent. We know what's best for everyone. Don't question authority. To do so is counterrevolutionary, and if you question us, we'll confiscate your home and car. Now go buy your five pounds of rice. We'll blame the circumstances on the United States and the Russians and everything will be peachy. But it's not. The people aren't stupid.

When Law 77, the Foreign Investment Act, was passed by the National Assembly in November 1996, the rules changed. Before Law 77, which was based on an older law passed in 1982, Cuba would entertain foreign investments as fifty-fifty joint ventures only. But in Cuba, a joint venture is not fifty-fifty capital. The international company provides the capital, and Cuba provides the land and labor. The profits are then split. The problem was that under the old law, foreign firms found Cuban investment unprofitable. By 1996, the government, desperate for income, passed Law 77, which opened the island to 100 percent foreign investment and offered tax breaks and incentives for venture capital. The only stipulation was that the internationals could bring only upper management and consultants to work on the island. All the labor would be provided by Cuba, and the land under the buildings would be leased, never owned.

The foreign firms who build and operate in Cuba pay the government directly for the labor, and the government divvies up the money however it sees fit. As for labor laws, before the Revolution, the old Communist Party controlled the labor unions. When Castro won the war, he quickly co-opted the old-guard Communists, and the Revolution itself became the labor union. Today, unions are illegal in Cuba, and any thought of forming one is considered illegal organization. Under this system, workers have little protection when it comes to wages and safety. If a worker is injured on the job, he or she receives free Socialist healthcare; and if incapacitated, worker's compensation is half the monthly salary. This means that if a worker earned 200 pesos a month and an injury occurred, he or she would continue to earn 100 pesos. There is no OSHA in Cuba, and no one to sue for safety violations besides the foreign firms themselves; but their safety standards are usually much higher than those of the government, and they often provide healthcare plans for their workers on top of the government's requirements.

One man I met who works for ETECSA, the formerly Italian and now Mexican-owned telecommunications company, had an eye problem that required a special operation in Havana. ETECSA paid the travel fare to Havana for him and his wife, paid for a week's stay at a hotel, including meals, and paid for the eye operation. The government has worked out deals with certain foreign companies; for example, if the multinational wants to provide extra healthcare above the Cuban Socialist medicine, the government will split the cost. Since the government equates the peso with the dollar, it provides its half in pesos and the multinational pays its half in dollars. If a surgery costs, say, $1,500, the multinational might pay $750; but the government still pays the doctor only 500 pesos a month, thus profiting even more. Besides Communists traveling on business, workers like this man are the only Cubans permitted to stay in the hotels; after all, the government can make a dollar profit on the room, the rationale being that 50 percent of $30 is better than 100 percent of nothing. Dollars are everything to the government. But few are fortunate enough to have a good job with ETECSA. In Cuba, there is no such thing as equal opportunity. Some say there is no opportunity whatsoever.

One day as I was walking past a hotel, a beautiful old '55 Chevrolet pulled up to the curb. It looked almost brand new. The chrome was perfect. Not a ding anywhere in the body, not a bump of putty, and it was obvious that much time and extreme care had been put into refinishing this relic. It was a taxi owned by the government's new GranCar taxi service. It's illegal for licensed peso taxi drivers to pick up tourists, and because the fine is 1,500 pesos, many won't take the risk. So the Ministry of Tourism thought it would be a good idea to provide a dollar taxi service for tourists who might want to experience the romance of riding in the ancient cars. I should mention that, in Cuba, it's legal to sell the old cars; new cars can only be traded or sold to the state, although Cubans do sell them amongst themselves illegally. The catch is that even though you bought the car and it's yours, because it's illegal to sell it, the first owner's name stays on the title. If you're ever pulled over by the police, you tell them that you're borrowing the car from your cousin, whose name is on the title. Cars have been sold nine and ten times in this manner.

The day I saw the '55 Chevy sitting at the hotel, I later met up with Francisco and Armando and told them how amazed I was to see this car in such excellent condition. Where did the government find these taxis?

"They confiscate them from people," said Armando. "They then refinish them, make them brand new, put them in the street for tourists and charge dollars."

"Who do they confiscate them from?"

"Let me tell you a story," said Francisco. "Back in my town, there was a guy who lived on my block. In the daytime, he worked as an auto mechanic for the state, and at night, he would fix up cars in his garage and resell them. He would buy broken down cars very cheap for $300 and take them home and make them perfect. Then he would sell the cars for $3,500. He used to travel everywhere to find the cars, and he did this for many years. He was an excellent mechanic and everybody in the neighborhood was friends with him. Well one day there was a knock on the door. Government officials from the town. They came to arrest him and confiscate all his cars. He had three cars at the time. One he had already completely finished, another he had just finished, and the third was a family heirloom handed down from his father when he died."

"Why did they confiscate his cars? What was the crime?"

"*Enriquecimiento ilicito,*" said Armando. "Illegal enrichment. They tried to take the car that was his father's, but the family won in court and was able to keep it. However, this man also had $2,500 in the bank and they confiscated that too. This is why we Cubans never keep money in the bank. Because they'll think you've attained it illegally and will just confiscate it."

"Not only did they take this man's $2,500," said Francisco, "but they also sent him to prison for four years. It destroyed the family. All because he bought cars and fixed them up and resold them. But here's the best part of the story. A week after they took him to prison, I was standing out in the street and I saw one of his cars coming towards me. I thought to myself, 'Who could this be driving the car?' I couldn't believe it. I looked and looked, and as it got closer, I noticed it was one of the town officials who had made the arrest. We later found out that they purposefully waited until he was done finishing the car before they came to confiscate it. The official is still driving that car around today."

"All dollars belong to the state," added Armando. "Nobody is allowed to make any money here. If you do, then you're stealing from them. They want every single dollar for themselves."

13

The Search for *Cubanidad*

P op Tarts, Marlboro Lights, Sprite, Green Giant green beans, Jell-O
pudding mix, Chiclets, Tabasco sauce, Bayer aspirin, Jack Daniels
Whiskey, Fruit of the Loom T-shirts, Tampax tampons, Revlon Flex
shampoos and conditioners, Brut cologne for men, Kit-Kat, Reeses
Pieces, Pringles potato chips, Gerber baby food, Dole canned pineapples,
Pepto Bismol, Dial bath soap, Dum-Dum lollipops. The list goes on and
on and on.

These are just some of the U.S. products manufactured either by U.S.
foreign subsidiaries or in the United States, then shipped through a third
country, such as Mexico or Canada, to Cuba. It isn't as if you could enter
any store and stroll through isle upon isle packed with American brands.
But each store carries a few items, and every time I stumbled across a
new product, I'd jot it down in a small notebook, along with the price. If
a Cuban bought all his monthly rations at a *bodega*, everything would fit
neatly into two plastic bags. If that same Cuban bought one each of
every American product available on the island, he would need three or

four shopping carts. Chef Boyardee canned ravioli, $3.85. S&W sliced peaches, $2.85. Creamette lasagna, $3.95 for a 16-oz. box. Popeye spinach, $2.50. Besides American cigarettes and the Pepsi and Coke products sold to tourists at $1 a can, the bulk of U.S.-made goods are shipped in for Cuban consumption.

When Armando said, "They want every last dollar for themselves," this highway robbery on the cost of dollar goods is one of the things he was talking about. Juan the *jinetero*'s crime was not for hustling but for tapping the money pipeline that runs straight from the tourist's pocket into the regime's. He siphoned off a few bucks, and he was punished. The man who repaired cars in the black market also tapped into the regime's profits and was punished. Had he followed the rule, he would have worked for 200 pesos a month fixing up those same cars, but the state would have used his talents to earn tourist dollars, none of which he'd ever see. With Armando, although he was there first, the state built its own food stand next door and forced him out by attrition and bogus inspections. New entrepreneurs are prevented from opening shops through licensing controls and over-taxation. Established entrepreneurs are forced out by tax hikes. And average Cubans are so underpaid that they'll never be able to accumulate the capital they need to become independent entrepreneurs; nor will they be able to purchase toaster ovens, hairdryers, or other simple appliances.

This is Cuba. And the rules are simple: You do not compete with the state, and you do not tap into the regime's money pipeline. Period.

The wisdom in the street is this: Don't get caught. In Cuba, essentially 10 percent of the population makes and enforces the rules, and 90 percent work overtime to find ways to bend or break them. Why? Because if you don't break them, you don't survive.

Much like Capitalist ideology, Cuba's Revolutionary ideology is all about selling a product and then keeping consumers on a string. In the United States, Macintosh computers are donated to school districts across the country. Every time a student boots up, a short Macintosh advertisement pops up on the screen. This is commercial indoctrination, and it will inevitably produce future consumers of Macintosh products. In the same manner, Cuban students are spoon fed anti-U.S. rhetoric while being showered with pro-Revolutionary propaganda. But what kind of mixed message is sent out when the Communist-controlled dollar stores sell products that say "Made in the USA" on the wrapper? And what about the genuine green U.S. dollars, complete with the faces of U.S. presidents, that Cubans use to buy U.S. goods? Finally, what happens when the people begin hearing that appliances are marked up by the government 100 to 300 percent from their real value to obtain these dollars?

When in 1492 Columbus dropped anchor at Holguín in Oriente, he noticed the aboriginal Taino Indians smoking these things called *tobacos,* which they pinched between their pinkies and ring fingers, fist cupped; then they would inhale the smoke through the thumb hole. These were the first cigarettes, and through five centuries, the tradition has stuck. So many Cubans smoke that cigarettes are part of the monthly ration. Younger Cubans prefer to smoke dollar cigarettes because they are a little more chic than the cheap rationed tobacco. In 1996, needing foreign capital, Cuba partnered with Brazil's Souza Cruz tobacco corporation, forming the Brascuba multinational, which manufactures six or seven brands of Cuban cigarettes. Today, Brascuba's hottest names are Popular, Vegas, Romeo and Juliet, and Monterrey, which cost $.50 a pack. In Cuba, the difference between smoking the standard rationed cigarettes and Brascuba's brands can be likened to the difference between smoking Marlboro and generic cigarettes. Not only is generic tobacco inferior but it carries the social stigma of poverty. The Cuban youth will scrape up that 50 cents somewhere, anywhere, to buy the brand-name tobacco. Brascuba's highest priced cigarette is called "Hollywood," its crème de la crème, and they cost a dollar a pack. As friends told me, Brascuba's idea was to create a Cuban cigarette that rivaled Marlboro, much like Cuba's *Tu Cola,* which was designed to rival Coca-Cola.

If you drive south on Calzada de Diez de Octubre towards the Lawton section of Havana, right around Coco Street there's an ancient pre-Castro Coca-Cola mural fading away on the side of a building. Apart from the Rex theater, the old Schwinn bicycle shop, and the RCA Victor building on Neptuno, few of these remnants remain from the U.S. neo-colony. Except for the cars and other odds and ends, most symbols of the United States were immediately destroyed following the victory, and others simply vanished over time.

I asked Armando about classic commercialism in Cuba, and he dug a yellowed newspaper from his attic, dated one day after the *La Coubre* explosion in Havana Harbor, March 1960. When *La Coubre*, a French freighter filled with Belgian arms mysteriously blew up, Castro and Che Guevara had the ammunition necessary to launch the first propaganda campaign against the United States. Alberto "Korda" Diaz's famous photo of Che, "Guerrillero Heroico," was taken the day *La Coubre* was destroyed, the same day Guevara accused the United States of this terrorist act, which killed and injured hundreds of Cubans. The photo was first published in this edition of the newspaper *Revolución,* of which Armando showed me a copy.

"Look at this," said Armando, carefully turning the yellowed pages. *"Aqui esta un anuncio por Texaco.* And here is a Gillette razor advertisement."

Page after page, there were advertisements for U.S. brands. And beside the advertisements were page jumps for the *La Coubre* feature which, as in all Latin newspapers, showed gruesome graphics and carnage. On this day in March 1960, the world changed for Cuba; and this is when classic Western commercialism and the new Cuban Revolutionary commercialism clashed.

"Soon after this event, there were no more advertisements," said Armando. "Ah, and look here. Here's an announcement that the national lottery would be suspended on this day because of the explosion."

"You had a lottery in Cuba, even after Castro?"

"Sure," said Armando, who was around twenty years old at the time. "Even after Castro. Back then, a peso and a dollar were equivalent, and for one peso, you would pick four numbers, and there was a woman whose name I have forgotten who would draw the numbers and announce them over the radio. The national lottery ended a few years after this date. Aha, and here is an advertisement for a mattress company.

You know, at one time, a train would travel around the country full of this company's mattresses, and they would give anyone credit who had a job. These were good, solid mattresses. And now look at the mattresses today. They want 4,000 pesos for some garbage that will last only a few years. Besides, nobody has 4,000 pesos."

When Armando spoke, he flashed back and forth between memories and a subtle bitterness. He talked about the magical day when his father brought home his family's first television, which he'd bought on credit. Then he'd shift into pessimism.

"Back then, a peso was equal to one dollar. If you worked five days a week for as little as one peso a day, you were earning around $250 a year. Today, forty years later, you work six days a week and earn only $120 a year."

"So are you saying Cubans are worse off now than before? Was Castro necessary?"

"Yes and no," said Armando after a long pause. "Let us say the revolution was necessary and Castro was the one who realized it. There was corruption. The poorest people could not afford shoes. They had no medicine. The *campesinos* had no education and were forced to work at a young age to feed their families."

"It doesn't sound much different from today," I said.

Armando just looked at me, and I could see about forty years of his best and worst memories rushing through his eyes. Fifteen years ago, he had no doubts about Castro. The system worked. During the 1980s, he was a well-paid school teacher earning 280 pesos a month; this was when the peso fell around five to a dollar. He was living large. Then came the Special Period. Then came the dollar. With the dollar came all the contradictions that Armando and many other Cubans are now either fighting to understand or have given up on altogether. And with the dollar returned the old commercialism, which had to reunite with the Revolutionary commercialism forty years after its bitter divorce following the *La Coubre* explosion.

Capitalist advertising in Cuba today is mainly geared for tourists. Revolutionary advertising is geared for Cubans. But the two enmesh with

Brascuba cigarettes and Che Guevara postcards, resulting in what I'll call the new Revolutionary commercialism. Korda's famous image of Che is one of the biggest-selling postcards for tourists in Cuba at $.50 apiece. To sell this postcard is the highest form of Revolutionary act, because the survival of the Revolution depends on tourist dollars, and a $.50-postcard is another dime of profit for the cause. A photo of Che is not only an advertisement of indoctrination for Cubans but one for tourists as well, who will send the postcards abroad and lure in more vacationers.

Throughout the island, the only capitalist advertising targeted specifically at Cubans is Brascuba tobacco products. Everywhere you look, there's a sexy new ad promoting these cigarettes. Before Korda died, most of his photography assignments were for Brascuba; one in particular was for the Romeo and Juliet brand, an erotic black-and-white image showing a man kissing the back of a woman's neck on a balcony overlooking the Havana twilight. In a Revolutionary sense, Korda's photo for this advertisement was as commercially powerful as his image of Che. The implication is that to smoke dollar cigarettes is a Revolutionary act because it puts dollars in the regime's pocket, and thus sustains the Revolution.

On my last visit, Hollywood was running a major ad campaign in Havana, and the posters were everywhere. Inside each cigarette pack was a small certificate representing one "Hollywood Buck," sort of like Camel Cash in the United States. If a smoker saved so many Hollywood Bucks, he was entitled to one of several prizes, perhaps a Hollywood baseball cap or a pair of Hollywood sunglasses. On a special day, those who had saved their Hollywood Bucks were to report to the El Rapido hamburger stand located next to the Western Union at the Carlos III dollar shopping mall. Western Unions in Cuba are always located at the dollar stores, much as ATM machines are located at the far ends of the casinos in Las Vegas. The day of the prize giveaway, the line for the Hollywood cigarette contest was longer than the usual line at the Western Union. Over a hundred young Cubans were waiting to claim their sunglasses.

Throughout the several weeks before the Hollywood giveaway, I would stop occasionally in a Central Havana park to eat a cheap *bocadito,* a Cuban sandwich. I used to see an old man who had a small goat-pulled cart, complete with jingle bells; he would circle the park with a wagonload of children, for which he charged a peso per child. I particularly remember two of the kids, whose father worked at a nearby café. This was during summer vacation, and while the parents worked, like many Cuban children, these two played in the streets. They were brother and sister, about seven or eight years old, and the first time they saw me, they ran up and asked whether they could have my cigarette pack.

"You don't smoke do you?" I played.

"No. It's for a game. We want to win a prize."

I removed the last two cigarettes, handed them the empty pack, and they excitedly ran under a tree where each pulled a handful of other empty packs from their pockets. The little boy took my old pack, ripped the top off, tossed the rest onto the ground, and began counting with his sister. It's always amazing to watch how much mileage Cuban kids can get out of something as novel as empty cigarette packs. They were playing their own version of the Hollywood game.

Future consumers. Future Revolutionaries. Fifteen years ago during the Rectification, if some functionary had posed the idea of a Cuban cigarette brand called "Hollywood," he would have been jailed as a fascist. Then the Special Period came. The dollar came. And the rules changed in the battle between ideological purity and absolute rationalization where the end justifies the means.

Besides Cuba's proliferation of cigarette advertising posters, I asked Armando about classical commercialism. Did the state-controlled television networks ever run commercials? I was interested to know whether he'd even seen one in the last forty years.

"Yes," he said. "During the Panamerican Games in the 1990s there were some television commercials. I remember there was a *Tu Cola* commercial, and there were car rental and hotel commercials from some of the foreign sponsors of the games. But after a few days, Fidel put a stop to it. He said this kind of trash didn't belong on the people's television."

DROPPING INTO ARMANDO'S APARTMENT one day, I was greeted by his daughter, who usually visits about twice a week. She's a street-savvy, willful young woman, highly outspoken and opinionated. On this day, I walked through the door for the ritual *besitos* with a friendly *"Compañera."*

"Why did you call me *compañera?"* she asked, slightly insulted. "Why not 'friend' or 'sister?' Here in Cuba we never use the word *compañero* when we greet friends. In America, do you call each other *compañero?"*

"Of course not," I said. "You know this."

"Well, then."

Her problem was one of pure semantics. *"Compañero,"* companion, was the word Castro, with his early utopian vision, had hoped all Cubans would come to use when addressing each other. It was a word meant to bind the masses together behind the Palm Curtain, much like the "Comrade" of the former Soviet Union. But the term *compañero* failed to become an element of the popular language, and the only time it's heard today is when some leader quotes the comments and stats of *"Compañero Fidel"* during speeches. Occasionally prostitutes and petty criminals use it smoothly and manipulatively when trying to talk their way out of a predicament with the police. But you'll rarely, if ever, hear the word used in the streets; and some people, Armando's daughter among them, are insulted when it's insinuated that this Revolutionary dictum even remotely applies to them. Refusing to use the word *compañero* is, then as now, a means by which dispossessed Cubans resist a Revolution they've been shut out of.

Other examples of this phenomenon occur constantly. At the outset of Cuba's 1959 rebirth, the government swept across the island and renamed the streets with Revolutionary themes. In Havana, Teniente Rey became "Brazil Street." *Galiano* became "Italy Avenue." Reina, the Queens Way, became "Simón Bolívar Avenue." Monte became "Máximo Gómez." Revolutionary fever gripped the nation. It was a romantic and exciting time. But by 1968, the magic had worn off. Today, nobody in the street uses the new names, preferring, as nonconformists, to adhere to the old ones. Ask somebody in the street where such and such restaurant is on Italy Avenue and, after a pause, he'll likely say, "Oh, you mean Galiano."

Today there is a lot of discussion about *Cubanidad,* or *Cubanía.* What exactly does it mean to be "Cuban?" Does to be Cuban mean being a Revolutionary? How do the old colonial symbols fit into the picture? When Castro seized control in 1959, the big theme was in redefining what it means to be "Cuban." A culture is always identified by its symbols. In Cuba, the symbols were colonial, first from Spain and then from the United States. This search for *Cubanidad,* for Cuban cultural essence, for solid identity, had always been part of the island's struggle.

Today, this struggle for *Cubanidad* can be seen in the arts, the music, the seeming confusion of the island's rhythms. Castro was fundamental in throwing off the chains of the former colonizer's symbols and giving the island its first stab at creating its own identity, this *Cubanidad.* Few Cubans will disagree with this. Even Cuban Americans understand that the revolutionary war was not only necessary, it was destined to occur. Whether Castro was the man for the job is still being debated. Many Cubans, whether living in Cuba or in exile, feel that Spain was defeated only to give way to the U.S. neocolony, later to be occupied by the Russians; and that today, Cuba is being colonized by Castro himself.

Today, to be Revolutionary is not to question the thinking of the government. To be Revolutionary is to be an obedient worker, take your pay, collect your ham, and be a contented part of the machine. The machine is the Revolution, and the Revolution has become twisted into the equation "Tourism equals economic power equals *La Victoria.*" But the biggest question is: the victory of what? The people? The idea? The *Cubanidad?* The regime? There's a lot of confusion about this.

At the the dawn of the Special Period, Castro faced a dilemma: Should we throw in the towel or fight it out?

"Some people think," Castro addressed his cadres at the 1991 4th Communist Party Congress, "that the sacrifices we have to make are because we want to save the Revolution and that, if we didn't want to save the Revolution, we wouldn't have any problems and wouldn't have to make any sacrifices."

Castro continually says that Cubans need to be *"Soldados de la Economia,"* economic soldiers. But even the toughest soldiers can withstand only so much war before they break. They begin to question why there is a war. And seeing little progress in the economic war other than monthly hotel-room reports—while the rations and salaries have been frozen for the past eight years—the soldiers begin jumping the fence.

Was the revolutionary war to end Cuba's racism, discrimination, and exploitation necessary? Some Cubans I talked to didn't believe so, thinking it only held the country back from its already progressive course. As one black scholar told me, "The problems we were having with racism in 1959 were exactly the same as the racism in your country's Southern states. It would have been a matter of only a few years before Malcolm X and Martin Luther King brought their internationalist struggle to Cuba. Today we still have racism in Cuba. All the rich whites who owned the biggest mansions in Vedado still own those mansions, and all the poor blacks in Cerro and Luyano are still poor blacks in Cerro and Luyano. There is less racism, yes. The government has mostly eliminated institutional discrimination in employment, in wages. But the people are still racist. At home there is a lot of private discrimination."

The problem with Cuba's current racism is that the government is constantly boasting to itself and the world that racism in Cuba has been eliminated; so now, if people such as this scholar began to spread awareness, it would be an admission that racism still exists and it would undermine the government's alleged successes. The police profiling of blacks in Cuba is a major issue that has yet to be discussed. There still exist the stereotypes of lazy blacks and industrious whites. When I asked Enrique, who is black, about racism in Cuba and police profiling, he told me, "Yes, there is racism in Cuba. All this talk about having eradicated racism is a farce. If you go out after 10:00 P.M., who is in the streets? It's all blacks. The whites are at home studying, sleeping, getting ready for work. The blacks are the delinquents. This is how the police think. A few years ago, there were statistically more whites than blacks becoming doctors, so to make it look nonracial, the government lowered the test scores for the blacks. They raised them again a year later. But you understand my point. Just having to lower the test scores tells you that the system is racist, but it's not something that's discussed."

One of the biggest ways that Cuba is still institutionally racist is in the *remesas,* the family remittances sent from Cuban exiles living abroad. To date, around 1 million, mostly white Cubans, have emigrated to the United States. One-fifth of these were the white middle-class profession-als who emigrated between 1959 and the 1962 Missile Crisis, and who today represent the first-generation Cuban American Miami establish-ment. Between 1985 and 1991, when Cuba experienced its most stable migration patterns, 92 percent of legal migrants were white, and only 2.2 percent were black.[1] The reason the majority of immigrants are white is because one of the U.S. stipulations for legal immigration is that the Cuban applicant must have family in the United States; this in itself is a racist policy because it immediately raises the odds against black immigration. On the other hand, the Communist regime is racist because it allows the largely white exile to send dollar remittances to white Cubans living on the island, thus putting them in a higher class than the blacks who have fewer family members abroad, and thus fewer means of obtaining dollars. Thus blacks also have fewer chances to leave the island, whether legally, or illegally, because they can't put together the money necessary to fund such an expedition.

In 1993, when Cubans such as the Ibáñezes were allowed to open *casas particulares* and private dollar restaurants, a lot of the initial start-up money for the businesses came from white relatives in Miami, creating a new unequal distribution. In 1995, about 457 million dollars flowed into the island from Miami; this came either through family remittances or through Cuban Americans traveling to the island and represented half of the island's tourist earnings and about one-fifth of Cuba's gross income for that year. The direct remittances from the largely white exiles and the white entrepreneurs who own the private dollar businesses provide incalculable profits for the government by way of heavy taxes and uncontrolled government pricing for dollar commodities. The government has instituted a lawfully racial inequality and unequal distribution system whereby the white minority (37 percent) still receives most of the material benefits and mobility, either domestically or through immigration, and the majority of blacks (51 percent mulatto, 11 percent black) have less access, and all for the survival of a Revolution that claims racism and exploitation in Cuba have been eliminated.

I don't mean in any way to trivialize the honorable aspects of the Cuban Revolution and what it has accomplished in its battle against racism, because it has accomplished many great things. But these are the facts. How the regime will contend with Cuba's new classism and racism in the future has yet to be determined. To date, these things simply haven't been discussed because the government insists on staying on the old track of finger-pointing at the rest of the capitalist world while domestic issues are largely ignored. Before 1993, classism and racism had all but disappeared from Cuba. Now they're back, and growing.

14

Still Isolated Behind the
Palm Curtain

The Cuban government prints three national newspapers, *Granma*, *Juventud Rebelde*, and *Trabajadores*, plus regional papers for the capital of each province. One morning I was sipping on a café under the stained glass transom of Enrique's *solar* when the newspaper man hobbled by. As always, I jumped up and chased him down, returning with the morning edition of *Granma*.

"I can't believe you read that stuff," said Enrique. "Nobody reads the daily papers in Cuba."

"Then why is everyone buying them?" I asked.

"We use it for toilet paper," he said. "It's cheaper. Everybody buys the dailies to clean their asses. That's all it's good for. The toilet paper at the stores cost 4.5 pesos per roll. With this many pesos, I can buy twenty-two newspapers, *mas o menos*."

That this was how Cubans valued their national news media struck me as an hilarious irony. So much for "The Official Organ of the Communist Party," *Granma*'s theme line.

"I never buy *Granma,*" Enrique chuckled. "I wait until Monday and buy the weekly *Trabajadores.* It has more pages. Your *Granma* there has only two pages folded. *Trabajadores* has twice as many pages at the same cost."

I described the hefty, five-pound Sunday papers sold in the United States. "¡*Cojones!*" he said. "You must bring me one the next time you come."

One of my most amusing memories of Cuba is an incident that occurred during a week in south central Cuba on a trip to the Escambray mountains with a friend. After a killer four-kilometer hike straight uphill in the national park, we stopped at an old woman's shack to buy a glass of iced mango juice. My friend asked to use the woman's bathroom, and afterwards, he emerged with a smile on his face. As we wound back down the road to Trinidad on the south coast, he kept grinning, until finally he said, "Oh yeah, I almost forgot your souvenir." With this typical preamble of Cuban drama, he eased some folded book pages from his back pocket. I pulled over and unfolded the makeshift toilet paper, which turned out to be several pages torn from the collected letters of Vladimir Lenin written to Russian friends and functionaries circa 1922, translated into Spanish.

"Noooooo," I said, looking him straight in the eye.

"Yessssss," he laughed. When we returned to Havana and told the Lenin story to a roomful of people, we incited a seismic laugh.

"Yes, it's true," said a rural cousin visiting from a distant province. "The *campesinos* use book pages. When we visit the city, we always bring a good book along. And when the *habaneros* visit the *campo,* they always bring us a supply of *Granmas.*"

Ten years ago, *People Magazine* and *Rolling Stone* were contraband in Cuba. Today, you can buy practically any popular Western magazine at the upscale hotels. Foreign magazines and newspapers are an accommodation to the tourists that began in the mid-1990s. Cubans who know a hotel worker or have a friend in the hotels can get their hands on these magazines. The problem is that they sell in Cuba for double their regular newsstand prices, again, putting them out of reach of the average

Cuban. If you keep the population's income down to 200 pesos a month, then receive half of this back at the *bodega,* knowing the other hundred will be spent on a bottle of shampoo, it limits the people's economic power to access controversial information, which threatens the regime's control.

Another item on the government's forbidden list is the VCR. Although there are two video stores in Havana that rent films for $1 a night, VCRs are not for sale in Cuba because, as a friend related, "they are a luxury that the state feels we don't need. So they don't order them, and they're not sold." More likely, the VCRs are forbidden because of the black market rise in underground video pornography, which in Cuba is absolutely illegal, thriving, and difficult to dismantle due to the people's own current, and overdue, sexual revolution. Visitors are permitted to bring VCR gifts along if they pay the 50 percent duty of the new price at customs, and often family from Miami and others who understand the rules will stash them, along with a few pounds of fresh beef, deep in their luggage to avoid the tax. The airport experience always turns into a big game of hide-and-seek between customs officials and visitors.

"Will they discover the VCR buried under my shirts and question me? Will I be followed? Will I be arrested?" These are the questions that bore into the minds of visitors trying to side-step the control. And there are always the piercing eyes of the guards, which seem to say, "We know what you are up to." So you shoot straight toward the customs agent who looks as if he might take your $10 bribe, just in case the VCR and beef are detected, praying that it won't turn into a big scene. Later in the evening, when you're plugging the new VCR into the back of the television, Cubavision will rerun its Revolutionary infomercial yet again, explaining to the people how Cuban customs agents are setting an example with their honesty and proficiency.

Cell phones are the latest concept in Cuban communication, but rarely, if ever, do you hear them jingle in public. Castro and other important functionaries have them, but the technology is limited to news organizations, foreign businesspeople, and tourists who want to pay for the luxury. Some foreign companies on the island provide their Cuban employees with cell phones, and sometimes you'll see them in the streets making a rare call off hours. But average Cubans—the regular workaday proletariat, cannot obtain cellular service, and even if they could, the price is out of range at $130 a month.

As for the Internet, Cuba's first official Internet site was launched in 1995 through a Canadian server; but it wasn't until 1997 that the island opened its own gateway through the newly established National Center for Automated Interchange of Information (CENIAI), when Cuba went online. Today, CENIAI operates four Internet providers and dozens of sites, from the Communist newspaper *Granma,* to tourist sites where even U.S. citizens can discreetly purchase Cuban-sold package tours through third-country banks in Canada and the Bahamas. But for 99 percent of Cubans, Internet technology is strictly forbidden.

The reasons Cubans are forbidden access are never discussed, any more than the specific reasons for the Special Period, who's to blame, and what could have prevented its dire outcomes for the Cuban people, which after ten years are still not talked about in public forums. For the Internet, it's simply another civil liberty denied the people. Anyone who owns a home computer is permitted to have an e-mail account with one of several state agencies, which charge $10 a month for the service. Out of a population of 11 million, only an estimated 36,000, or one in 305, had Internet access in 2000.[1] The few permitted Internet access are journalists, computer technicians, Web-site designers for state Internet sites, certain scientists, university students, and, of course, celebrities, who bring the island prestige and essentially have carte blanche access to anything they want. These few who have legal access can surf the Web liberally, and they are trusted by the state to stay away from pornography and counterrevolutionary information. Spain's cultural center on Prado Avenue once had its own Internet lab with two computers, where average Cubans who were members could browse. But only a few knew about its existence, and it has since been shut down.

At Cuba's first official cybercafe, which opened in May 2000, I continually asked the managers whether Cubans were permitted to plug in.

"Why do you want to know? Are you a foreign journalist?" they would ask. After some prodding, I would finally get an embarrassed shrug of the shoulders and a slow shake of the head. The response was never an outright "No, Cubans are forbidden Internet access." It was always a stunned, apologetic look.

During the Special Period's paper shortages, business cards were a luxury none could afford. Today, though, everyone seems to find it in their means to scrape up the $3 fee their computer-owning contact charges for a batch of fifty. Computer owners in Cuba are the most prestigious, most hotly sought-after people on the island because there are so few have them, and because, in the information age, computer technology is almost impossible to live without. I've had dozens of requests to smuggle computers in, and the reasons were always the same. Cubans know that by owning a computer they can earn an illegal, nontaxable fortune by making business cards, bootlegging the CDs of popular U.S. music, which is unavailable in Cuban stores, and charging a fee to let other Cubans receive and send e-mails abroad.

"How much do they cost?" one woman who wished to become a CD bootlegger asked. "If you can do it, I have a friend at *la aduana,* customs, who will sneak you through. We can arrange to know which flight and time you'll be coming, and then we'll get him to check your bags."

"Yes, but there are three checkpoints if you have electronic equipment," I told her. "They'll surely catch me, and I'll be forced to pay an extra $500 for the tax. Plus they'll want to document who the receiver is, and since it's a computer, they may want to hold it until the receiver can sign for it."

It was a dilemma. I'd brought a photo scanner through once and was forced to pay the penalty. The problem again is one of control by outpricing. At the dollar stores, Cubans can order from a catalog of new computer equipment, which is marked up by 100 percent. I had seen the catalogs, and a basic Compaq or Hewlett Packard, which in the United States or any other country cost around $1,000 on sale, runs an easy $2,000 in Cuba. Photo scanners that cost $150 anywhere else were even more outrageous at $450.

"The price doesn't matter," the woman told me. "If they cost $1,000 in your country, even if trying to sneak it through *la aduana* fails, it's still only $1,500. With a computer, I can make easily the money in three months to pay you back."

There is no way of knowing exactly how many Cubans own computers, but the number is minuscule since few can afford them. The majority of nongovernment people who do have computers in their homes are making up to $500 a month. Many are relatives of Miami exiles, who send the money just for this purpose. They know that wiring the $2,000 for a computer will essentially start a son or daughter in a small business, even if it is illegal.

With this giant income, PC owners can then afford to pay for illegal Internet access, and charge other Cubans $5 an hour to surf. One couple I know, both young professional doctors in residence, simply pays a technician $100 a month to make the connection. We always talked about computers and the Internet because they liked to converse with someone who knew the lingo, terms such as "Java" and "C++" and "interface," which are like Russian to the average person. The couple explained that they pay a state technician each month to run the illegal Internet to their home.

This couple actually has a Hotmail account, which, like the Internet, is highly illegal contraband. If they were ever caught with the Internet connection, on top of contraband charges, the couple would be cited for stealing from the state for not paying the $10 monthly e-mail costs to CENIAI. If the history of their past Internet activity revealed Web sites that are in any way anti-Castro, it might buy them twenty years in prison, and at the very least, the loss of the computer, the house, everything. When I mentioned these possibilities, the couple played it down. They know that the laws surrounding computers are very loose, for now, mostly because the state hasn't figured out how to control the Internet bandits. Because there are so few computer owners, the issue hasn't yet become a serious threat.

"We don't want one of the state e-mail accounts," the husband replied when I asked him, "because, primarily, we would have to enroll, and then they would know we have a computer and it would be more difficult to get onto the Internet. And besides, we don't want them monitoring our mail."

Cubans will likely be able to plug in once the government finds a way to filter and regulate the information, but in 2002, they're still waiting. The biggest problem with the government's ban is that, by limiting information and providing no outlet for non-Communists to market their ideas and talent, it causes the Revolution to lag behind and stagnate at a faster rate as more and more look to the outside world for ways to fund and develop their ideas. Some distrust the system and hoard their ideas even if they have a contact inside the system because they fear that someone else might steal and develop them, taking all the credit. I was approached constantly by people who hoped I could locate entrepreneurs in the United States looking for ventures. On one occasion, a highly specialized communications tech approached me with a brilliant idea.

"I've already designed the technology, and I only need an investor," he told me. "My idea is to launch Cuba's first Internet phone service. Cuba doesn't have this service now, and I think it would do very well, because people could talk for free. Do you think you might know someone who would be interested?"

"Isn't there someone you can explain the idea to at the Cuban phone company or in one of the ministries?" I asked.

"I've tried all of that," he said. "I've exhausted all of my contacts. No one will listen to me, and even if they did, it would take three years to get it developed. There is no time to wait three years. This technology is important now."

Unfortunately for this man, and many like him, the system is geared against this kind of ambition because it promotes only selflessness and nonindividualist, uncompetitive conformity. If it weren't for this constriction of thought and self-isolation, Cuba would be much further ahead than it is today. It could even be a burgeoning technological environment. However, disinherited by the groupthink bureaucracy, nonstate Cubans with talent and ideas are forced to search desperately outside the Revolution for ways to develop them.

LOAFING AROUND HIS APARTMENT watching the news, Enrique engaged me in an animated discussion about the Helms-Burton bill. On March 12, 1996, President Bill Clinton passed the bill in retaliation to the Cuban air force's shooting down of two Brothers to the Rescue planes that had entered Cuban airspace without consent. The mission of the Brothers to the Rescue, founded by Bay of Pigs veteran José Basulto, was to scan the Florida Strait for rafters on the high seas and radio speedboats to assist them in fleeing Cuba. However, they also made over-flights of Havana to drop subversive anti-Castro leaflets, hoping to ignite an insurrection. The debate is whether the U.S. planes were over international waters or within the twelve-mile limit of Cuba's national airspace. To date, neither country has been able to provide convincing evidence one way or the other. Under pressure from the Miami exile community, Clinton passed Helms-Burton, which essentially froze the embargo—formerly only congressional resolutions—into law. The ultimatum was that the United States would not do business with Cuba until the Castros and Communism were gone, and the debt of $3 billion—incurred from the confiscation of foreign holdings during the 1961 nationalizations—was paid in full. To date, Cuba has worked out debt repayment plans with every country affected by the nationalizations except the United States. With Helms-Burton, Clinton essentially signed over all executive authority on Cuba to the U.S. Congress.

Today, Helms-Burton is discussed in the Cuban media as much as it was in 1996. Few Castro speeches go by without mention of it, and the law not only destroyed the average Cuban's hopes of the embargo's ever being lifted but also increased the pessimism felt toward the Cuban government and the United States. In Cuba, most all of Cuba's economic woes are blamed on the Cuban-American National Foundation (CANF), the Miami exile's political powerhouse, known in Cuba as "The Foundation," the de facto instigator of the embargo and Cuba's continued isolation. The predecessor to CANF, and the earliest known anti-Castro organization, was actually La Rosa Blanca, founded by Rafael Diaz-Balart, Castro's exiled brother-in-law, and a former statesman in the Batista cabinet. Rafael's two sons, Lincoln, a U.S. Republican congressman, and

Mario, a Florida state representative, are two of the most staunch sup-
porters of the embargo on U.S. soil. Ileana Ros-Lehtinen, another Cuban-
born exile, is Miami's other anti-Castro voice in Congress, and all three
are deeply entrenched in any new legislation involving Cuba.

In 1981, the late Jorge Mas Canosa founded CANF, which became
the political muscle of the exile's anti-Castro faction, born right when
the United States started softening on Cuban relations. Mas Canosa and
the Diaz-Balarts, besides authoring the Helms-Burton bill and pushing it
through Congress, are responsible for maintaining the current political
climate with Cuba. Because Florida is a swing state for presidential elections, they have the White House in their back pockets. And it all goes
back to a bitter family dispute between Rafael Diaz-Balart and his sister,
Castro's ex-wife, Mirta, and their son, Fidelito, over whom Castro and
Mirta had a vicious custody battle during the 1950s. One of the biggest
reasons why both Castro and the Diaz-Balarts became so personally
involved in the Elian González crisis was to relive vicariously this ancient
custody battle through Elian. In many ways, the entire embargo boils
down to bad family blood.

I explained to Enrique that, back in 1996, Helms-Burton had been in
discussion for an entire year before it was signed into law, and that it had
all but died before the Brothers to the Rescue tragedy gave Clinton the
fuel he needed to sign it.

"The bill was dead in Congress," I said. "Clinton, Congress, the business community, none wanted to isolate Cuba even more. Then Castro
shot down the planes, and *la fundación* pressured Clinton into signing
Helms-Burton, which he did a week later."

"This is news to me," Enrique gave me a stunned look. "This is not
what we've been told. If this is the case, then Castro *knew* when he shot
down the planes that the United States would pass the law as retribution.
So perhaps, if Castro had not shot down the planes, there would be no
embargo today."

Enrique shook his head, almost in disgust, his mind searching back
to March 1996. It all seemed to become very clear, and none of it jibed
with his past five years of understanding. "We were never told that

Helms-Burton was retribution for *Los Hermanos del Rescate*. And we were never told that Cuba owes $3 billion."

"Do you remember the Brothers to the Rescue planes coming over and dropping the leaflets in the streets?" I asked him.

"Yes, I remember," he said. "I can't remember what they had written on them. No one ever paid attention. It wasn't as if we all ran out into the street to chase after the papers. If I'm busy peeling yuca, am I going to drop everything for this? As if we would start another revolution and fight Miami's battle for them. We all thought they were just crazies from *la fundación*."

Enrique's reaction about Helms-Burton, or at least a different viewpoint, didn't surprise me. Few Cubans understand how the United States functions. They don't understand its domestic laws or its international relations, how Congress or the electoral process works. It's all a big mystery. Likewise, few Cubans really understand the process of *el dialogo*. Most Cubans I met knew only the government's portrayal of the United States as the bad guys who are out to strangle Cuba, and who write laws and pass them without examination and debate. Many Cubans sense that *la fundación* controls the entire U.S. political system, because everything Cubans are fed about the United States directly involves the embargo and the so-called Miami Mafia.

In reality, the embargo is already being lifted. It's not something that's going to happen overnight. It's a process that began on January 5, 1999, when Clinton reopened the negotiations after discussions were closed in 1983. At that time, Reagan was slamming the door shut from one side while Castro was pulling it shut from the other. The new door of *el dialogo* is wide open today, and discussions are in full swing. Each year since 1998, dozens of bills to lift parts or all of the embargo have been floored in Congress, and *la fundación* continues to foil them. *El dialogo* is not an open forum; rather, it's a series of actions that set a political tone between the Cuban government, the exile, and Washington. Senators from the United States visit Cuba, and, in a trade, Castro tones down his anti-U.S. rhetoric. Sometimes the music is harmonious, sometimes it's dissonant. But Castro is clearly playing ball, and every diplomatic move he's made, beginning with the Pope's 1998 visit, has been geared towards getting the embargo lifted.

In Miami, *"el dialogo"* is a commonplace word heard in living-room discussions involving the homeland and Castro. However, in Cuba, if you start talking about *el dialogo,* you'll likely get a puzzled look. When the United States began shipping al-Qaida prisoners to the Guantánamo naval base in eastern Cuba, Castro told global news networks that not only would he not be objecting to the U.S. move but that he would cooperate with the United States in any way possible. This is *el dialogo.* Everybody gives an inch, and we all get one step closer to lifting the embargo in its entirety.

In the Cuban media, there was no mention of Castro's pledge of cooperation with Guantánamo. Just as there was no mention of Castro's buying $30 million in U.S. grain and agricultural products in November 2001. In Cuba, there is little mention of anything regarding diplomatic trade-offs with the United States; certainly, by keeping such knowledge from the people, the Cuban government appears to remain strong at home.

Enrique is a newshound, mainly because for a sixty-year-old, there's little else to do besides play dominos, maybe go to the *peña deportiva,* take a walk, visit neighbors, and look for food. The thing that set Enrique apart from everyone else was his pure skepticism on everything he saw and heard. In Cuba, there is an evening debate on television each night called *La Mesa Redonda,* The Round Table, for which the government handpicks a forum of specialists and analysts on any given topic. One night it may be "The Future of Religion in Cuba." Another night it will be about the arrest of smugglers in Cuban waters. Sometimes there would be an entire block roped off in Vedado and under heavy guard at M Street. On such nights it meant that Castro would be joining the discussion. Enrique always watched the *Mesa Redonda,* and I briefly described CNN's *Crossfire,* in which opposing specialists and politicians wheel-spin and hotly battle out their views.

"Here," said Enrique. "Here in Cuba, we have the same thing, *La Mesa Redonda,* with Randy Alonso, only everybody *agrees* on everything!"

15

Marches for Justice

T he old Russian Lada crawls in first gear up Prado, a massive bullhorn strapped to the roof, rim mangled and straightened through
the years. The woman's small brown knuckles tighten around the wheel,
one hand hoisting a microphone to her mouth, crimson lips astir with
Revolutionary fire in a fractionary delay with the snout of the tuba.

"¡Mañana! Cada uno para la Tribuna Abierta Antimperialista José Martí.
For the victorious Pueblo Cubano! For Elian! Against the murderous
Cuban Adjustment act!"

Past the Hotel Sevilla she drifts, eyes scintillating, determined, possessed with purpose. Then onward, brushing by Hotel Inglaterra. Next
the Payret theater, and finally the Capitolio, where she spins a U-turn
and begins the process all over again.

A '53 Chevy darts around the Lada, nearly scraping fenders, and then
a '44 Ford wagon, and a '51 Dodge coupe, people's taxis jammed panel
to door panel with Cuban flesh. A steady stream of ancient U.S. iron. A
melting pot of skin tones, faces, and routine destinations. The woman in
the Lada, a devout Communist, makes a point of stopping at Parque

Central, where the typical hundred or so men roil in that special brand of Cuban machismo so vibrant you can see it floating in the air.

"Tomorrow we march to the protest dome!" the Lada rolls up to the curb. "Read today's *Granma* for details."

The men pause to absorb the woman's chant, but they already know about the march, just like the march last Friday and the Friday before, and they launch back into their arguments.

"*¡Oye chicos!* Did you hear me?" barks the bullhorn. "Take some of that energy from your mouths and put it into your legs tomorrow! *¿Me entienden?*" A few men wave in acknowledgement as the woman floats off and hangs a left on Neptuno.

I would see this woman almost every Thursday morning, barking for the weekly Friday marches for Elian's return and various other gripes with the United States.

Her basic function was to be "The Reminder," that repetitive voice that would psychologically stir streets into armies of protesters, just like the daily reminders in the newspaper *Granma,* or the reminders on *Cubavision* television that yes, tomorrow we will be 200,000 strong, 450,000 strong, 1,000,000 strong in our march for justice against the imperialist *yanquis* who want to invade Cuba and take her back.

No doubt, Cubans hold the record number of protests against Uncle Sam's policies, rivaling even U.S. activists on the home turf. The real momentum of these sporadic invasions of the U.S. Interests Section by flag-waving, slogan-chanting Cubans started around 1985 to demand the return of the Guantánamo naval base, an issue that is still unsettled in 2002. By the mid 1980s, with perestroika in full swing, it was becoming obvious that Castro couldn't count on the Soviet military shield. Because of the imminent pressure of a possible Reagan-Bush invasion—using the War on Drugs as a pretext—Castro shifted his style from radical to leftist. Rather than maintaining his position as a direct U.S. national security threat, he began staging "peaceful protests," which would show Cuba as the innocent victim should an invasion occur. Castro was looking for every conceivable smoking gun to throw back at the United States. Until that time, the United States was considered *part* of the problem in

Cuba's woes, but not *the* problem. This is when Cuba began emulating more of the "victim of imperialism" role. The marches were a centerpiece of this shift, but it took another fifteen years and one Elian González for the world media to train its cameras on them, leading many to believe the protests are new Cuban phenomena.

Viewers in other countries who followed the Elian crisis were fed a constant barrage of nightly news clips showing streams of Cubans storming the U.S. Interests Section—and it hurt Cuba's tourism. But the money lost as a result was made up for in points gained on the political front. Dozens of bills were floored in the U.S. Congress to lift the embargo, to open trade with Cuba, to remove the travel ban, to normalize relations between the two opposing governments. Many Americans and Europeans were coming to Cuba to see for themselves, trying to determine exactly why this outlaw culture was still being bulked in with rogue nations such as Iran and Libya. For Fidel, it was a no-lose situation; the longer the United States kept Elian, the better Cuba looked, and if they kept him forever, it would result in a permanent stain. If the United States returned Elian, Castro would also win, because 1) the United States would be admitting he was right, and 2) the comandante would then rope in fledgling Cubans who had lost faith during the Special Period. But, more important, by personally orchestrating the Elian crisis, Castro pulled off the biggest coup he'd been struggling for in his tenure as Cuba's prime minister: He won the world's sympathy.

For seven months, they marched, and marched, and marched. And I marched with them. Every week it was a different theme. One week Castro would round up a couple hundred thousand Cuban grandmothers to coincide with Elian's grandmothers' Washington visit. The next week there were throngs of elementary school kids, the *pioneros,* marching to coincide with Elian's classmates' visit to the United States. A week later, it was the *trabajadores,* the factory workers; next, the tourism workers. From province to province across the island, Castro would snap his fingers and protests would be held to bring Elian home; they were held on the dates that commemorate important historical events, of which Cuba has no shortage, such as the Bay of Pigs victory, the day Che's bones were returned from Bolivia, the day the Cuban Communist Party was born, the day Antonio Maceo delivered his *Juramento de Baragua,* the 1878 declaration to continue the Ten Years War for independence from Spain. Castro even rewrote Maceo's protest and focused most of this article of war on Elian's return; he then gave one of his four-hour harangues at Mangos de Baragua on February 19, 2000, the 122nd anniversary of the event.

The May Day celebration is one of Cuba's most cherished pastimes. It takes place each year, highlighted by a Castro speech in the Plaza of the Revolution. The 2000 May Day march with Fidel was the big salvo for Elian; it lured a record 1 million *habaneros* (half the population of the city) into the streets, along with thousands more Cubans from across the island. It was an historic event, and I asked Ramon to join me and Armando's son Lucas at the march to help explain what was going on. In Cuba, you say 7:00 A.M. sharp, and everybody rolls in by 8:30 or 9:00 and there are no apologies or questions, it's just the way it is. Cuba runs on a give-or-take-an-hour clock, and you just get used to it. We all met up at Armando's apartment for coffee. But no matter how hard we tried to persuade him and Carmen to come along, they would have nothing to do with it.

"*Papi no sale la casa nunca,*" Lucas antagonized his father with a chuckle. "The only time he leaves the house is if there's a special price on food somewhere. If there was rice for two pesos at the plaza, he would have been there, the first in line, even before the sun came up."

"Nah," Armando retorted with a grunt. "*Ese no me interesa.* That nonsense doesn't interest me. You know, in every other country in the world, the first of May is when the people protest their governments. But not in Cuba. Here we celebrate. If we protest we go to jail. Don't you have a day in your country for the workers?"

"It's called Labor Day," I said. "On September 1, and everybody takes the day off."

"I thought so," said Armando. "Here May 1 is the day of the workers, but instead of relaxing for the day, we march. It's just more work. You guys go ahead. I'll watch it on TV if I get bored."

Although he didn't say so, by refusing to march, Armando was resisting the government in his own way. His nonparticipation may not have meant much in the big picture, but it meant a lot to him. I could see the self-empowering satisfaction in his eyes, his determination to resist in any small way possible. On top of this, the noise and lines and people constantly invading Armando's space in downtown Havana are the things he hates most about the city; May Day is one of the only days of the year when the streets are barren, when Havana is a ghost town, when there are no signs of police, no horns blowing, no traffic, no buses. It was a day of peace and quiet for a million *habaneros*, including Armando and Carmen, and they were going to enjoy every succulent moment of it. If it weren't for me, Ramon and Lucas probably would have stayed home, too. Why crawl out of bed so early to march in the baking heat? But, as a lot of marchers reasoned, there was nothing else to do. It was a good place to look at girls in the crowd, maybe bump into a friend and catch wind of a party happening later in the evening.

Rolando and Martina Ibáñez weren't marching either. Instead they were having their apartment painted by a Bay of Pigs veteran who did most of their construction work.

"We have to stay here and care for the house," said Martina. "Marching doesn't put food on the table."

"To hell with those marches," added Rolando. "Those people you see march, all of them are robots."

"So how does Castro get so many people to march at the snap of his fingers?"

"It's like a fiesta," said Rolando. "Like a vacation. Fidel decides he wants the workers to march. So the organizers call up all the factories and tell the bosses that the work order for the next day is to march. As an *estimulo*, the workers receive maybe half a sandwich and a glass of lemonade. The next morning there will be 200,000 workers marching along the Malecón. A week later it is 500,000 school students. They march for four hours, and get the rest of the day off. It's like a fiesta."

May Day is different, though. It's Cuba's second biggest national holiday, paled only by July 26, which celebrates the 1953 date Castro failed at his ambitious attempt to launch the revolutionary war by attacking the Moncada military barracks in Santiago. With a few cars full of rag-tag rebels, Castro charged into the barracks, certain that the rest of Cuba would pick up arms and follow his lead. Cuba at the time was ripe for revolution, but none heeded the call. July 26, 1953 is commonly known as the day the revolution started, ending in the 1959 victory six years later. Yet here is Cuba, celebrating May Day, the day of Russian independence, eleven full years after the Berlin Wall crumbled and the Soviets stormed through Moscow destroying their own Communist symbols. What's more, only 10 percent of Cubans are actual card-holding Communists. So why does 50 percent of the population of Havana join Castro in this celebration?

Armando ran up to the attic, where he keeps his goodies such as the 1960 newspaper stashed, and returned with a small history book.

"Parts of history," he said, "that they wanted to erase."

Dusting off the book, he flipped it open to the middle and showed me a picture taken in the Roaring Twenties during the tenure of President Machado, who led one of the most brutal and corrupt regimes in Cuba's history until his 1933 ouster.

"Look at this," said Armando. "This picture was taken at the Presidential Palace. Do you see how many people have come to listen to Machado give a speech?"

In the photo, thousands of Cubans were gathered in the antique tropical heat of the palace square; they wore the art deco fashion of the day, the men in their white, long-sleeved shirts and black ties, the fedoras and wool slacks, and smoking the hot new Punch cigars; the women in flapper-style dresses and racy straw hats.

"*No es facil,*" said Armando. "In Havana, when Fidel gets one million to march, there are one million who stay home. Look at this photo and how many supported Machado. Fifty percent were for him, fifty percent against. These numbers are historical for politicians in Cuba, and it's the same with Castro. Half of the people profited under Machado, and half profit with Castro. Not everyone thought Machado was a bad president. Not everyone thinks Castro is a good one."

〜〜

You HAVEN'T LIVED until you've witnessed the irony of a young *pio-nera* screaming obscenities about the evils of imperialism through a monstrous stack of U.S.-made JVC speakers to a swelling hive of 1 million flag-waving Cubans. The electricity, the beauty, the presence of this degree of Revolutionary energy is staggering. Behind the people, a six-story bas-relief of Che Guevara looms from the side of the Ministry of the Interior over the baking pavement of the Plaza of the Revolution. And in front, the monolithic statue of the revolutionary apostle José Martí stares down on the people with his permanently chiseled stare of approval and wisdom.

The Plaza of the Revolution is a military zone. The entire island is a military zone. Everywhere those green uniforms, those cold suspicious glances, all permanently engraved into the Cuban rhythm. How normal those green uniforms become over time, how easily they blend into the language of the streets. All of Cuba is the streets. All of Cuba is a military zone. It's so easy to forget this. But there are the reminders. The green uniforms. Revolutionary billboards on every corner. Flags and slogans so omnipresent that eventually they become invisible. Once I asked Armando whether a day ever went by in which he didn't think about Castro. After a moment of thought he pointed to the television and said, "For the past forty years, we've seen him every ten minutes, all day long. He's everywhere. It's part of the Cuban psyche now. I can't remember a day when I didn't think of Castro."

"*¡Viva Fidel!*" screams the child through the ear-splitting sound system.

"*¡Viva!*" chants the crowd.

"*¡Viva la Revolución!*"

"*¡Viva!*" A million flags shoot toward the sky.

"*¡Patria O Muerte! Venceremos!*"

Then comes the silence. In great symphonies and plays, the silence immediately following the action gives the experience dimension. Space is as important a tool as the sound, and the silence allows the mind to wrap itself around and digest the impact of what has occurred. Cuban national acts function the same way. Repetition and harmony, disso-

nance and tension, pursued by a finale of euphoria, immediately followed by that stark curtain of silence. Then comes rest and music, perhaps *"La Bayamesa"* or *"Guantanamera,"* followed by a Silvio Rodriguez
folk song. And then the next speech.

On this May Day, an inspiring keynote address was given by special
guest, Hebe de Bonafini, the Argentinean founder of the Mothers of the
Plaza of May, who spoke against neocolonialism and exploitation in the
impoverished third world. Soon after, Castro took the platform in his
new Adidas tennis shoes and delivered a typical but unusually short
thirty-minute speech; he went through several grievances against the
United States, predominantly about Elian González, and used the alle-
gory of David and Goliath. At the end of the speech, he pulled out a cell
phone and wrapped it up with a call to Elian's father, Juan Miguel, at the
Wye Plantation in Delaware. There is some debate about whether Castro actually placed the call, but for 1 million Cubans, it was sensational,
charging the crowd with a shot of nationalist pride.

"Every year before this year," said Ramon, "the people just came to
the plaza, listened to the speeches, and went home. Today, we start at the
plaza and march to the Interests Section. This is the first time of marching in this manner."

The reason was Elian González. On former marches that began
along the Malecón and ended at the plaza, many Cubans would skip the
march and head up to the speeches; or they would simply straggle into
file when they got around to it, so the wall of flesh that passed the U.S.
Interests Section was spotty and full of holes. The march organizers no
doubt thought of this when planning the 2000 demonstration. If you
have all the people marching at once, it shows greater strength, especially if the march is paced so that everyone is sandwiched together. For
Castro, it was brilliant guerilla theater in the media war over Elian,
knowing that CNN and the rest of the global news networks would be
waiting at the protest dome for the showdown.

This kind of media strategy is nothing new to Castro. He's a master
at the game, and the press has always been his number one weapon for
winning support at home and from allies abroad. During the war in the

Sierra Maestra, it was reported that Castro had been killed by the Cuban military, a lie that the dictator Fulgencio Batista boasted to the world media. In 1957, shortly after the rumor of Castro's death, *New York Times* reporter Herbert Matthews was invited into Castro's camp for an exclusive interview. At the time, Castro's rebel army amounted to about twenty poorly armed soldiers. Castro shrewdly duped Matthews by ordering pairs of soldiers to march back and forth during the interview to create the appearance of staggering numbers of troops. He also had ordered one soldier to interrupt the interview with urgent news from fictitious "columns" in the field. When Matthews returned to the United States and wrote his story, he called Castro's army "a force to be reckoned with."

When the march began, my friends and I jogged ahead twenty blocks on a street parallel to the main route, hoping to cut off on a cross street where we could run to the front and take photos of Castro in the lead. Through police cordons and along alleyways we zig-zagged, finally getting ahead, and bolted to the front of the line just before Castro passed not ten feet away. Interestingly, in street after street after street, at the end of each block stood an impregnable human cordon of muscular volunteers who stood tightly together, shoulder to shoulder, facing the marchers.

"Why do they have these volunteers posted here like this?" I asked Lucas and Ramon. "Do they want to prevent people like us from entering the march?"

"No," they both laughed. "After a few blocks, the people get tired of marching in the hot sun. They want to go home and watch television. The volunteers aren't here to stop us from joining the march. They're here to prevent the marchers from leaving. If they didn't have the volunteers here, by the time the march reached the Interests Section, Fidel would be walking alone."

16

A Day At School

Fidel would be walking alone. . . . That was a new one. One of the big slogans for the Elian crisis was *Regresa Elian a su pupitre,* "Return Elian to his school desk." This was the big debate. What exactly was Elian returning to? Back to the tyranny, the brainwashing? Or back to the Revolutionary struggle where he belonged?

The grade school *pioneros* were unarguably the largest group of Cubans affected by the Elian crisis. But despite the poverty, with today's *pioneros,* the Revolution has produced some of the happiest kids in the world. They missed the worst years of the Special Period and have known nothing but a relative stability.

At a local school near the Ibáñezes, there was no gym or playground. The administration simply roped off the street for half a block each day at recess, where the kids could play under supervision. They play in the streets, the streets are safe, and the people look after them. The children are unquestionably the most successful aspect of the Cuban Socialist experience.

Most of these kids have very little in the way of material things. Most of the parents have a hard time scraping enough together to purchase a new school uniform; but without the uniform, the child is forbidden to enter the building, so it's always a familial priority. Pencils and notebooks must also be provided by the parents, and since the Ministry of Education usually provides only one textbook and chalk for the teacher's use, the students learn by note-taking and fill up the notebooks fairly quickly. During the height of the Special Period, there were few notebooks due to the paper shortage. Today, because there is a uniform shortage, the children take very good care of their one or two uniforms. They are washed and pressed each time they're used.

I'll never forget a special day I stepped out into the street and the *pioneros* were leaving school for the day. As in any country, towards the end of the school year, the volume of screams and laughter when the kids hit the streets usually turns up a few notches, but on this day, the merriment was extra loud, so I walked down to see what the stir was about. On the way out of the building, each child was handed a small packet, something like a greeting card, and within the packet were several prints of Elian González. It was just after the reunion with his father in the United States, and every photo in the packet showed Elian smiling. The new photo was different from all the photos on the billboards, which had shown a sad Elian, an Elian behind bars, for the preceding five months. And on the front flap of the card was a quote by José Martí in an elegant script about the importance of children to the struggle.

Naturally, the kids were overjoyed. For most, who usually entertain themselves knocking around a ball of duct tape in street baseball, or play marbles, or might have one doll, such a colorful little gift from the government was a new possession in a world of few possessions, and the children showed them off to each other in their quirky way, completely consumed with their good fortune. Usually, when the government gives gifts, they're typically reserved for the kids in Old Havana to create the illusion to the tourists that the children are provided for. This time, all of Havana's *pioneros* received the little Elian cards, which must have been an enormous expense. And for Castro, no expense is too large when it comes to the Revolutionary indoctrination of the *pioneros.* After all, they will be the ones inevitably sustaining the machine.

Months later, I spent an entire day at one of Cuba's middle schools, meeting with the superintendent and attending a few 8th grade classes. Afterwards, I went to see Francisco the sausage maker and Daysi to hear their own clear-headed, common sense impressions of the Revolutionary school system. Cuba's schools are basically the same as those in any Western country. There are morning classes, followed by a recess for lunch, after which classes resume. The Cuban school system is simple in structure: The children enter their first grade education at age six and are called the *pioneros,* the national pioneers of Cuba's Socialist future. At age eleven, they graduate from sixth grade and enter secondary school; this is when their uniforms change from Cuba's national colors of red, white, and blue to simply white and gold. At age fifteen, the students enter a year of evaluation in the classroom, when testing and performance decides their future classification. At sixteen, they enter Cuba's *beca* system, the pre-university high school that preps students either for a working trade or higher education, depending on grades and family decisions.

The future depends on what needs the regime has in the professions, and the grades of the students. For example, if there are demands in the government for bridge engineers, then a dozen slots will be opened for future studies at the university level for this profession. If there is little demand in, say, a linguistic specialty, perhaps only two slots will be open at the university for this profession. Competition is stiff for university studies, and only the top 5 percentile of Cuban kids with the highest marks are eligible to compete for the open slots and enter the university. If a child gets straight A's on his report cards and good marks for obedience, he is groomed for the professions. However, he can't simply say, "I want to be an artist" or "I want to be a chemist," and then enter the university and study whatever he wishes. It all depends on the demand. And if a child is brilliant at physics, for example, and has good marks but turns in work slightly inferior to that of another student, he will perhaps lose the competition for the few slots in physics open at the university and be forced to decide on studying bridge engineering or sewer inspection, wherever the regime projects a future demand. Honor students are placed highest on the Revolutionary pedestal of superiority; they enter special vocational schools, which groom them for the highest positions in the country, by the best professors.

The other 95 percent of students have more choices, and they'll enter the pre-university as future *trabajadores,* workers, in the trades of their choice. Their choices include careers in the building trades, law enforcement, bookkeeping, auto repair, hotel housekeeping, the military, agriculture, nursing—there are many possibilities. At sixteen, everything is decided. The kids then begin their career tracks in the *beca;* this is when they spend half the day in classes and the other half working in the trade or profession of their choosing. There are a few variations on the *beca,* but the above essentially describes the system. After three years in the *beca,* two mandatory years are spent in the military, after which the 95 lower percentile of youngsters enter the Cuban workforce in their chosen fields. The superior students spend only one year in the military, and then go on to the university, where they earn a 30-peso monthly stipend, later entering their professions. Before 1995, Cuban university graduates were forbidden to hold licenses and enter the new sector of self-employment. But when the university enrollments fell and absenteeism increased as a means to protest this restriction for dollar-hungry Cubans, the regime was forced to alter its stance and pass a law that allowed graduates to become self-employed. Currently, only those graduates entering the medical professions are still restricted from self-employment. These students, after their five years of training, will never be able to leave Cuba. Once they finish their studies, they are stuck on the island unless the government sends them on an internationalist mission.

Cuba's schools have two essential functions: to enhance critical thinking through education, and to indoctrinate the child into the Revolutionary program, which in turn translates into society. To deviate from the Revolution is to be antisocial, contrary to the cause, a hindrance to the progress of Cuban Socialism. The schools are the systematic tool used to embed this logic into the child. Undeniably, though, the ultimate goal of Cuba's school system is to prime children for future membership in the Communist Party, and the superintendent admitted this at the end of my day at the middle school.

"What is the purpose, the function of Cuba's school system?" I asked her.

"To provide the students with a Revolutionary education, giving the basic knowledge of the world. Here the children acquire the education necessary to advance the Cuban Socialism."

"Yes, this I understand," I said, "but in reality the school system is designed to groom good Communists, right?"

She looked at me suspiciously when I framed it in this way. "You're not a reporter are you? You ask questions like a reporter."

"No, I'm just curious," I said. "In my country, the schools systematically groom the children to grow up and be good capitalist consumers. To me there is no difference, capitalist, Communist, they are only two ideologies."

"Since you put it that way," she said, "yes, the Cuban school system is designed to produce good Communists."

The Cuban superintendent, essentially the school principal, also teaches classes; this woman's specialty was computer science, which she studied at the university. Her school was one of the first in Havana to have a computer lab installed, and she was very excited about being instrumental in bringing the Cuban youth up-to-date in computer technology.

"In my class, the children learn Windows, Word, Excel. We use a Windows 98 operating system. We have only five computers for all the students to share per class, but we are one of only five schools in Havana that has a computer lab. Right now the government is working on getting them installed in every school."

The typical Cuban school has a shrine on which sits a bust of José Martí, a Cuban flag, and a Martí quote, such as: *"En la escuela se ha de apprender el manejo de las Fuerzas con que en la vida se ha de luchar,"* which essentially means "In the school, one must learn how to use the tools necessary for the life struggle." Martí was not a Communist but a patriot in the vein of George Washington or Thomas Jefferson, yet the regime has revised history and twisted all of Martí's wisdom, along with that of the rest of Cuba's liberators, into the Communist format. In Cuba's schools, no distinction is made between the struggles of Martí, of Antonio Maceo (who lived two centuries ago), or of today's Communist Castro. A cyclical history is ingrained into the children at a very young age. The struggle of Maceo is translated into today's struggle by means of the U.S. embargo, even though the revolution has indeed been won. And although Martí or Maceo would likely never approve of a Communist administration in Cuba, the children are led to believe that these liberators were Communist. From the ages of six to fourteen, Cuba's children undergo rigorous indoctrination. Each morning the day begins with the singing of *La Bayamesa* and the *March of the Guerrilla,* two of Cuba's national anthems. Then before each period, a *lema,* a slogan, is rehearsed by the entire class, such as, "To be a teacher is to be a creator," or "The child's role is to study, to work, to learn, to conquer the future."

Yet even though the system is rigid in structure, kids will be kids. During the English class that I attended, one child slept through class. One girl, an honors student, took pride in throwing the teacher curves on words that even she couldn't translate, such as "hyena" and "jaguar." Two boys would throw paper balls at each other when the teacher's back was turned. These things are universal with young students around the globe when they are thirteen or fourteen years old. Yet in Cuba there seems to be a residual hesitancy for students to take the English language seriously because it's the native tongue of the *yanquis.* Cubans have been taught to abhor Americans, if not in the rhetoric, then in policy and social attitude, despite the appeal of American influence in the popular culture. Most Cubans I know had already forgotten the language two years out of high school, and many are now relearning it on the new tri-weekly hour-long television program, *Universidad para Todos,* "University for Everyone." The newspaper *Juventud Rebelde* prints and sells tabloid-sized workbooks for 20 centavos that viewers use when watching the programs. Many Cubans are realizing today that a second or third language can be the key to acquiring contacts and dollars. *Casa particular* owners, taxi drivers, *jineteros,* and prostitutes—many Cubans are taking advantage of these state-broadcast telecourses, which include basic English, intermediate English, advanced Spanish grammar, and world history. Martina Ibáñez and Armando both liked to throw a few English words at me to see whether they were saying them properly, and I would often hear Martina practicing this new phenomenon of Cuban Spanglish with such phrases as, *"Necesito limpiar my house,"* or *"Me voy al shopping comprar una esponja por my kitchen."*

At the middle school, the geography class I attended was more structured than the English class. The students paid closer attention, and it was interesting because the geography of the United States was never mentioned. The lesson covered regional climates around the globe, including Europe, South America, and parts of Europe. But when it came to North America, it was Mexico, and then Canada, but nothing in between. Armando later told me that before Castro, it was just the opposite. The United States was covered, though sparsely. Today, in Cuba's world history classes, the only American discussed is Abraham Lincoln; when you get into a conversation about pre-Kennedy U.S. presidents with the average Cuban, the most you are likely to hear is some trivia about the Civil War and Lincoln's role as an American liberator. My Communist friend Ana, a university art history professor, explained that in high school and university, artists from the United States are never studied. Most focus is placed on Mexican arts and the European modernists. She'd never heard of Andy Warhol. The absence of North American culture, geography, and history in Cuba's school system is part of the "we're right, they're wrong" structure of the program, which is highly selective of the things being taught. Politics are taught to Cuban children, but because the structure of the system is political in itself, it limits the critical thinking that Fidel himself promotes. Ultimately, this results in the homogenization of thought and the people's growing hunger for new information.

After my day at school, I went to Francisco's home to discuss the experience, and to ask his thirteen-year-old son, Daniel, to give me the inside scoop. Parents are universally concerned about their children's educations, and Daysi and Francisco's opinions were important to me. But my friends were more interested in hearing my own comparisons between the schools in Cuba and those in the United States.

"What do you think about the schools in Cuba having no running water?" Daysi asked me. She was very direct in her approach, and I could tell she had a mountain of opinions.

"I'm not sure what to think about this," I said. "After all, it's Cuba, and it's the third world. These conditions seem normal considering the circumstances."

"Well, I think the conditions are terrible," she said. "The children have to carry the water to flush the toilets. There's no place to wash their hands. The bathrooms stink with urine."

"But on the other hand," I said, "all of Cuba's schools are now being equipped with computer labs. The government knows that technology is the future."

Daniel was listening as we talked, which concerned me, and I asked whether we should talk in private, and then I could ask him a few questions later.

"No, it's okay," said Francisco. "We don't hide anything from him. In the past, the Cuban parents would wait until the kids went to bed, and then we'd discuss everything quietly. But things have changed. Today, everyone talks honestly about the government in the presence of their children."

When I asked Daniel questions about his own school, he shrugged his shoulders a lot.

"I don't like school that much," he said, answering several of my questions. "I don't like the teachers. For me it's a place to see my friends. I'm not sure yet of the future. I like martial arts and music. I like the

Back Street Boys and N'Sync. Some of the kids smoke in the bathrooms. That's the biggest problem."

"Isn't that terrible?" Daysi added. "That there are kids smoking in the bathrooms? Do the kids do that in your country?"

I explained that it all sounded normal to me, but by the look in her eyes, I could tell I wasn't very convincing. The interesting thing was how Francisco and Daysi, like all the Cubans I know, compared everything in their country to conditions in the United States. When they talked about Cuban healthcare, transportation, sewage, anything, it was held in reference to the north. Partly due to the tourist explosion, when new information began trickling into Cuba for comparison purposes, and partly from the pre-Castro tradition, Cubans typically compare themselves to the United States. In the media, the regime only selectively compares itself to the United States, both with the value of the peso to the dollar and when it can outdo the *yanquis* statistically; an example of this occurred in the year 2000, when Cuba bragged about a 7.4 to 1,000 infant mortality rate,[1] the same U.S. infant mortality rate for that year. "If the capitalists can do it, the Revolutionaries can do it better," the *lema* goes. When it talks about poverty and the economy, the government always compares Cuba with Mexico and Haiti, placing itself somewhere between the two. However, when it comes to lifestyles, average Cubans almost instinctively compare theirs with those of the United States. "They have this, we should too," is the attitude in the streets, and the newest question today is this: "Without Castro, without the Revolution and *la lucha*, would we have it too?"

Even Daniel, a shy thirteen-year-old Cuban kid who, like most boys of his age, has his eyes set on girls and music, thinks about the incongruent life on the island. He, too, lives the paradox of what it means to be Cuban. He spends half the day in the rigid structure of the system's indoctrination, yet at home he is treated as an equal and openly questions the wisdom of the Revolution.

It is strange to hear Cubans utter the word "Castro." They could be flying along, explaining a thought, but the moment the word gets to "Castro," the voice drops almost to a whisper, the eyes look suspiciously back and forth, "Castro" is spoken, and the voice resumes its normal volume. It's the unutterable word. Fluid thinkers simply pull on their chins as if stroking an invisible beard when the sentence comes to the word "Castro," and they often replace the chieftain's name with *El Dios* or *El Hombre*, "God" or "The Man."

I was in Armando's living room and heavily into a political discussion when he caught me doing this, too. I came to the word "Castro" in a sentence, paused, looked out the window, dropped my voice, said "Castro," and then finished the sentence. This habit of dropping the volume had become natural to me by then. I had simply become accustomed to doing it myself through the course of many conversations.

"Why are you whispering?" Armando stopped me cold. "What are you looking around for?"

"You know exactly why I did that," I said. "You also do this all the time, so why are you criticizing me for doing it?"

"I'm not," he said. "But it's funny to see you doing it."

When I was talking with Francisco and his family about the school system, this happened again, only it was Daniel who lowered his voice. In the past, Cuba's children had always been sheltered from the criticisms of Castro, and it wasn't until they reached the eighteen-to-twenty-one age group that they were suddenly thrown into the confusion of losing their innocence and sorting out the contradictions.

"Castro doesn't care about the kids," Daniel whispered.

"The problem," added Daysi as she looked around, "is that Castro is more concerned about being able to say we have computers in every school than he is about the children having running water. Which is more important? The teachers are awful. They get paid so little that they don't concentrate on the kids anymore. They leave school early. They only think about how they're going to find dollars. It wasn't this way when we were young. The quality of the education has declined."

The Cuban teacher shortage could be comparable to the problems in North American inner-city schools, where the teachers are generally underpaid and the hiring standards are sacrificed to keep the positions filled and the doors from closing. According to Armando, who taught school from the 1970s until the early 1990s, teachers with a university degree in education start out at 180 pesos a month. Teachers without the degree start out at 148 pesos. The superintendent who guided me through the middle school earns 450 pesos a month. In the mid-1980s, the Revolution's best years, 148 pesos wavered between $30 and $45 in value, which at that time was a reasonable wage in Cuba. A decade and a half of stabilized inflation later, 148 pesos is worth $7.40; to live comfortably in Cuba in 2002, a family needs to earn about $100 a month. In 1994, when the Special Period reached crisis levels, 148 pesos were worth $1 in real value. Armando explained that there is a current restructuring of teachers salaries to contend with the decline in the quality of Cuban education. University grads will now earn 220 pesos a month; but this is only $2 more per month and will unlikely curb the need for Cuban teachers to earn money outside the school.

Christmas with the Castros

When I asked average Cubans what they thought about communism, with a wave of the hand, sick of hearing about it, they would say, "Bah! Haven't you heard? All Cubans are Communist." Others would say, "Communists? In Cuba? When you find a Communist in Cuba, let me know."

One man, a Communist Youth Party member, told me with a chuckle, "Cuba is not Communist. Cuba is not Socialist. Some parts of our country are Socialist, just like in the United States. Your public transportation system is Socialist because it's administered by your government so that everyone will have fair and equal access. Ours is the same. Our economy is not Socialist in its entirety. It is a free market economy with Socialist elements. However, the Cuban society and economy are administered by the Communist Party."

In reality, only 10 percent of Cuba's citizens are registered Communist Party members. Half those belong to the UJC, the Communist Youth Party, a powerless organization that grooms ambitious young people between fourteen and twenty-seven for membership in the higher Communist Party of government functionaries and decision-makers, who in turn administer everything on the island through the various branches and ministries.

Enrique, who has read numerous Marxist-Leninist texts, said outright, "Fidel is not Communist. Neither is Raul Castro. Nor was Che Guevara." I'd heard the same blasphemous statements more than a dozen times in my travels. Even during the Cuban Missile Crisis, Soviet Premier Krushchev told U.S. officials, "Castro is no Communist, but you are turning him into one."

On April 16, 1961, Fidel Castro stood atop a grave in the Colón cemetery in Vedado and announced to the world that the Cuban Revolution was Socialist in nature. At the time, the United States was preparing to invade Cuba with a small army of CIA-trained exiled Cubans living in Florida. The *New York Times* had broken the story that the CIA was covertly planning the operation, and Castro had received intelligence reports that a U.S. invasion was imminent. Feeling defenseless and knowing that the Cuban armed forces had no chance of surviving against the military might of the United States, Castro declared Cuba Socialist in a desperate attempt to thwart the attack. He was hoping to send the message that the United States would be contending with Soviet forces if it invaded Cuba.

On April 17, the 2,000-troop Cuban-exile army, fresh from their Nicaraguan training camps, launched the attack. The plan was to secure a beachhead and declare a provisional government. Immediately, the U.S. government would recognize the provisional government and send in the navy and the marines, who were waiting with destroyers and aircraft carriers just outside the twelve-mile mark of Cuba's national water boundary, to destroy Castro. At the last minute, John F. Kennedy decided to renege on the U.S. commitment of military aid to the invading force for fear that the attack would create an international scandal. Without air cover, the invasion was doomed. The beachhead was never secured, the operation crumbled, and the rest is history. Then and now, the defeat of the exile army is called "The Victory" in Cuba. It's the biggest page of history in all of Castro's tenure.

Fearing another invasion and knowing that merely standing on a tomb and declaring Cuba Socialist wasn't enough, Castro took measures to attain Moscow's military shield by entrenching the Soviets in Cuban affairs. On December 2, 1961, Castro declared, "I am a Marxist-Leninist and will be one for the rest of my life." Neither he nor the Cuban people wanted the Soviets, but it was a necessary trade-off. Today, very little remains in Cuba to show for the thirty years the USSR was entrenched in the island. Besides the Eastern European cars and buses, some statues of Lenin, and a few Russians who stayed behind after marrying Cubans, you'd hardly know the Soviets had been there. It's a chapter the regime would rather forget about, mostly because the Soviets abandoned Castro and left him hanging out to dry beginning in the mid-1980s. During his Special Period speeches, Castro bitterly chastised the Soviets as sellouts to the United States. But underlying the rhetorical finger pointing was Castro's anger with himself for leaning the entire Cuban economy on the Soviets to begin with. The Cubans I spoke with about the Soviet epoch said they had always seen the Soviets as a necessary evil to be approached with indifference and a healthy distance because they were a reminder that the Cuban dependence on one superpower had been traded off for another. Cubans would consistently say, for example, "Back then. . . . Yes, back then. When Cuba was *Russian*." The emphasis was always placed on the word "Russian" and accompanied with a grimace, as if the word itself had a foul taste. But even with the Soviet Union gone, communism, at least in title, remains.

Enrique, a brilliant thinker, perhaps framed it best.

"Cuba is not Communist. And it's not Socialist. Cuba is centralist. . . . Communism. . . . Hmmph," he would grunt. "Look around. Communism does not allow Christians in the Party, but here in Cuba it's now allowed. That's not communism. And take for example these young Communists who get all the good jobs as cashiers in the tourist market.

The government won't trust anyone but Communists to count the money. Yet all Communist cashiers are thieves, short-changing the customers. They join the Party to obtain the better jobs, a nicer house, a free car, unlimited gasoline, prestige. Do you think in their hearts they are truly Communists? No. There are no Communists in Cuba. They are centralists and opportunists."

As soon as Cuba entered the Special Period, membership in the Party increased dramatically, an event that supports Enrique's observations. For the full decade of the 1980s, annual membership had increased by only 4 percent. Yet between 1990 and 1997, membership increased from 550,000 in 1990 to 780,000 by 1997, more than 30 percent.[1] The impoverished 1970s had, like the Special Period, seen similar increases in membership. Two factors weigh into this pattern. One, during the Rectification of the 1980s, Castro wanted to cleanse the party of opportunists, decisionmakers with too much autonomy, and ambition, so the rules were changed, making membership more difficult to attain. Second, when Cuba's economy is thriving, as it was in the 1980s, there is less reason for people to apply for membership because they don't need to join the club to receive the benefits. At the 1991 Communist Party Congress, the standards for admission were again lowered to gain members; no doubt this was a political maneuver to buffer the leadership against a possible counterrevolution. In a necessary trade-off, the opportunists flocked to the call and lowered the integrity of the Communist Party. There's no question that as soon as the regime feels the island is again economically empowered, membership standards will again be redefined. But the pattern is obvious: During hard times in Cuba, people race to join the party. During boom years, membership dwindles.

The only true feature that makes Cuba Communist is the organization of the central government. The Central Committee and the Political Bureau, which make and execute all the big decisions, are all modeled on the bureaucracies of the former Soviet Union. The National Assembly of People's Power, heralded as the parallel representative voice of the people, is an essentially powerless body that rubberstamps the decisions of the party and the ministries into national law. Higher than this body, the various ministries are charged with executing the laws and administrating the island with varying degrees of autonomy and persuasive powers to get laws passed and changed. This is the Cuban government in a nutshell. What makes Fidel Castro such a power-wielding force is his position as the president of the Republic of Cuba, first secretary of the PCC's Central Committee, chairman of the Council of Ministers, and commander-in-chief of the Cuban Armed Forces. It's Quixotic, but with this kind of lock on the power bodies, Castro has kept the island's fate sealed in the palm of his hand. The only real threat has been the wavering faith of the people, which the regime has been able to contain through a variety of control mechanisms and laws.

As far as Revolutionary culture goes, to be Communist is to sit at the pinnacle of Cuba's pyramid of power. This pinnacle widens when it reaches the average, obedient Cuban, and progresses downwards, the bottom strata being composed of janitors and the elderly, followed by deviants. Today, the Communist who brings the island the most money or prestige by making the right decisions is a national hero. The rest of the Communists are cogs in the machine, expected to work toward those goals, and they understand that these are the new themes for the Revolution's survival. Non-Communists who bring the island prestige and money from abroad (such as members of the Buena Vista Social Club) are not recognized as national heroes—just the Communist decision-makers who so brilliantly thought of taxing these Cubans for 50 percent of their foreign earnings.

I've met a lot of Communists in Cuba, and have even befriended a few. The important point about communism is that it's merely a political religion based on the principle that "each person receives equally according to his need." The principles of Socialism say that "each person receives according to his labors." The current Cuban reality and the super-human standards of Communist dogma, however, are rarely in harmony. Francisco told me once about his brother-in-law, a devout Communist. "He never buys anything in the black market, never," Francisco explained. "He always complains about how the criminals in society and the parasites and black marketeers are destroying the Revolution. No, he never buys in the black market. He sends my sister out to do it!"

All the Communists I know in Cuba are regular people who live a regular existence. They stand in the lines, earn low wages, believe in and never question their leader's vision. Some were less idealistic than others, but at the core there was a moral value and the mission to promote it. They weren't stereotypical coldhearted robots, but self-righteous humans with a perspective that, to me, reflected the values of all the world's great religions. And like the Christian *Bible,* the *Koran,* the *Bhagavad Gita,* or the *Tibetan Book of the Dead,* with their moral standards, the Communists had Karl Marx's *Manifesto* and the doctrines of Vladimir Lenin.

One of my best friends on the island was Ana, a twenty-five-year-old member of the UJC. An art history professor, she was a devout Communist with an unshakable dedication to the Revolutionary program. At the same time, she wasn't an old-school Communist, but a next-generation administrator who was on her way to full Communist Party membership. Like other Communist women I know, she dresses conservatively in dresses down to her calves and buttoned blouses tucked into formal skirts. Of the other Communists I met, many were patronizing toward me. As soon as they realized that I was an American, or that I was skeptical about Cuba's brand of communism, they went on a mission of persuasion and subjected me to hours of the gospel. When I argued about the hypocrisies and double standards, they always seemed to have an answer. Ana was different, though. She respected my views, and although we disagreed about a lot of things, we heard each other out and remained friends. She was a common-sense person who realized that the world, and especially Cuba, is gray with contradictions.

Ana is bona fide *Guantanamera,* a country girl from Guantánamo. In Cuba, everything leans toward Havana, and like many of the island's internal migrants, so did she. After receiving her degree in art history at the provincial university in Santiago, she waited for a job opening in Havana and moved as soon as one opened. She left the *campo* behind, fortunate to have obtained the legal documents necessary for the move to the capital. But the move had its price. She had been in Havana a month when we first met, and now month two was looming up, but there was a possibility that she might have to return to Guantánamo because Havana was unaffordable.

"You don't know how hard it is," she said, tears welling up in her eyes. "My dream is to teach, but all the odds are against me."

She was living with an older cousin in Centro, who was charging her 150 pesos a month for a tiny bed in a ramshackle little storage room. The daylight of the streets shined through the cracks in the walls, and there was no running water; but meals were included in the monthly 150, which evened things out. She walked the twenty blocks to and from the university because she couldn't afford the luxury of taking the bus, which cost 40 centavos a day.

For Ana, and transplants like her, steep fees and endless paperwork are involved in the move to the city. A mechanism was launched during the migration crisis to discourage people from moving to Havana, where there was access to income. Only 20 percent of Cubans live in rural areas, and during the Special Period, the mass land exodus was causing even more shortages in produce and urban housing. The crisis was so overwhelming that the government was forced to curb it by levying heavy fees on anyone who wanted to move to the capital. Today, although the migration has been stabilized, the fees are still used to discourage domestic movement.

"My cousin is very difficult to live with," Ana told me. "She's always complaining. She calls me *La Palestina*. She's a bitch, and I can tell she wants me to move out. And now I must come up with the money to pay to transfer my address from Guantánamo. The whole thing costs about 500 pesos. First, you have to have an attorney to handle the paperwork. This costs 200. Then there's a filing fee of another 150, and the stamp for the identity card costs 50 more, plus a few other charges. Where am I to come up with $20? After this week, I'll be living in Havana illegally."

In Cuba, people from Havana call transplants from the east "Palestinos." It's one of the most derogatory slanders, and the domestic migrants bear the brunt of the jokes. In Havana, most of the police are from Oriente; not only does the government like to keep the force diverse to prevent corruption but people from Havana will have nothing to do with policing their own and arresting their neighbors. Across Cuba, the police are always stationed in other provinces and municipalities. It's an old trick that goes back to Roman times, and in Cuba it's still used, both in the police force and in the military. I asked a cab driver one day why the migrants are called *Palestinos*. "Why do we call them *Palestinos*?" he laughed. "Because they come and come and they never leave!"

The system is now geared to discourage anyone from coming to Havana legally. But Ana was determined to stay, no matter the cost, even if it meant going without shampoo or food. Her determination to succeed was as devout as her faith in communism.

What makes Ana part of the new Communist order is that she's not only a member of the UJC but also a member of the Seventh Day Adventist church. Her father, who rolled cigars for a living in Guantánamo, and her mother, a housewife, were both diehard Catholics, and I asked Ana why she had switched to the Seventh Day Adventists.

"Because all the Catholics in Guantánamo smoke marijuana and drink," she said. "They're not truly Catholics in their hearts, and when I saw these contradictions, I began looking for a different church."

She visited the church every day, and she took me along a couple of times to meet the people in her parish. But Ana's dual faiths seemed more contradictory to me than those she saw in her former Catholic church. For one, the Seventh Day Adventist denomination isn't an officially enrolled religion on the island, and her church operates clandestinely under a different name. Technically, Ana is breaking the law of illegal organization. Her church refuses to ask the government for the official recognition that would enable it to practice openly. Instead, it practices under the "Baptist" banner, which is accepted by the Revolutionary government.

The idea of Christians enrolling in the Communist Party is still controversial on the island. The decision to begin allowing Christian membership was announced at the emergency 4th congress held in October 1991. Before this time, anyone who was a member of a church was discriminated against and forbidden entrance. There were a couple of reasons for the PCC to change its attitude toward Christians. A papal visit would legitimize Cuba in the eyes of the Catholic world, which had constantly condemned Castro for his religious repression and the inability of church members to participate in government. In 1991, at the Special Period's doorstep, this need for the Pope's validation was becoming almost imperative, not to mention the new need to polish up the island's image in hopes of garnering some of the world's tourists. Allowing Christians to enter the PCC was a political maneuver that eventually made the Pope's 1998 visit possible since the Vatican refused to authorize it until the regime's religious stance was modified. Another benefit to allowing the religious into the Communist Party was that during economic crises, traditionally, humans turn to religion for answers. In Cuba, religion and communism have always been opposing forces for this reason. The Communist Party has always seen the church as direct competition. When he essentially banned religion in 1961, Castro was merely eliminating the competition. Religion's new acceptance in Cuba in 1991 and again in 1998, was a way to pull the competition into the Communist fold at its weakest hour, when God was gaining ground in Castro's own war of faith.

The Christmas following the Pope's January 1998 visit was the first Christmas officially declared a national holiday since 1961. Today, all Cubans get December 25 off from their forty-eight-hour workweek. Moreover, in 1999, a new item was featured in Cuba's dollar stores: artificial Christmas trees. Big trees, small trees, strings of lights, tiny nativity sets, colored bulbs, and plastic stars. That same year, 8,000 Cuban Americans traveled to the island to celebrate Christmas with their families. In 2000, this doubled to 16,000, many of whom stayed in the hotels, legally sleeping in beds and eating from tables they were forbidden to use just years earlier. Why? Because they have dollars. Christmas in Cuba is nothing more than a profitable event, and by legitimizing it, the government has capitalized on Christianity in myriad ways. The state controls everything shipped into Cuba, and ordering artificial Christmas trees was just another means of pocketing those dollars wired through Western Union and earned illegally in the black market. On Christmas Day, the dollar stores stay open, as they do at Easter. By legalizing Christmas, the hard currency earned far outweighed the pesos lost by giving Cubans the day off.

There is nothing as sweet as walking or driving by a Cuban church the night before Christmas. The doors are flung wide open and the choir of children sing "Silent Night, Holy Night" in Spanish. When I walked with Ramon from Vedado to Central Havana on Christmas Eve, we passed several cathedrals and small Protestant churches and at each one I made him stop so that we could listen to the services for a few minutes. In every church, there were a dozen or so people standing around at the back. They had wandered in from the streets out of curiosity, and when one left, another took his place. I noticed the same thing happened during the Easter mass.

"Before," said Ramon, "the churches weren't allowed to have their doors open like this. The government didn't want people coming in from the streets. This is why the Jehovah Witnesses are forbidden to go door-to-door. They didn't want people having faith in anything but the Revolution. Before, the people sung more quietly. Are you listening to what the priest is saying?"

"He's comparing Christianity to the Revolution," I said. "He's talking about how the Cuban Socialism and Christianity have the same values."

"Yes, but it's only a front," said Ramon. "Just a minute ago, he was talking about how many governments in Latin America are corrupt, and how politics often lead people away from their faith in God. He didn't say Cuba, but you know he was talking about us. These people here, they read between the lines."

As we walked into the street, the priest began yelling *"¡Feliz el Año Nuevo, Compatriota!"* "Happy New Year, Compatriot," the official Cuban holiday cheer.

"Why don't they say *Feliz Navidad?*" I asked Ramon.

"Because they want to be able to keep the doors open," he said. "It is a trade-off."

Centuries ago, the Afro-Cuban religion Santería was born in similar circumstances. When the Catholic church outlawed the Yoruban tribal religions in sixteenth-century Cuba, the slaves resisted, fooling the priests by pretending to pray to Catholic saints. They were secretly talking to their own deities, Los Orishas. For instance, Changó is Santa Bárbara; the goddess Ochún is the Virgen de la Caridad del Cobre; and Babalú Ayé is San Lázaro. Although it has no national holidays, Santería has always been tolerated by Castro. It is Cuba's traditional street religion, the religion of yesterday's resistance. Today, Christians have become the new religious resistance. And while they bury the faith under a thin mask of Revolutionary rubric, the Communists serve as the new priests.

I spent the Christmases of 1998 and 2000 in Cuba. I wanted to watch the evolution of the island's religious celebrations, which had been suppressed for almost four decades. In 1998, there was still a lot of residual hesitation to celebrate because of the past stigmas associated with religion. Christians had always been treated as second-class citizens, often harassed and made to feel like counterrevolutionaries. In the windows here and there you could see an occasional Christmas tree or perhaps a string of lights. It was a pathetic attempt to try and reconnect with those roots from so far in the past. During the Christmas of 2000, however, the air was denser with merrymaking, mostly because people could purchase Christmas trees in the dollar stores.

I hopped from celebration to celebration at the homes of Enrique, the Ibáñezes, and Armando. The families had their own miniature Christmas trees, which cost them $7 apiece. The year before, Armando told me how he had cut out a Christmas tree from green construction paper and pinned it on the wall, his first Christmas tree in thirty-eight years. But this year he sprung for the miniature from his savings. Like Armando, many Cubans had forgotten how to celebrate Christmas, but they're relearning the old tradition. Before 1998, claiming to be Christian was a way for Cubans to protest. A Christmas tree lit up in a living room today still carries these connotations. It is a form of protest. A form of individual self-expression. A holiday to celebrate that isn't Revolutionary.

A new ingredient in the stagnant morass of the Revolutionary culture. It's new information.

About half of my time in Cuba I rented an illegal apartment from a woman named Amelia. Her brother, who was out of the country, asked her to rent it out while he was away to earn the family a dollar income. Had Amelia been caught renting this apartment to me, she would have been fined $1,000. Had she been unable to pay the fine, the apartment would have been confiscated. Why does the government impose the fine of $1,000 rather than confiscate the apartment right away? Obviously to get its hands on the money earned from the apartment because simply confiscating the apartment would be of no value. As long as the government can profit from these illegal acts, they are ignored.

The apartment was a nice one bedroom in Vedado. It was a block away from one of Castro's headquarters, which was the former apartment of Celia Sánchez, Cuba's highest example of the new Revolutionary woman. Sanchez was Castro's assistant in the Sierra Maestra during the war, and his closest confidante until her death of cancer in January 1980. Fidel still likes to stay at her apartment on occasion. The entire block surrounding the place is always under heavy armed guard. There are cameras on the rooftops, likely snipers in nearby buildings. About twice a month, I would wave as Fidel zipped by in his black Mercedes on Linea Avenue en route to Celia's or his other place in Playa. Each day as I walked past the guards at Celia's to grab my peso taxi downtown, they jumped to attention and saluted me. I had no idea why. A friend explained that maybe they thought I was a Cuban military inspector.

I loved the apartment. It had atmosphere. And for me there was something serene about knowing I had my head on a pillow only a block away from the comandante's place. Whenever there was a march, the president of the CDR and his wife would stand at the bottom of my apartment building, writing down the names of those who were marching and those who weren't, and when I walked by, they would always look at me quizzically, wondering who I was. I was always afraid that I'd be caught because it would likely result in my deportation. But again, avoiding capture is part of the rhythm, and to understand the culture is to operate in it.

Over time, I got to know the people in the building fairly well, and Amelia would drop in on occasion for some coffee and talk. One day she said, "You know, I'm very confused these days. I'm really having a hard time understanding who I am. I just feel unhappy."

I asked her why she was unhappy. After all, she had a dollar income from this apartment, as well as a good job as a translator and a great young family.

"I don't know," she said. "Maybe it's my age. I went to church last week. It was the first time. Because I think what I need is a faith in something. I need something to believe in. It feels to me as if I have nothing solid in my life. I have no social group or community."

"What about Santería?" I asked. "Have you ever believed in that?"

"No," she said. "We were brought up to believe that Santería is the worship of the devil. We were taught that it was bad, that it was witchcraft. I'm not sure yet if Christianity is for me, but I think I'm going to attend church again."

The legality of religion and the disappearing persecution associated with it is creating a lot of confusion in faith. The Ibáñezes also had their first Christmas tree in 2000. They consider themselves Catholic, but don't attend mass. Throughout their home are little religious items such as calendars with prayers written in Spanish and little pocket prayer cards with colorful illustrations of the Virgin Mary and Christ. In the corner of one room sits the common ceramic statuette of San Lázaro, who represents the amalgamation of Santería, the Afro-Cuban religion, to whom they pray and give offerings when a family member is sick. When I asked Martina about this, she said she likes to keep him around "just in case." This inability to adhere to one faith, whether it be Christianity, communism, or Santería, seems to be a dominant trend.

Christmas has never been the culture's principal Christian holiday. Although Christmas is celebrated each year, the old Spanish holiday, *El Dia de Tres Reyes Magos,* the day of the three kings, is the most dominant observance; like the rest of Latin America, Cubans celebrate it on January 6. On January 6, 2001, the Spanish cultural center hosted a bonanza. It rented a luxury horse-drawn coach and drove through the streets of Havana: down Prado, west on San Lázaro, and along the Malecón. Three Spaniards were dressed up as the three kings and threw handfuls of candy out to the poor Cuban kids in the street. After this extravagant display, a long line of Cuban children formed at the Spanish cultural center. Once inside, hundreds of toys were handed out by the kings. I was in Cuba at the time, and this act created a serious national uproar. That night, a furious Castro made a speech denouncing Spain for its behavior.

Spain is always challenging the government in this way. It offers Cubans privileges that the Revolution forbids, and the government can do nothing about it because Spanish investments make up a large percentage of all foreign capital on the island. The former colonizers are moving back in. Out of the 404 foreign enterprises now operating in Cuba, 99 are Spanish companies, which makes them an unchallengeable, influential shareholder. Today, Spain is Cuba's greatest antagonist, always creating tension, always looking for ways to prod Cubans into asking hard questions.

Castro's biggest problem with Spain's action was that if there's not enough candy for all the Cuban kids, then none should get any. On top of this, Spain had stolen the dignity of the children. Reviews in the streets were mixed. In a lot of ways it was very sad, in others it was heart-warming. Here were hundreds of Cuban children who never get a piece of candy suddenly scrambling through the streets, chasing after Spanish sweets, yet it was nice to see the sheer magic and excitement in their eyes from this new sparkling force in a drab life.

In the evening, a big spectacle was made of it on national television: endless reruns of the kids and the kings, the toy giveaway, Castro describing what had occurred and pointing out the cruelty of it. The emergency news coverage was even more sensational than the act itself. I watched the program with Armando and Carmen. Both had grown into their late teens before Castro, both disagreed with Castro on many fronts, but both agreed that Spain had violated the Cuban dignity with this one.

"It's terrible," said Armando. "Those children are poor. How dare Spain taunt them like this with candy, making them beggars. They don't even understand what's happening. Suddenly there's a coach in the street throwing candy. They've never heard of *los tres reyes magos*. It's confusing for them."

"When we were kids," said Carmen, "we would put a handful of grass under the bed for the kings' horses, and then in the morning the grass would be gone and there would be a piece of cake or some candy. Every year we did this."

"That's not how it was at our house," said Armando. "We would just look under the bed and there would be candy, maybe a toy. There was no grass."

As they both explained these things, a warmness came over their eyes as they drifted into memory. They were thinking about "the good old days," which they often did when the present was too hard to accept, and they would delight in giving me or anyone else then-and-now comparisons at almost any chance they got. Their children, more concerned with their own destinies and the reality they face today, really didn't want to hear about it. "Yeah, yeah, the way it was. That's all you two ever talk about. The way it was."

You'll hear these kinds of things in Cuba and in Miami. The older generations say, "The young people, they just don't remember how it was." The new generations are living in a different world today with new symbols, far removed from the struggle of their forebears.

"By throwing the candy," said Armando, "Spain just wanted to create a conflict with the government. They're always doing these kinds of things. They still haven't gotten over our independence. Castro is afraid of this, because people will begin wondering what it was like before him and that maybe it was better. That maybe without him there will be more candy, a better life. Today after this act, a child came up to me and asked me about the magic kings. He knew I was an old guy and could remember. He wanted to know everything about it. People are becoming more curious. They're beginning to wonder."

Spain's behavior created a new competition that the regime could not control. Until now, Castro was Cuba's bearded Magic King who had entered Havana on a tank rather than a wagon, and now he was being forced to play tug-o-war with his people. But because Spanish companies represent 25 percent of Cuba's foreign investment, the best Castro could do was to go on television and bark about it for two hours in an effort to strike a balance between Revolutionary adherence and this new information—which had nearly been erased from the *Cubanidad*.

It's all about Communist competition with Christianity, Castro versus Christ, and how the former can capitalize on the latter. In 2000, the state scheduled its national elections to occur on Easter Sunday. And not surprisingly, the regime has its own Revolutionary holiday for the children to compete with the day of the three magic kings. January 8, 1959, was the day that Castro rolled into Havana with his army to claim the capital and celebrate the victory. On the forty-second anniversary of the event in 2001, I was walking down Prado when I noticed that all the children leaving school were carrying small toys. Some had generic matchbox cars, others had marbles and toy guns, but one little girl had a toy robot, about the size of a Barbie doll. She stood there alone in her little *pionero* uniform with the robot in her hand and bent its arms and legs, then made it walk across the base of a Spanish colonial pedestal, the pastel paint weathered and soiled. I watched her curiously, knowing that in her mind, the streets around her had dissolved away and she was now floating in her own hazy world of imagination with her little robot doll.

Armando later told me that only the *pioneros* in Old Havana can take part in the toy giveaway. When I said it seemed hypocritical that Castro would chastise Spain for giving to a few when there wasn't enough for all, yet would turn around and do exactly the same thing—in the high-visibility tourist sector of Old Havana, yet not in Centro, only one block away where there were no tourists snapping photos of the regime's generosity—he simply shrugged his shoulders.

18

Reflections of the Parallel Culture

To delve into the mindless escapism of Hollywood any chance the opportunity arises is both one of the people's most savored pastimes, and, of course, one of the few things there are to do besides drink, dance, and stand in line. *Titanic* was a big hit among Cubans. They adore Kevin Costner films. They'll improvise poems about Julia Roberts's award-winning lips in one breath, and in the next, dish up descriptions in spades over their favorite Jack Nicholson scenes, running through his filmography in seconds flat. You'll often hear things such as, "Marlon Brando visited Cuba for the Latin American film festival. I remember Arnold Schwarzenegger walking past the Capitolio with boxes of cigars from the Partagas factory stuffed under his arms. Naomi Campbell was in Cuba last year. Keanu Reeves came for the festival. Morgan Freeman dropped in. I heard Brad Pitt is coming this year."

Every weekend, Cubavision runs two or three Hollywood films with Spanish subtitles over the national airwaves; Cubans love them, and it's a good way to keep people off the streets, safe at home, and occupied. Curious about their reactions, I've watched dozens of North American films with Cubans, sometimes seeing them myself for the first time. Cubavision reportedly pirates international satellite feeds, often showing the blockbusters free of charge before the U.S. video release.

As I watched some of the more violent films with sexual scenes, I was at first surprised that the content could slip through the censors. There is no official film rating system in Cuba, and the standard warnings spliced into the reel by the manufacturer are the only alert to graphic content. But most said outright, "No, they never edit for sex. The kids see it, too. It doesn't matter." For a young culture currently exploring its own sexual revolution, no doubt the erotic scenes fulfill the hunger. Violent scenes are never edited out, either. One of the reasons for this is that the state-run Cubavision, while occasionally airing off-beat camp and hip-level humor such as *There's Something About Mary* and *Three Men and a Baby*, leans toward serious movies that in some way criticize the United States or question capitalist policies and the negative trends of the Western lifestyle. As long as the movie doesn't cross the threshold of pornography, the state leaves the gritty stuff in for impact. The blood only enhances the message. Oliver Stone's anti-interventionist *Salvador* and *Platoon* are two examples. Stanley Kubrick's *Full Metal Jacket*. *The Last Don*. Denzel Washington in *Hurricane*. Al Pacino and Russell Crowe in *The Insider*. Anthony Hopkins in *Instinct*. These films are run to foster critical thinking and instill the idea that the United States are the bad guys, that North America is a violence-riddled wasteland of racism and discrimination, and that crime, particularly murder, is rampant. I can't count the number of times Cubans have asked me, "Is it really like that in your country? Is it really this dangerous?"

These films also send a mixed message to Cubans who think more critically than they're given credit for. Several friends have commented to me as the credits rolled, "I can't believe the U.S. lets these filmmakers get away with criticizing your government like this. We would never be allowed to make movies criticizing Castro or the Revolution." On one hand, yes, these films convey the message that the United States has problems, but on the other, they show the expressive freedom that North Americans enjoy. The Cuban government's censorship is therefore all the more obvious.

Aside from the biased social commentaries about the wicked ways of the United States, Cubans also indulge in more mainstream Hollywood fare. *Jaws* is as popular today, watched and savored for the umpteenth time on Cubavision's *Midnight Cinema,* as it was when it premiered for consumption on Cuban television in the 1970s. Because Cuba is an international seaport, Cubans love films that have anything to do with water. These, coupled with the Latin American *telenovelas* such as Colombia's *Café con Aroma de Mujer,* "Coffee with the Scent of Woman," or the latest Brazilian six-month soaps, *Rey del Ganado,* "The Cattle King" and *Fuerza del Deseo,* "Force of Desire," Cubans keep themselves entertained. Twice a week, behind every door in every barrio, the *telenovela* is blaring away from home to home across Havana. These programs are so popular that you can leave a friend's apartment in the Vedado municipality and walk all the way to Old Havana without missing a scene. Likewise, Cuba's children never miss the popular *Power Rangers,* recently added to the Cubavision menu, nor *Fragglerock,* both shown biweekly in after-school programming.

Young children in Havana have their own theater, the *Cinecito* at the corner of Consulado and San Rafael, where each week Disney favorites, from *Dumbo* and *Pinocchio* to *Alice in Wonderland* and *The Seven Dwarfs,* stir the imaginations of toddlers and preadolescents. Films for Havana's twenty-two mainstream theaters are handpicked by the Cuban Institute for the Cinematic Arts (ICAIC), which likes to present a nice variety of Cuban, Latin American, and European pictures, but leans predominantly toward Hollywood. I asked my Communist friend Ana, whom I regularly accompanied to the movies, and who often consults with ICAIC in her arts studies, why the Cuban theaters thread so many North American reels.

"Well, first," she said, "we have always liked Hollywood films here in Cuba, but I think the biggest reason is that North American films are cheaper to rent. ICAIC leases the subtitled reels from Mexico. European films cost a great deal more, so we can't afford to rent them. The technology is changing, too, and our outdated projectors won't work in the new formats. The new projectors cost hundreds of thousands of dollars. But what I recently learned is that ICAIC is going to install new video technology in some of the theaters. Maybe then we'll see more variety."

One of the films that Ana and I caught at the Payret was *Lista de Espera,* which criticized Cuban social bureaucracy and the endless *colas.* The film was the latest from Juan Carlos Tabio and it was widely discussed in Latin cinema circles and on the streets of Cuba throughout 2000 and 2001. Cubans love their own homegrown cinema because they need infusions of humor to stave off insanity, and the theaters were packed for two months. *Lista de Espera* wasn't a critically acclaimed smash, as Tabio's earlier codirections *Guantanamera* and *Strawberry and Chocolate* had been, but it was a brilliant film, and the final offering in a necessary trilogy of Cuban social commentary. I stood in the long *cola* at the Payret theater twice with Ana to watch it. We went Dutch; I bought the tickets for two pesos each and she covered the peanuts. Because Ana was an art history scholar and a member of the UJC, I valued her thoughts about the movie.

The film opens at a provincial bus terminal where a grumpy line of passengers waits for a coach to Havana that never arrives. However, the next bus in has one available seat, and the mob launches into a big fight over the fare. Suddenly, a blind man stumbles into the station, and with typical Cuban generosity, the group insists that he take the single ticket. When the bus is fully loaded and the blind man is in his seat, this bus also breaks down. Now some twenty people, caricatures of every type of Cuban, are stranded at the terminal in the middle of nowhere. There is the Communist functionary and his family, two gays, the blind man, a petty black marketer with boxes of stolen canned meat, a young woman heading to Havana to marry a foreign man whom she doesn't love, and the terminal boss. With this setup, as in his codirections with Gutiérrez Alea, Tabio creates a miniature Cuban society.

Being Cuban, everyone in the group, naturally, is a self-styled mechanic. After the group attempts and fails to repair the bus, the flustered Communist functionary goes on a rampage, impatiently making phone calls to all his cadres and demanding another bus immediately. None arrives, and he forces his wife and daughter to begin walking with him; he commandeers horse-drawn wagons and motorcycles to drive them, scenes that are cut to throughout the film. When the tale begins, everyone at the station is secretive, each hoarding little stashes of illegal foodstuffs, greedy about their possessions. As the story unfolds, they become close, and without the Communist functionary around barking orders, the miniature society begins to unify and work together. After several days, they all break out the food they've been hoarding, and enjoy a fabulous feast complete with illegal lobster, evaporated milk, *yuca*, rice, and pounds of canned meat. Later, someone locates a stored supply of house paint, and the group engages in painting the station. Someone else discovers a storage room full of antique books, so the people work hand-in-hand to launch a bookstore. Days later, everyone at the bus station wakes up, only to discover that everything had been a dream—but everyone had dreamed the same dream. The point of the film is that the people, in the dream, formed their own kind of Socialism that worked perfectly well without central control's slowing everything down. The movie implies that the bureaucracy is unnecessary and only disturbs the harmony that comes naturally, not just to Cubans but to the human race in general. Through these mechanisms, Tabio reflects upon the parallel Cuban society operating outside of the Revolutionary framework.

Ana agreed with everything in the film, laughing loudly at each witty scene, but framed her criticism as room for improvement: The bureaucracy needs to be minimized, efficiency must be increased, order must be restored—things that could be overcome with organization, effort, strong leadership. To her, the bossy functionary in the film represented the kinds of undesirable bureaucracy that the Communist Party needs to eliminate and could accomplish through reforms.

During one of my stays on the island, I was fortunate enough to meet Juan Carlos Tabio, the director of *Lista de Espera,* one of Cuba's top three filmmakers today. He began his career in 1975 at the ICAIC, where he made documentary films as a protégé of Tomás "Titón" Gutiérrez Alea, Cuba's all-time master screen director and 1959 cofounder of ICAIC. Titón's most well-known works in Cuba are his 1966 *Death of a Bureaucrat* and 1968 *Memories of Underdevelopment.* It wasn't until the critically acclaimed comedies *Guantanamera* (1994) and *Strawberry and Chocolate* (1993) were made, both codirected with Tabio, that the two filmmakers turned heads around the globe, giving the largely ignored Cuban cinema its much deserved corner in the global film industry.

"Before ICAIC we didn't have a film industry," Tabio explained to me over coffee at his Vedado apartment. "There was little cinema, and what did exist was very commercial. Sure, there were a few films, but there was no system. The film industry in Cuba was born after the triumph of the Revolution when ICAIC was created."

After seizing power in 1959, Castro realized the importance of visual communication in winning the support of skeptics. One of his first strokes was to establish a competitive Cuban film industry and focus it mainly on domestic consumption. Gutiérrez Alea would pioneer the industry and give it initial form and scope. ICAIC essentially had carte blanche control over what films would be produced, as long as they reflected the building of the Revolutionary society in a Revolutionary commercial sense, and the result, endorsed by both Castro and Che Guevara, was Cuba's unique Revolutionary cinema.

ICAIC's debut film was Gutiérrez Alea's 1960 *Historias de la Revolución,* the first war reenactment documentary produced in Cuba. For the first half of the 1960s these black-and-white productions were the rage in Cuba because filmmakers, and much of the populace alike, were still feverishly excited about the big changes sweeping society. Cubavision still runs this crackly old documentary once or twice a year for nostalgic purposes, along with the many others created during this epoch. But the genre lost wind, and by 1965, ICAIC began shifting focus into fictitious drama. As long as films didn't speak out against the Revolution and continued resonating with a moral code, the expressive parameters were permitted to expand and ICAIC could continue to enjoy carte blanche control. The new drama movement accompanied the documentary wave, and both lasted until the mid-1970s, when Cuba's comedy movement began and the documentaries fizzled out.

Tabio went on:

I don't think there is a fundamental difference between Cuban film and all Pan-American film. A lot of the distinctions depend on the individual characteristics of the artist, the director, the author. Titón was important, as were Santiago Álvarez and Carl Váldez. . . . Nicolás Guillén, the poet's nephew, made very interesting documentaries, very interesting. Sara Gómez, a black director who died very young of asthma, she was very important. And today there are many important Cuban directors who have different visions, but generally use Cuban themes. The means of achieving this is always unique, but all try to look deeply into our contradictions—the most important part of Cuban reality. Comedy is the current trend.

"Is it easier to mask criticism with humor?" I asked. "Is criticism shrouded in humor easier to digest in Cuba?"

"Well sure, and I have always thought it also depends on the habits of the personality and shape of the viewer's destiny. I don't think humor spites itself. I've always believed humor serves to inspire self-reflection in the people. Always."

That comedy is Cuba's current cinematic trend is no surprise considering the survival circumstances of the Special Period, and, heeding Wordsworth's "Artists are the antennae of the race," both Gutiérrez and Tabio have provided Cuban society with a series of mile-markers. The comedies are by no means tongue-in-cheek. They confront serious Cuban problems. The 1993 production of *Strawberry and Chocolate* (which today is still shown at midnight on weekends for film cultists, akin to North America's *Rocky Horror Picture Show*), looked squarely at governmental homophobia. In 1994, *Guantanamera*, the Jack-Kerouac-meets-the-Special-Period bedroom comedy, tackled serious questions of bureaucratic inadequacies and the mounting "good old days" denial that Cubans were, and still are, dealing with. Tabio explained that these films are not criticisms aimed at the government, but are criticisms of society as a whole, a means for the collective Cuban psyche to see itself, a vehicle for the Ego to see what the Id is up to. Tabio used the same cast from the two Gutiérrez Alea coproductions and dedicated *Lista de Espera* to the memory of Titón, who died of cancer in 1996. As a eulogy to the master, the film also serves as a redeeming conclusion to the Special Period.

"Although some ideas in the film stem from that epoch," says Juan Carlos, "it speaks to today's Cuba. The film provides a measure of contrast, a precise ceiling, creating the ability to clearly see the reality of then which is necessary to interact in the reality of now."

After the affluent 1980s, the Special Period with its shortages crushed Cuba's young cinematic industry. Although this period was a director's wet dream for material, filmmakers were forced to shop for foreign investors to fund Cuban productions. Often, homegrown island themes had to be filmed on location in European countries.

"In the last few years, almost all Cuban and Pan-American films have been coproductions with foreign associations, fundamentally from Spain," said Juan Carlos. "That's not to say that a Cuban or even Peruvian film, like the latest Lombardi, *Pantaleón y las Visitadoras*, based on the novel by Vargas Llosa, has somehow lost purity. The coproduced films are having great success. They are very Latin American in flavor, but have universal themes. Between distribution and publicity with the foreign associations, our films are brought to a wider audience in Europe and the United States."

Tabio's *Lista de Espera* is one of these, coproduced with Cuba, Spain, Mexico, France, and Germany. Another is the Cuban-Spanish production of 2000, *Hacerse el Sueco*, "Making the Swede," a comedy that questions the reality of Cubans' being treated as second class to tourists. This has been a huge and sensitive issue and it needs to be discussed. It's one of the unsettling truths that both Cubans and the government have been struggling, and failing, to face. *Hacerse el Sueco* not only brings a serious problem to the table in the digestible form of comedy but also serves as a yardstick for Cuba's current trend of film as public forum. Before this trend, nobody even knew where to begin. People usually ignored the problem and hoped it would just disappear. Relatively speaking, productions such as *Hacerse el Sueco, Fresa y Chocolate,* and *Lista de Espera* are as radical for conservative Cuba as, say, *Full Metal Jacket* and *Platoon* were for Ronald Reagan's 1980s United States.

"So who were your influences?" I asked Juan Carlos.

"I don't know," he said. "Many, many, many, many, many. Gutiérrez Alea of course. Buñuel . . . Chaplin . . . Robert Altman interests me a lot. Eisenstein. Everything he made was superb. Italian neorealism . . . Rosellini."

Cuban film, as experimental film, is its own unique movement in the Revolutionary context and in its Afro-Cuban nuances. The similarities to the Italian neorealist movement are apparent both in theme and character. The 1960s, when Cuba's film industry began, and the Special Period of the 1990s were emotional times of sweeping change, strife, and sacrifice, almost identical to the postwar rebuilding years of Roberto Rosellini's Italy. Both movements explore the idea of broken societies searching for a national identity. Both explore once-stable cultures now splintered and fragmented in the aftermath of war and poverty; Vitorio de Sica's 1948 masterpiece, *The Bicycle Thief,* could have easily been filmed in Cuba today.

Tabio and other Cuban filmmakers identify with Sergei Eisenstein's films on many levels. Foremost, Eisenstein was a world master of montage in his own right, a poet of light and fragment. Eisenstein was constantly scrutinized and harassed by Russia's 1930s and 1940s censors to the point that Stalin would even order guards onto film sets to intimidate the director. These conditions forced Eisenstein to discover ways of burying his messages and criticisms into the celluloid weave, a key factor that stimulated his imagination, only adding to his genius. Although the Castro government is leaps and bounds less restrictive with its creators, it is nonetheless very conservative, and the similarities are apparent. Cuban filmmakers are subject to limitations about what they can and cannot produce. The parameters jelled between the paranoid years of 1961 and 1975, and the almost innate self-censorship still exists today. Gutiérrez and Tabio have treaded ice with the government in some of their codirected commentary. In 1994, Castro panned *Guantanamera* nationally as immoral, a friend told me, although it received international applause, created some prestige for the island, and raised global awareness of Cuba and its issues—which is half the reason why the regime tolerates these kinds of social commentary films and gives the island's creators some breadth of leniency within the prevailing system. The films also provide average Cubans with that outlet to humor themselves and release some of the frustrations of daily life. The regime, no doubt, sees the healing qualities in this function.

According to Tabio, the jury is still out on the future of Cuban film. "It may change," he told me, "when its vision is unrestrained, and when filmmakers have moderate space, or a more liberal rest from the pressure. I consider Cuban cinema more roomy and more critical about its own reality than cinema of other Pan-American countries. Practically all Cuban directors of cinema try to penetrate and reflect on Cuban reality in a critical manner. Cinema in Cuba—as in every country—is conditioned by many effects, both economic and political."

Other personalities I met went into more detail after asking me to stop the tape, giving me a full understanding of the past and current political climate towards Cuba's creators. In 1968, when Castro created the Union of Cuban Writers and Artists (UNEAC), he was essentially launching the first organization of systematic Revolutionary commercialism. Like ICAIC before it, you didn't have to be a Communist to become a member, but both were controlled by Communists. Ethical guidelines were laid down about what kinds of content could and could not be included. In order to get published, have a film produced, or display an exhibition, you had to be in the club. And to thrive in the club, you had to pass the censors, and to pass the censors you couldn't challenge the regime or produce a work considered in bad taste. Thus developed the Cuban internal censor.

Throughout the 1960s, Cuba's creators chiseled away at the Revolutionary parameters, testing the limits. The initial foreclosure on Cuba's cinematic expressive freedom occurred in 1961, when a fifteen-minute experimental film called *P.M.* portrayed Cuban nightlife in a manner that the new rule found distasteful and counter to the new Revolutionary culture. ICAIC refused to endorse and license the film. But Guillermo Cabrera Infante, director of the literary magazine *Lunes de Revolución,* managed to air it on Cuban television. This act led to what would later culminate in the "Padilla Affair."

One of Cuba's most vocal creators was poet Heberto Padilla, who died in exile on September 25, 2000. Initially exiled in Miami during the Batista reign when he was twenty-seven, Padilla, excited about rejoining and molding the culture of the new Revolutionary society, returned to Cuba in 1959 along with other exiled Cuban intellectuals after Castro had seized control. He immediately joined Cabrera Infante and a few other writers and together they formed *Lunes de Revolución,* a weekly literary supplement to the newspaper *Revolución.* The new supplement published the work of authors such as Proust, Joyce, and Kafka. In June 1961, after the airing of the film *P.M.,* a summit was called for Cuba's writers and artists to outline what it meant to be intellectually "Revolutionary," and both Padilla, Cabrera Infante, and the Cuban playwright and poet Antón Arrufat were accused of being outside the Revolutionary culture, elitist *burguesa,* and anti-social. Castro intervened in the meeting and concluded the sessions with the theme, "Within the Revolution, everything; outside the Revolution, nothing." This meeting decided the underlying parameters of expression for all the island's writers and artists and they still exist today. *Lunes de Revolución,* only two years after launching, was immediately shut down; Antón Arrufat, then editor of *Casas de las Americas* magazine, was dismissed, and the film *P.M.* was banned.

An early supporter of Castro, Padilla had become disillusioned with the regime by the late 1960s. He published a book of poetry in 1968 titled

Fuera del Juego, "Outside the Game," which challenged the Revolutionary paradigm, and he won UNEAC's poetry prize of the year from an international jury. The same year, Antón Arrufat won the theater prize for his play *Los Siete Contra Tebas,* "The Seven Against Thebes." Again, both were scolded as bourgeois elitists, and the international juries were eliminated to prevent this from happening again. In March 1971 the whip lashed when Castro ordered a crackdown on Cuba's intellectuals because they were still pushing the limits. Padilla was arrested and jailed, which caused an uproar in the international smart set. Petitions of protest for his release were signed by the likes of Jean-Paul Sartre, Octavio Paz, Gabriel Garcia Marquez (a good friend of the comandante's), Mario Vargas Llosa, and Susan Sontag. Padilla was released five weeks later after being forced into a pseudo-confession of counterrevolutionary behavior.

Over the next decade, Padilla was excommunicated from his craft and prevented from publishing anything in Cuba. In 1981, when the writer was denied permission to leave the island, Senator Edward Kennedy and members of literature circles in the United States protested. Padilla was finally able to take political refuge in the United States where he went on to publish and teach until his death. But Padilla was a test case for Cuba's intellectuals. Not only could you not function creatively outside the Revolutionary framework, but the definition of "outside" was clearly established.

Many intellectuals responsible for helping the culture see itself and evolve have been shut out because of these inside-outside parameters. Although Castro states constantly that no one is forced to be a Communist in Cuba, Communist Revolutionary conformity is indeed imposed upon the ordinary people and the creators. Being more committed to their arts and themselves than they are to the Revolution, many have chosen to remain on the island, yet they exist outside the system, searching for an international audience where there are no censors. This phenomenon continues to grow because younger artists are learning that it is suicidal to be a commercial Revolutionary creator. When these artists finally do run into a little fame abroad, the regime gets right behind them with support, coopting their newly won prestige into the Revolutionary program with a "You see, you see what talent the Revolution produces!" For this reason, Cuban artists who do win international accolades on their own merits try to play it as low-key as possible in Cuba. They keep their names out of the spotlight for the simple reason that they feel they've earned their fame without any help from the establishment, and they're unwilling to share the glory. These artists also fear that they will become puppets of the government, dictated on every front, if they become too popular in Cuba.

One world-renowned Cuban artist—a friend who has had long-running exhibitions in New York, Paris, and Spain, and whom I cannot name for obvious reasons—said, "I'm going to be completely honest. I'm going to be straight with you, but you cannot write anything about it. You give me your word?" He continued,

I don't want my name spoken too loudly in Cuba, because then they'll get behind me. I have earned a beautiful amount of money selling my work abroad, and they can say, "The money that you've earned is necessary for the Revolution, so give it all to us, and now you must work for the Revolution and the Communists, blah blah blah." I don't want this shit behind me, so I prefer to be in the background. I'm young and single and I have my whole life in front of me. Right now I can go anywhere I want with my exhibitions. I can go to any embassy, even the American embassy, and they're going to give me a visa in five minutes because they know that I'm not an immigrant. I don't want to lose that. I want to be free. I want to be outside of the politics. Right now I could buy a tremendous house in the most expensive neighborhood in Havana. Easy. But I won't do it. I have a beautiful apartment, and no one knows where I am. I'm in the background, and that's the proper thing because it could be dangerous with the kind of regime we have in Cuba. I don't want the attention. Probably that's stupid, but the only other choice is to live maybe in San Francisco or New York or something. I don't want to be living there. I want to live in my own country. And if you want to live here and are successful in a sense, you have to be very careful. Nobody can be bigger than Fidel. You have to know how to live here, because otherwise they'll take you as a kind of enemy of the government, and in the name of the Revolution, they're going to crucify you.

When the Special Period struck in 1991, the regime was simply repeating its 1970s actions to reinvigorate the economy and win back the people's dwindling faith. Today's musical pioneers are Charanga Habanera; they play Cuba's latest musical form, *timba,* which is essentially high-speed, aggressive salsa, the Cuban equivalent of rap, and a direct reflection of the Special Period. The difference between Charanga Habanera and the earlier pioneers—for example, the 1970s music groups Los Van Van and Irakére, which were controversial but tolerated—is how blatantly they challenge the Revolutionary paradigm lyrically rather than in form, and in doing so represent the continued liberalization of the culture. In one song, "El Mango," although the lyrics can be enjoyed for their typical Cuban simplicity, the underlying message obviously addresses Fidel Castro and his inability to change with the times: "Hey you, mango, we loved you when you were green. Now that you're yellow and ripe, isn't it time to fall from the tree?"

Because of the messages buried in the music and because the lyrics question today's Cuba, Charanga Habanera has been a thorn in Castro's side. At the 1997 Youth Music Festival held in Havana, Charanga Habanera took the stage. Midway through the set, the band's singer began climbing onto a speaker tower, gyrating his hips and unfastening his pants. The teenage crowd went ballistic. The censors pulled the plug, quickly ending the performance, and later banned the group from playing live in Cuba for six months.

Because of the group's daring, and because they address today's issues and speak the new youth's language, Charanga Habanera has become the hottest band in Cuba today. The older people I know, most of whom are conservative, find the music in bad taste, much as the regime does. The young people love Charanga Habanera, but the group must play a balancing act; they know that if they push it too far lyrically they will be banned altogether. For now, the band is pushing it to the accepted limits, which again are constantly changing according to the strength of the economy. Today, Castro is also forced to play a delicate balancing act. Before, he had to give Charanga Habanera some space because the group tours abroad and brings hard taxable currency to the island while alluring tourists. Now that the band has grown a huge fan base and become a notorious legend as the people's outlaws on the island, they are allowed to continue because pulling the plug would be seen by the youth as a betrayal.

Cuban rap music is, like *timba*, today's hottest music for the island's youth. It, too, speaks directly to the streets and the Special Period. The hip-hop band Los Orishas, a powerful group of Cuban expatriates in France and Spain, opened this door by playing their rap-son hybrids, and you'll often see groups of kids spinning on their backs in this rhythm new to Cuba. Los Orishas's discs aren't for sale in the dollar stores, but the bootleggers have saturated the streets with them. After their debut disc, *A Lo Cubano,* was released in Europe in 2000, the Cuban youth grabbed hold and quickly made rap part of the mainstream culture; consequently, Los Orishas were able to play in the government-sponsored 2001 New Year's celebrations. Oddly, the state scheduled the performance, along with that of Charanga Habanera, far on the outskirts of Havana at Arroyo Naranja, near the airport.

"It is because they want fewer people to attend," Ramon told me. "If they put it way out there, it will require transportation. The people will have to ride a bus two hours to get there. It was done to discourage attendance. They don't want to encourage this music, but they also can't refuse it."

19

Cuba on the Fringe:
A Revolution of Ink

They are everywhere. Pixies surrounded by daisies, floating in a wind of color across the small of a woman's tan back. The face of a hungry lion roaring triumphantly from a man's arm. A small prong-tailed *bruja,* jet black hair whipping violently across a twenty-something's shoulder blade. The bold words "Love" and "War" stained across a hard rocker's knuckles. A tiny red scorpion crawling into the hairline on the side of a teenage girl's neck. Dragons and devils, wizards and warlocks. Pierced ears, noses, eyebrows, nipples, belly buttons, sterling silver shouting loudly from the daring skin of next-generation Cuba. If the conservative government owns the television networks, the new Cuban youth own the streets, and block after block, zone after zone, they're staking claim through an explosion of body art. It's a new revolution, a new language, a new rhythm of the flesh, throbbing to a tempo the bureaucracy will never grasp. "This is our time," shouts the flesh of the youth. "Our ideology, our bodies, our minds, our destiny, and our Cuba."

As one of the only seven professional tattoo artists in Cuba, Yovany Cabañas is a living legend. And because he's a non-Communist living legend, he has to play it low-key. On Obispo Street, a wall beside a darkened doorway leading up to his parlor holds a tiny, almost unnoticeable sticker that reads "Tattoo." It's the only advertisement in the street acknowledging his existence. But through the Cuban word-of-mouth circuit, he's known throughout all of Havana's municipalities, and they come from far and wide for his coveted services. It's just one of those things. It's all about the network, the *contacto*. Someone in Cerro wants a tattoo and starts asking around. Someone else says he knows of an artist on Obispo, and soon, the seeker and Yovany are face-to-face, haggling over designs and prices. He's a mystery to the older people in the barrio, and is commonly referred to as simply *el tatuador*. But with his trademark ponytail and a thin Fu Manchu dripping from his chin, all the young people in Old Havana know and admire him.

Everyday, Cuban folk-rocker Carlos Varela plays over Yovany's boom-box as a cluster of five or six initiates lean into his workspace, watching carefully as he works away, his mind, hands, and the tattoo machine a complete unit, spraying colorful designs onto clean brown flesh. The bystanders stare fascinated, flipping through wrinkled copies of foreign tattoo magazines, either juggling ideas for future designs when they can scrape together a few dollars, or seeing how badly it hurts before rolling up their own sleeves.

The day I met him, Yovany was just finishing up shading in a small marijuana leaf layered with black tribal brush strokes. As the blood was wiped away and the tattoo given the final inspection for flaws, the customer grinned with complete satisfaction. Reaching his once-virgin forearm into a brown paper sack, he pulled out a black silk shirt emblazoned with white dragon prints, tossing it to Yovany as payment. It was strange to see a Cuban guy getting a tattoo of a pot leaf, and I caught him on his way out the door to snap a photo of the work and ask him why he had chosen that particular design.

"*¡Porque me encanta!*" he said, looking me squarely in the eye, zapping me with the electric gaze of his life's passion. "Because I love it!"

His attitude surprised me as much as the pot leaf design. After all, wasn't this Cuba, home of the repressive regime? Where outspokenness was forbidden? Where this kind of antisocial behavior could result in punishment? When I returned to the parlor, Yovany was sliding into his new shirt.

"Normally, a tattoo that size would cost about $10 for Cubans, $20 for tourists," he explained. "The guy didn't have any money, so we negotiated a deal beforehand. But to be honest, I was drooling over this shirt as soon as I laid my eyes on it. You can't get clothes like this in Cuba."

Negotiating is one of those things Cuba's body artists, indeed all Cubans, are accustomed to. The young people have little money, but they have the itch for ink, often settling for smaller tattoos costing $3 or $5, perhaps trading a bottle of rum or owing a favor for the work.

"If I didn't bargain, I couldn't stay in business," said Yovany, the smooth, vegetal words rolling from his tongue. "Everybody wants a tattoo, but nobody has the money, so I try to be generous. As long as I make enough to buy more supplies and have a little extra, I'm satisfied. I'm not doing it for the money. I'm just content that I can make tattoos, the thing I love most. Not everyone can say this."

Yovany led me into the street, introducing me to a few of his clients clustered in the barrio, all Gen-Xers between twenty and thirty-five years old, asking them to show me examples of his past work. His style is naturalist—portraits, stills—and his specialty is shading. On one young guy's shoulder sat an enormous tattoo of Bob Marley; on one young woman's lower belly, a massive black-and-white tribal design; from a young arm sprung out yet another palm-sized pot leaf, highly detailed, glowing with Yovany's meticulous touch.

At first, this pot-leaf tattoo trend struck me as fantastic. But Cuba's Gen-Xers are bent on pushing the envelope of expressive freedom. In conservative Cuba, where the establishment forbids voicing frustrations too loudly, body art is quickly becoming the new high-decibel street language. After seeing millions marching against the U.S. embargo on international television, and after years of notion-feeding propaganda, many would be swayed to think that all Cubans are diehard Communists who should have, if anything, tattoos of Fidel Castro and Che Guevara etched into their foreheads. However, a Cuban getting a tattoo of Che would be comparable to an American punker getting a tattoo of Christ on the cross. This comparison is important, because Che is very much Cuba's Christ figure, the chief martyr for the Revolution, and communism is Cuba's equivalent to Christianity. To the young people, bent on challenging the establishment, the stagnant Revolutionary symbols represent the isolated language of the past, and an undercurrent of angst is rising from the youth culture. Because they feel a shade rebellious by visiting the outlawed island, only tourists are getting souvenir tattoos of Che, the Cuban flag, and Revolutionary symbols. Cubans, with their flair for the exotic, are striking a different route, emulating more worldly designs, pushing the limits of the establishment's acceptance.

"One time I did a tattoo for an Italian girl," Yovany said. "All she wanted were the words *'Hasta la Victoria Siempre'* on her shoulder. You know, how Che used to sign his letters. I couldn't understand why an Italian girl would want this. Once in a while Cubans ask for tattoos of Che or the flag, but almost never. Cubans like other things. Asian lettering is very popular right now. The tribal designs. Science fiction and fantasy designs, it depends on the person. A lot of times people will come in and say, 'I just want a tattoo. Give me something nice, and make it color.' They don't know what they want, they just want something."

In 1996, tattoos in Cuba were virtually nonexistent, mainly because there was no professional equipment, the tattooists were still amateurs, and the people were still nervous about challenging the establishment. You might have seen a muddy jailhouse tattoo of the Statue of Liberty or of Che on a rare arm, but Cuba was essentially vacant of body art. With the tourist boom came plenty of ink on the appendages of foreigners, and the Cuban tattoo rage began. Today, body art is the hottest new trend, just now boiling over the cusp of the underground into the mainstream culture as more and more young people take the plunge.

The advent of skin ink in Cuba is one of those distasteful side-effects of tourism that the government still isn't quite ready to digest. At the outset, it was treated like some malignant social ganglia. The initial reaction was disgust, and the official attitude, as it is toward any offspring of the underground culture, was nonacceptance, a distant tolerance with a gaping chasm of misunderstanding between. The effect was the same in the United States when the punk scene descended on the conservative mainstream in the late 1970s, and even when the Love Generation appeared in the 1960s. No one quite knew how to grasp these weird mutant youths with their pierced flesh and spiked hair, their need to express themselves so loudly.

But the similarities of the American youth of the 1980s, and Cuba's new tattoo infatuation is essential in understanding the generation gap between the Castro regime and today's Cuban youth. It's natural for young people of any culture to challenge the fundamental values of the status quo, and Cuban youths are no different. The only real difference is that in Cuba, Fidel isn't just a figurehead. Fidel *is* the system. Fidel is the father of the people. You could say, as Cuba's expressive freedom blossoms, that today's youth is now in its early teens, taking the wisdom of papa Castro's outdated modes to the mat. The tattooists are the new pioneers of the rising voice of the next generation.

New trends have always been a hard sell for Castro's Cuba, which is trying to adapt to people's changing tastes while toiling with the residual Stalinist conservatism leftover from the 1960s. Emerging arts are always met with indifference simply because they can't be controlled or understood, and this makes them some of the most valuable ingredients in Cuban culture. Many consider Castro and the Cuban government a repressive force, and to a certain extent this is true. But when the street places demands on the regime, the regime is forced to bend to the will of the people. Cuba has constantly evolved in this direction, especially since the tourist boom began and prestige in the world media became imperative to attracting guests. Castro knew that cleaning up the image of Cuba's so-called tyranny was essential to winning the world's trust—and it's money. Today's Cuba is a far cry from extremism of the past. The government is more tolerant than ever before, and even the Cuban American exile knows that the island is a different place now. But out of an ingrained fear, the people don't realize how much power they truly have in swaying the system. Today, when the government acts in a repressive manner towards a trend, suddenly that trend becomes an instant hit with the people. The people are constantly looking for ways to challenge the system. Oddly enough, tattoos have become one of these important mediums. For these reasons, the regime has learned to tread lightly on anything it finds unacceptable. It adopts more covert, sometimes even cynical ways of controlling the people. Tattoos are an example of the latest modes of repression.

I asked my friend Ramon why, if the regime detests tattoos so much, are they becoming so common. Why doesn't the government outlaw them? And he simply put his hand over his eyes.

"They pretend they don't see it, and then it's not a problem," he said. "They ignore the tattoos because they don't know how to deal with it."

One day Yovany took me to meet another of Cuba's seven *tatuadores,* a twenty-eight-year old tattooist named Che, who runs his tattoo parlor in Vedado. His forte is sketching Salvador Daliesque designs—called "tattoo flash" in the trade—while learning English listening to a Miami classical rock radio station. We got into a conversation about the arts in Cuba. Why is there an infatuation in the Cuban youth to become artists, poets, musicians? Almost every young person you meet on the island is trying to develop some sort of talent.

"Sure, everyone is an 'artist' in Cuba, but not everyone has talent," said Yovany. "All of the young people want to be heard. *Quieren ser misticos.* They want to be mythical and important. They want to be noticed."

It made a lot of sense. Younger Cubans are almost desperate to find any way possible to express themselves. The Revolutionary program doesn't make them feel important. They want to be respected as individuals, but the regime is still stuck in a Marxist-Leninist rut that rewards only the vanguard cogs in the machine. Which worked fine with previous generations. But to be an individual is still frowned upon today. The system is geared toward producing good and obedient workers, and individualism doesn't mesh.

"It seems as though it's the same everywhere in the world," I said. "There is this element of prestige associated with being an artist in every country." I began telling Yovany and Che about a certain chain restaurant in the United States that uses the term *artist* loosely to give the minimum-wage workers a feeling of individualism and self-worth in their roles as "Sandwich Artists."

"Ah, *sí, sí, sí, sí*," said Che, searching his memory. ". . . Subway!"

"How do you know about Subway restaurants?" I asked, surprised, and he jabbed his thumb toward the radio.

"I hear the commercials all the time," he laughed. "I've always been curious about that restaurant."

Tattoos, naturally, are the dominant, global, street-level means of artistic individualism today. With a tattoo, you have something to say about yourself, a permanent symbol that reflects who you are and what you believe in. Cubans are just now hooking into this idea. Yovany and Che are two of Cuba's seven mediums to this coveted individualism, which places them in a threatening position with the government's non-individualistic program. But it also makes them heroes to the people, who are quick to champion anyone with enough nerve to publicly question the Revolutionary paradigm.

Yet even though the government is turning a blind eye to tattoos, there are means of repression. In any other country, the government would already have formed fifteen committees on tattooing to find ways to tax the income; tattoos would even be promoted as a way to generate a new source of revenue. In Cuba, it's quite the opposite.

"There is no license to make tattoos," Yovany explained. "And we went to the Ministry of Public Health to try and obtain information on sterile conditions for tattooing, but they really knew nothing. So we're mainly forced to pick up information here and there from wherever we can, visiting artists, magazines, word of mouth."

By not accepting and helping to develop the tattoo trade in Cuba, the government is creating hurdles for the artists to jump through. When artists exchange their services for dollars, they're are actually committing the crime of illegal enrichment because there is no license available for tattooing. No doubt the government will crack down when it feels too threatened and decides to stop ignoring the growing tattoo rage. Even though the law against illegal enrichment is not enforced yet, tattooing in Cuba could indeed be construed as a petty crime, and some of the *tatuadores* have been raided, all of their equipment confiscated. Another means of controlling the spread of tattoos in Cuba is by making the necessary equipment and supplies unavailable to the artists. The government controls all dollar commodities shipped into Cuba for sale to the public. Tattooing supplies are not on the rosters, nor will they ever be, and this creates yet another hurdle.

"You can't buy anything here," said Che, "and we can't mail order since Cubans are prohibited from having credit cards to pay for it. It's very difficult. We have to rely on people from other countries to bring us what we need."

Like the rest of Cuba's tattooists, neither Che nor Yovany acquired professional equipment until the late 1990s. Before then, tattooists were forced to use either the standard jailhouse needle and thread or some jerry-rigged electronic contraption. All the *tatuadores* I spoke with told me charming stories about their first equipment, typically a large hypodermic plunger with a single needle powered by a small motor from a tape recorder. A lot of amateur tattooists still use this kind of equipment. Another *tatuador,* Central Havana–based Junior Pérez, a Cuban heavy metal fan, explained with a chuckle how he had once put together a system whereby he pedaled a bicycle to pump the needles. He also found a broken sterilizer from a hospital, repaired it, and still uses it today.

Despite the Third World setting, the *tatuadores* maintain ultra-high standards for sterility. Gloves are never reused, and fresh needles are employed as often as possible. Stolen latex gloves are often purchased in the *bolsa negra,* and acupuncture needles, lifted either by a doctor or medical supplier, are sometimes used as a cheap and clean alternative to standard prefab tattoo needle bars. Because such a wealth of petty crimes are associated with the industry, the *tatuadores* stay on their toes and in a mild state of paranoia for their passion. They know that at any time the hammer could come down, putting them out of business, while the sickle chops away their lives in one clean sweep.

All of Cuba's *tatuadores* want to gain the state's approving nod and official recognition. They also need an official license under which to operate. They want to grow the fringe scene into a mainstream industry, and Yovany and Che explained passionately how all of Cuba's seven professionals would like to form a real Cuban tattoo association so they can organize international tattoo conventions, have a Web site, and open a school to train new artists in the genre of skin. But in Cuba, these kinds of changes, which must first run the gamut of bureaucracy with its votes and discussions and committees, take forever to develop. It will likely be several years, maybe even a decade for the *tatuadores* to achieve their goals, if ever.

In the mid-1990s, as a first step toward official recognition, the seven joined Cuba's official Communist-controlled youth arts organization, *Associación Hermanos Saíz,* which is the precursor for Cuban National Union of Writers and Artists (UNEAC). The association is for youngsters who wants to groom themselves for future membership in UNEAC, which they apply for when they turn thirty. If they don't apply and aren't accepted into UNEAC before their thirty-fourth birthdays, they can never join. When I asked my artist friends on the island what they thought of UNEAC, the reply came back, without exception, "UNEAC is a farce." Ramon went as far as calling it "a mafia," a tightly controlled club of back-slappers in which those in power dictate the upward mobility of younger artists. Unless one can somehow wiggle under the umbrella of favoritism, the possibilities are nil. Most younger Cuban artists see UNEAC this way. To them it is just more of the establishment, and they choose to strike it out alone, desperately hoping to make enough international contacts in the United States and Europe to stumble into an exhibition abroad, where the majority of Cuba's artists, frustrated with the system, are turning their focus.

The *tatuadores* no doubt understand these dynamics, but official recognition is important to them because their genre is confined to the island. They are not selling oil paintings that can be placed on exhibition in New York. It's street art. Body graffiti. A purely domestic art form. And in Cuba, acceptance is necessary to operate to full capacity. After joining the *artes plasticas* division of *Hermanos Saíz,* the seven named their group *Lienzos Vivientes,* Living Canvases, and began developing the meager foundation of a national industry. The Cuban government, and Castro in particular, has an infatuation with what are called *proyectos de artes,* community art projects. The idea is that the art, in order to gain official support, must benefit the community, whether a barrio, a zone, or the entire Revolutionary culture. Castro's 1961 saying concerning the arts and media, "Within the Revolution everything. Outside the Revolution nothing," still rings true today, and it became the task of the *tatuadores* to prove that tattoos were an art form having cultural value. The same year, they held their first national tattoo exhibition in Havana, where they showcased photos of Cuba's finest tattoo work. The regime looked on, letting them do their thing. But the following year, when a tattoo of a U.S. flag won first prize in the competition, a Miami newspaper printed a scandalous anti-Castro story and created a fiasco for the *tatuadores.*

"The headline went something like this," said Che: "'In Fidel's whiskers, the youth are rebelling against the government with an opposition of tattoos.' It was a Cuban American who wrote it. Of course it created problems for us."

"There were inspections," added Yovany. "We had to explain that we didn't know anything about the article. That the writer was a nobody making propaganda against Cuba and we had nothing to do with it. And we didn't. This particular tattoo won because it was excellent work, the line quality, the shading, not because we're counterrevolutionary."

Occasionally, you'll stumble across a Cuban with a U.S. flag or Statue of Liberty tattooed on his arm in a more rebellious attempt to lock horns with the establishment. And it's amazing how many Cubans you'll see in the streets wearing clothing decorated with U.S. flags and symbols. Every day you'll run across these daring individuals, who no doubt received the garb from Miami relatives, who no doubt love the idea that a cousin, nephew, daughter is in Havana tromping around in a full U.S.-flag T-shirt. But these people are a minority. And as the *tatuador* Junior Pérez put it in plain Spanish, speaking for all Cuban tattooists, "We're artists, not politicians, and if someone wants an American symbol tattoo, that's their business. As tattoo artists, we create what a person desires. We're only the medium, and we're neutral."

One day when I went to visit Yovany, he said, "Hey, you're in luck. Perfect timing. I'm just about to make a tattoo of Che Guevara."

Excellent. I'd been wanting photos of a Che tattoo, and capturing one in progress was even better. As Yovany sketched a freehand stencil of Korda's famous print *"Guerrillero Heroico"* onto a shred of paper, I noticed that the customer was a Cuban. With his long ponytail and two-day stubbled chin, he explained to Yovany that he wanted a small black-and-white tattoo of the Che portrait in his upper left arm. Yovany proceeded to talk the guy into letting him make the tattoo much larger. After some debate, the man agreed, and the work began. As Yovany turned on the fan and launched into the task, the man remained silent, wincing occasionally to the bite of the needles. He didn't know me, and it was apparent that he was nervous in my presence. Everyone else in the room continued talking except for the guy getting the tattoo. After an hour he felt a little more comfortable with me. When he heard that I was a journalist, he looked at me square in the eye and said, "Guess who's the most famous *campesino* in Cuba right now?" His words were rapid, as if he had an urgent story to get off his chest. "I am," he said, turning his head away, retreating into his former silence. This is a common Cuban way to begin a conversation. Many calculate their words, and then with one good Spartan sentence, they bait the listener into dire curiosity.

"So why is the most famous *campesino* in Cuba getting a tattoo of Che?" I asked.

He looked at me again, and with the same rapid pace he unloaded a fusillade of words on me.

"Because I'm just like Che. I believe in his ideals, and I live by his example," he said proudly, explaining how he's a dairy farmer who owns a ranch and two hundred head of cattle on the outskirts of Havana. He had just traveled forty kilometers to Yovany's shop to get his Che tattoo, and he was on his way, right now, to do an interview with a reporter from CNN's Havana bureau.

"I just spent the night in jail," he said. "I wasn't charged with anything, but they made me stay the night." On and on, he baited me like this, pulling me into his story.

"For what?" I asked.

"Well, you see I have my two hundred head of cattle, and everyday, I have two hundred gallons of surplus milk leftover after I make my sale to the state. It's good milk, this two hundred gallons, and you know there are a lot of people in Cuba who can use this milk, but the state makes me throw it away. Week after week, I've been asking the boss, 'But this is good milk, why can't I sell it privately, or why can't I give it away?' and he would say just to go ahead and dump it over here in this ditch."

In Cuba, beef and dairy farmers are restricted from selling their products to anyone but the state. Selling it privately is against the law and butchering a steer will result in a seven-year prison term for the crime of "illegal slaughter." Those who sell beef or milk on the street in small quantities face a six-month stretch on a government work farm. The man getting the tattoo explained that he was so fed up with being forced to dump good milk into a ditch that the day before he had taken his dairy truck loaded with the two hundred surplus gallons and driven to the Plaza of the Revolution, opened the spigot, and loudly began giving away milk to anyone who had a container. The police immediately intervened and arrested him for this act of civil disobedience.

"So now CNN is going to interview me," he said, "and they told me they're going to interview Fidel later today and ask him why I was arrested for giving away free milk instead of throwing it away when there are so many children who could drink it. That's why I'm the most famous *campesino* in Cuba today. And I'm getting the tattoo of Che because Che would have done exactly what I did. I'm just like Che."

As the guy paid and left, Yovany and I followed him downstairs and out into the blazing sun of the street.

"You know," said Yovany as the farmer drifted away, "he could have just kept quiet and given the milk away and he would have had no problems. You don't just pull a truck into the plaza and make a big scene like this. He just wanted to make a scene. To make a statement."

We stood and watched, both speechless, as the man walked east, soon tossing in Obispo's tumultuous sea of bodies as the continuous stream of moving flesh devoured him. Another fleeting ghost dissolving into Cuba's perpetual flux of history.

20

Cuba, Drugs, and the
Curse of Tio Sam

One of the most thrilling and dangerous times I had on the island was plunging into the underworld of Cuba's marijuana growers and illicit drug dealers. This realm is the fringe of Cuban fringes. It is completely outside the Revolutionary culture and it's the blackest part of the black market. For me, the task became one of finding the dealers and the pot growers, the people daring enough or hungry enough to break one of the Revolution's biggest commandments. I'd been approached by petty drug peddlers in the streets. With the right contacts and some caution, it's fairly easy to score a couple of joints, or even a gram of cocaine for $25 in the black market; but I wanted to get off the streets and into the next level and discover the process, where the stuff comes from, how it circulates. When I first told one of my black market contacts, a guy named Faustino, that I wanted to do this, we were at Playa Santa Maria across the harbor, sitting under one of the weathered palm-thatched umbrellas and passing a bottle of cheap rum with another mutual friend.

"I want to meet the marijuana growers," I told him. "I want to meet the dealers, and I want interviews."

There was an immediate tension. Both men turned ghost white, and a nervous pause ensued. They simply stared at me, but their eyes said a thousand things. Surely I was some demon cast from fate, here to bring misfortune into their lives. Maybe I was being followed. Maybe I was a state agent posing as a tourist to set up a black market sting.

"You're with the CIA or maybe the DEA, aren't you?" said Faustino, breaking the silence. "You only want to make bad propaganda against Cuba."

"Yes," said his friend. "We know you are one of them, it is certain."

"You know that's not true," I said. "I only want to investigate Cuba's drug culture. Look, the truth is the truth. People want to know what's going on in Cuba."

"*No es facil,*" Faustino loosened up with a shot of rum. "It's not easy. You never know when you're talking to an informer. You could be an informer. He could be one. So could I. The growers will think you're CIA. Why else would a *Norteamericano* want meet with the growers?"

"*¡Esta loco!*" the other said, eyes reclining. "This guy's nuts!"

"It won't be easy," Faustino repeated.

"*La vida de aventura,*" I mumbled. "The growers can blindfold me, whatever is necessary."

After an hour of convincing them of my good intentions, they explained the dangers. By helping to aid a foreign journalist creating counterrevolutionary propaganda about Cuban drugs, they were risking ten to twenty years in prison. Doing my research in Cuba without state permission for months at a time was already risky, and this only upped the ante. For Faustino, it gave him an opportunity to live on the edge and take some chances in ways he had never imagined. But if convincing him was a difficult task, convincing the growers and dealers themselves would be a nightmare. I became "*el periodista de Alemania,*" the German reporter, and Faustino began cautiously putting out the feelers. There were rumors of a man in Santo Suarez who had seven big plants. Rumors of another in Guanabacoa with a small marijuana plantation.

The networking involved in tracking these people down was horrendous. Faustino would exhaust his contacts, and then these would query yet others; finally, someone entrenched in dealing large quantities or growing was contacted. For every dealer located, there was a week of waiting for an answer, usually a "no," followed by "The plants have already been killed, forget everything you've heard."

Their fears were understandable. The first rule for pot cultivators anywhere in the world is "Never show your plants to anyone, not even close friends." In Cuba, this precaution is tripled. During the January 1999 crackdown on prostitution and petty crime, I had watched a Communist shaming that was broadcast nationally over Cubavision, essentially a Revolutionary crucifixion of a man caught with an ounce of cocaine. As part of his prison sentence, the man was forced to admit publicly that his possession of the cocaine was counterrevolutionary while a mob of older, more conservative Cubans hurled insults at him in the streets. Throughout the 1980s and 1990s, Cuba was on full military alert because it feared the United States would launch an invasion using the War on Drugs as a pretext. Because of this, drug sales are one of Cuba's biggest crimes and taboos, dealt with more harshly than anything else.

Cuba has always been a haven for contraband and smugglers. In the eighteenth and nineteenth centuries, pirates and gunrunners knew every hidden key, islet, and obscure beach across the island. During the Prohibition, Cuba was a port of call for rum-runners from the United States. And today, a few drug traffickers and human smugglers carry on this salty tradition. Low-flying planes from Colombia, Mexico, and Jamaica make the drops within Cuba's twelve-mile national water boundary, and 100-kph speedboats from Haiti, the Bahamas, and Florida, able to dance circles around Cuba's outdated Soviet vessels, make the haul. While 60 percent of all illicitly imported drugs enter the United States via the Mexican interstate and desert mules, 30 percent enter through the Yucatan and Bahamian sea channels, and Cuba is stuck right in the middle. When the boats miss their rendezvous, or the Cuban coast guard intervenes, some of the goods float inland.

"Some years ago," said Castro in a 1999 speech devoted solely to drug trafficking, "if they washed up on the keys or the island, people handed them over to authorities voluntarily; there were no dollars here then. Now, much persuasion is required to obtain the people's cooperation. Sanctions against domestic trafficking had to be tightened."

Castro refers to the Cuban penal code modifications of February 26, 1999, which doled out from eight to twenty years in prison for anyone caught fishing drugs from the sea and failing to report them: a tempting sin for seaside peasants living in subsistence-level poverty who stumble upon a bale and decide to sell it. All the previous penalties for anything involving drugs were simply doubled. Four to ten years and state confiscation of all property involved for unauthorized trafficking or growing marijuana. Eight to twenty years for aiding international traffickers to use Cuba as a drug hub. Eight to twenty years for sales to minors. And two to five if someone knows about one of these crimes and fails to report it. Before 1999, petty drug possession in Cuba was legal. Now, petty possession, distribution, and consumption carries a penalty of six months at one of Cuba's work farms to two years in the penitentiary.

But the big change was Castro's adding death by firing squad for Cuban officials aiding in the smuggling of relatively large amounts of drugs. The message was clear enough; drugs would not be tolerated in Cuba. The National Assembly, in its introduction to the 1999 penal code modifications, said plainly that the changes were largely due to the deterioration "of the international image of our country." Interpreted between the lines, the meaning here is simple: "The United States has been accusing us of money laundering and drug smuggling as a reason to uphold the embargo. If we take these reasons away, then they look more like the bad guys while we look more like the victims."

The Cuban people clearly understand these dynamics. To harm Cuba's prestige is now seen as more counterrevolutionary than drugs themselves. The worst counterrevolutionary act that any Cuban can commit today is to give the United States even a dribble of fuel to launch a new smear campaign; such a campaign would slow down the U.S.

travel ban's lifting and hinder tourism, both of which Castro needs almost imperatively at this time. In my exploration of Cuba's drug culture, I was one of the guys Cubans had been warned about.

One day I picked up Faustino in a rental car and we drove to a distant barrio to pick up his contact, a guy named Tomás, who sold and fronted marijuana by the ounce to others, who in turn peddled single joints in the street. After promising Faustino that I'd buy an ounce and give it to him for the trouble, he made me drive around in circles, trying to purposefully get me lost. Finally, after what seemed an eternity of dodging rubbish piles and skirting kids on bikes, Faustino said, "Pull over to the curb," and as I did, a guy popped out of nowhere and jumped in with a sweaty *"Vámonos."* He was the man who was going to take me in, but first he wanted to check me out. After driving out to Parque Lenin and drinking a couple beers over a game of billiards, we went to his house, and he broke out one of several ounces.

"This was grown on a plantation in Guantánamo and smuggled to Havana by truck," he said, cracking open the *paquete,* the package, explaining that the little bulk pot raised on the island originates in easternmost Oriente with its mountains and hills garbed in alpine jungle. I told him about marijuana in the United States, how before the 1980s it was always smuggled in from Colombia and Mexico, but that now most of it is grown domestically and is very high-grade stuff.

"Hah!" Tomás chuckled with a macho grunt. "If you think the American stuff is good, wait until you try *la Cubana.*"

I couldn't believe that this proud idea of "If the capitalist can do it, the Revolutionaries can do it better" translated even to the depths of Cuba's underground drug culture. In Cuba, plastic bags are nonexistent, as are rolling papers, and the guy simply tore a corner from the paper wrapper and rolled one up. It was loose, leafy pot at $40 an ounce. Heavy on the stems. It had never been pressed into bricks and was obviously grown at a small domestic plantation with perhaps a five- or ten-pound yield.

"Most of our marijuana comes from Jamaica," he said. "The Jamaicans toss it from boats on the south coast and it's picked up on shore."

The pot was mild and had a sweet perfume. As the joint sailed around, I framed one of the amphibious operations in my mind—the night signals, the lucky pargo fisherman who stumbles across a forgotten bale tossing in the waves. In Castro's July 1999 speech on *narcotrafico,* he admitted that drugs are dropped five to twenty miles off the Cuban coasts for pickup and transport to the United States via the Bahamas. But the Cuban coast guard, making do with old Russian tubs that lumber along at a snaillike 25 kph, is paralyzed in dealing with international traffickers who use the island as a transit hub.

The magnitude of Castro's dedicating his entire forty-sixth annual July 26 Moncada speech to *narcotrafico* is evidence that his country is so stable that he can swat flies like this old but significant pest. But for him, drugs were the next point of order in *la lucha;* a problem, like the U.S. immigration problem, that had caused years of strain on the Revolution and was still smudging Cuba's poise. A problem he was personally sensitive about.

Just when President Carter was lifting the travel ban and taking steps to lift the embargo, the "Castro Connection" story first broke on the CBS program *60 Minutes* in 1978, in which allegations were made tying Castro and Cuba's highest military leaders to the Colombian drug cartels. Every year since that time, the media has diced up a new breaking story about Cuba's drug smuggling and cited "new evidence," usually testimony to a federal grand jury in which, to lighten his sentence, some convicted smuggler has cooked up an unfounded and bizarre story tying the Castros to Medellín. During Manuel Noriega's 1991 federal hearings in Miami, charges were raised indicting Castro's brother, Raul, for aiding the Colombian drug cartels. Coincidentally, the "new evidence" always seems to arise right before U.S. presidential elections, when campaign statements are typically made in Florida regarding a candidate's stance on relations. And even more coincidentally, after every media slur in the United States, the Cuban media seems to make a series of drug arrests, quickly trumpeting a success in their own domestic war on drugs. On December 3, 1998, when a seven-ton shipment of cocaine was seized in the Colombian port of Cartagéna, the newswires went berserk. The smoking gun everyone had been scrambling for linking Castro to *narcotrafico* had been found; Havana was listed as the next port of call. It turned out to be just more unfounded and embarrassing hype for Castro. Then on December 5, in a stroke of good counterpropaganda, Cuba's paper *Granma* ran its own front-page article announcing the arrest of eighteen foreign nationals at the José Martí airport, mules attempting to smuggle 120 pounds of cocaine in coat hangers to Britain and Canada through Cuba.

The patterns are so obvious that they seem almost ludicrous. On January 5, 1999, President Clinton, in an obvious attempt to open dialogue with Castro and thaw relations, announced new measures to "step up contacts with the Cuban people." In a trade-off, on the same day, Castro commenced with his crackdown on Cuban delinquency, prostitution, money laundering, and drug trafficking to polish up the island's image and make Clinton's decision, a first step towards lifting the embargo, look good. And on the same day—coincidentally, of course—Ileana de la Guardia, the daughter of a Cuban colonel executed by firing squad in 1989 for his involvement in a Cuban smuggling ring called "Case #1," filed suit in Paris; she claimed that Castro had been the actual mastermind behind Cuba's drug smuggling operations throughout the 1980s and that her father was Castro's scapegoat. This, of course, may or may not be true. However, with the strength of Cuba's economy during that decade, it seems unlikely. Both Bush and Reagan were no doubt hungry for any crumb of evidence linking Castro to Medellín, and had they found one, there would have likely been an invasion, but it never occurred. To date, no one has yet been able to provide hard evidence linking Castro directly to *narcotrafico*.

The year 1999 was pivotal for the alleged "Castro Connection" and for the embargo. It was the year that the idea of lifting the embargo began to surface in Washington. But before moves to lift the embargo could proceed, the drug smuggling business had to be cleared away first. In no way would the United States find itself in the embarrassing position of waging a war on drugs while tabling business with an alleged *narcotrafico* nation. And Fidel knew it was one of the primary obstacles. On January 14, after the above mentioned foray, Colombian President

Andres Pastrana was invited to Cuba to sign a new bilateral anti-*narco-trafico* accord with Castro. Colombia, then and now the primary partner of the United States in the war on drugs, was added to Cuba's global honor roll of twenty-three similar treaties. The implications of this move were far reaching. It was clear that Cuba was playing ball, and Clinton was listening. Understanding full well what was happening, in April, Representative Lincoln Diaz-Balart (R-Fla.), a vocal anti-Castroist representing the exiles' interests, retaliated, delivering a speech to the House of Representatives titled, "The Need to Maintain the Embargo Against the Castro Dictatorship," dedicating a good chunk of the message to the alleged drug connection. However, it wasn't enough, and in May, White House drug czar Barry McCaffrey stated that he had seen no evidence of the Cuban government's involvement in the international drug trade during the past twenty years.

In June, the DEA and U.S. Coast Guard officials met with Cuba's antidrug authorities in Havana to discuss ways of coordinating antitrafficking operations. It was as if Cuba was quickly invited to be an honorary member of the War on Drugs club. This flung the door wide open for further negotiations, and in August, Senator Tom Daschle and Senator Byron Dorgan visited Castro on a feeler mission to discuss possibilities of future trade with Cuba. They were the highest statesmen to visit Cuba for this purpose since the emplacement of the embargo in 1960. These were baby steps, but it was becoming evident that the embargo was on its way out the door. Then, on Wednesday, November 17, less than a week before Elian González was fished from the Florida Straits, the Bureau for International Narcotics and Law Enforcement Affairs announced that Cuba would not be penciled into the "Majors List" as an international drug trade threat to the United States any longer. It was a major victory for Castro. For the exile it was a defeat. And for the "Castro Connection"? Case closed.

Only six months later, I would find myself sitting with Faustino and Tomás the drug dealer, buying an ounce of good Cuban pot, passing a joint, and talking about how marijuana is grown and smuggled into the island from Jamaica for Cuban domestic and tourist consumption. Cuba doesn't keep statistics on alcohol and drug abuse, so there are no numbers on societal patterns. However, it's safe to say the Cuban drug culture is very small, mostly because the majority of people have no money for food, let alone for recreational drug use. Cuban pot smokers I know can usually scrape up a dollar or two for an occasional joint, but few smoke daily; not only is the drug out-priced by the low state wages but the fear of arrest runs deep. The people I met who grew marijuana were amateurs, and their knowledge about cultivation was limited to word of mouth, perhaps a contraband book smuggled in from a Miami cousin with illustrated growth methods. These were people who liked to smoke or wanted to grow a small quantity to sell for a dollar income, deciding to take the risks usually out of the need to find some kind of euphoria to mentally escape the poverty. Besides the four-to-ten-year prison sentence, the *confiscacion de bienes* clause in the penal code, state confiscation of the house and cars, was the biggest deterrent. For the pot growers, the seizure of even one plant would break a family. Regardless, most of the growers had two or three, and up to ten plants going at a time. They were homeowners who had good cover, an enclosed driveway, or a big fenced yard with foliage where they could hide their operations.

Getting in to see those operations was another matter. In the following weeks, Faustino would drop in sporadically at my illegal apartment, sweating and nervous with an "Okay, we've found someone who will meet you." We'd then go pick up Tomás at a prearranged location in some distant barrio, park at another barrio, and then walk two kilometers or take a bus to yet another. As we were walking, Faustino and Tomás would say, "Okay, keep walking," and they would veer off across the street, walking parallel to me. A quarter mile later, they would cross back over, explaining that one of the growers was standing back at a certain bus stop, and he wanted to check me out before he approved of my meeting him. Then we'd reverse our tracks, and the grower would be at another location to give a prearranged hand signal to Tomás, either a yes or a no. Sometimes it was no, at others it was yes. When it was a yes, the dealer would say, "See that guy standing over there? Just go over to him and he'll take you." I would walk over to the stranger and together we'd walk a few blocks where the actual grower was waiting to take me to his house. It was a foolproof procedure, and I was impressed by the details that had been worked out beforehand.

One of the cultivators I met grew his stuff about a mile away from Ernest Hemingway's ranch, Finca Vigía, in San Francisco de Paula. After going through the routine, I was led up to the second floor of an apartment where a very nervous family was waiting to greet me. On the back breezeway, next to a massive pig stuffed into a small pen, sat a large milk crate holding three unimpressive plants. Vintage Cuban stuff. The tension was stifling, and the grower was petrified by my presence. There was time only for a few basic questions, and with each one the stress intensified. Our stomachs were in knots, which, in the black market, is a sensation the people are accustomed to. But these were big, gnawing knots, and after fifteen minutes, with no sting in progress, Faustino and Tomás felt it was safe enough to come in and quickly whisk me away.

"Look," I said to them. "These plants are okay, but I'd like to see better plants. Bigger ones. And some relaxed conversation would be nice."

"Of course," Tomás assured me. "We know of more, but the people are afraid. They know about you, but they wanted to wait and see if you were a cop. Today was the test case. After a week, when they see that nothing happened here, they'll be less reluctant."

In the underground network, word was circulating about me, which made the operation more dangerous. There is a black market kinship among the growers, who are also dealers and petty smugglers, and through the ring, they'd heard about my interest in their clandestine crops. But there were many things to consider. Certainly the consequences would be disastrous if I innocently led an investigator to them. Assisting a foreign journalist in spreading negative propaganda would result in a one-to-three-year prison sentence for illegal association, and another one-to-four for harming Cuba's international prestige. This on top of the four-to-ten for growing, loss of the house, and another two-to-five for not reporting other dealers who happened to get caught in the web. A total of twenty-two years in prison was at stake. Although it was unlikely that the maximums would be given, you never knew when they were looking for an example, who they would throw the book at and ostracize publicly in a national shaming. Everything depended on the current tolerance, which hinged on the economic weather, and in Cuba, the weather is constantly changing.

"I see Fidel is in Panama this week," I said to Enrique one day after reading a notice in *Granma*.

"Yes, he's never in Cuba," Enrique explained.

He's always on internationalist tours, building amistad. And when he's gone, everyone sighs. There is more celebration. The people can get away with more. Then just before he comes home, there are arrests, the streets are cleaned. If he decides to take a tour of a certain building, they'll spend a week making it look perfect before he arrives. Castro knows nothing of what's going on in Cuba. He's kept in the dark. He'll ask one of his assistants, "Are the crime rates on burglary going down?" And his assistant will answer, "Yes, *comandante*, of course, because your actions last year on dealing with burglary were brilliant and exemplary." Fidel thinks everything in Cuba is always okay, because the people close to him tell him lies. Then he goes on another internationalist mission. He is kept distant from the realities the people live in.

The reality of Cuba's domestic drug trade is, like everything else, a means of survival. Drugs are a dollar commodity in a world where it's impossible to live in pesos. Packages of cocaine and marijuana that wash up on shore are a means to instant wealth on an island where wealth is for a tiny minority. And the people using these drugs have found a way to escape both the poverty and the accompanying mental weight of living in it.

Castro wouldn't understand this, because for him the entire world is a statistic. In the 1999 crackdown address, he announced that "in the past, marijuana was the predominantly consumed drug. However between January and November 1998, this tendency has changed with the confiscation of 106.49 kilograms of cocaine in 101 incidents, while only 80.52 kilos of marijuana were taken in 978 incidents."[1]

He ignores the evolving patterns of the international drug trade, which are reflected in his statistics. He doesn't mention that marijuana has slowly become a domestic crop for the United States, that the demand for imports has decreased, and that international cocaine trafficking has increased. Nor does Fidel mention that the cocaine confiscated in Cuba is largely bound for his own dollar-carrying tourists as a means for average Cubans to earn a highly illegal income on an island where it's impossible to survive in a worthless peso economy. I have yet to meet a Cuban who can afford cocaine at $25–$35 a gram. For a state employee, this equals four or five months' wages. The *jineteros* score the cocaine for tourists and receive a monetary commission, perhaps a line or two for the trouble. But the problem, as Castro sees it, is not that the new wave of tourists are creating the demand, nor that the state of the economy forces Cubans into taking these risks. Rather, the problem is the Cuban people. The delinquents. The undesirables who fail to step up to the task of superhuman expectations and starve like good Revolutionaries. Castro says that in the past, pot was the biggest domestically "consumed" drug. And it still is.

At another distant barrio in a hilly Havana suburb, Tomás led me to the home of one of his main suppliers, a man who with his small family lived in a tiny house with an enclosed driveway wrapped in rusty corrugated sheet metal. The front gate was kept locked and had to be opened with a key, even during the day. Before the Special Period, few of the homes had security gates; but by mid-1993, burglaries had become so rampant that most scraped together what small savings they had to purchase bars and padlocks for their doors and windows. But the man we were going to meet kept his home secured to protect his drugs. As we approached, Tomás yelled out, "*Oye,* we're here," and the wife came out to greet us. Everything was casual. By now, everyone in the network knew there had been no busts. The nervous tension and paranoia were gone. The guy appeared from the back yard and handed his baby to the wife.

"We're as close as brothers," Tomás said to me, making the introduction. "We're like family."

The dealer took us to the back driveway. Cicadas buzzed away in the summer heat, weeds grew up through the cracked cement, an ancient Oldsmobile sat on blocks, no doubt a family heirloom dating back to the decade before the victory. Although it didn't run, the car was obviously washed and polished once a week. The guy waved us over to the back corner of the lot, where a fifty-five-gallon drum sat rusting in the humidity. Inside the drum was the man's pride, an impressive two-foot plant reaching maturity, the green top bursting out over the mangled rim of the barrel. Near the drum sat a few seedlings, recently germinated in small plastic bags holding that sweet, red Cuban soil. Unlike the other growers I'd met, this guy knew how to grow healthy plants that produced bulk and potency. The leaves were pristine, and the shade of green revealed experience in balancing the soil.

"I'm getting ready to kill this one, when I'll transplant these others," he said with a warm smile. "It's just about mature."

"But Cuba has a year-round growing season," I said. "Why don't you let them go longer?"

"In Cuba, this is impossible," he said. "Someone might notice. You have to kill and cure them as soon as they mature. Sometimes you can't even wait this long. We have to follow our instincts. Many times I've had to kill them and throw them away because another grower, a friend, was arrested. Other times, they are killed just on a premonition. Maybe you feel that there is trouble coming. Maybe it comes, maybe it doesn't, but you can't take chances."

"Do you grow to sell?" I asked.

"No. I grow for my own use," he said. "It's too risky in Havana to grow those kinds of quantities. Sometimes I'll sell a little of what I grow, but the *habaneros* like to keep only a few plants. Most of the bigger plantations are in the mountains in Oriente. The marijuana is packaged and shipped to Havana, and this is the stuff I sell."

I bought a couple of joints, and they were surprisingly wrapped in genuine contraband rolling papers. Most Cuban smokers use a pipe made out of old fittings rummaged from a *derrumbe,* or a beer can with holes poked into the aluminum. As we passed the joint, he broke out a few photos of exiled family and friends in Miami. The pictures were smeared with fingerprints from excessive handling. Another vintage Cuban scene.

"My sister and her husband," he pointed to the people in the image. Then after a thoughtful pause, the next photo. "My brother, and these are my two best friends. They all went in 1994."

"*Balseros,*" I said. "Were they taken to Guantánamo Bay first?"

"Yes, they were stuck in Guantánamo for a year."

"*Estas bromeando,*" I laughed. "A year? You're kidding."

"Can you believe it?" he said. "Many of those people couldn't last three months down there and they wanted to return home. I come from determined blood."

"Why didn't you go to Miami with them?"

"I had a spot on a boat, but I couldn't leave my wife and kids behind. My first child was just born, and it would have been irresponsible. Cuba may be the biggest prison on earth, but family comes first, you know how it is."

As we talked, I posed the same ritual question I asked all the dealers and growers I met: "How many people do you think smoke marijuana in Cuba?" I'd heard as low as zero from a hard-line Communist, and as high as 75 percent.

"Ah!" he said with the standard Cuba gesture, a twist of the wrist above the head to exclaim infinity. "Everyone smokes here. Even the *comandante* used to smoke. He and Che used to roll up in the Sierra Maestra during the war. Camilo, too. You know, Camilo Cienfuegos. They all smoked."

"Yes, it's true," Tomás emphasized.

"Where did you hear this?" I asked, almost shocked.

"Come on," said the grower. "Everyone knows it. I mean look at them. Long hair. Beards. Fidel, Camilo, Che. . . . Did they smoke marijuana or not?"

"Now that you mention it," I said. "But it's not something you'd read about in the history books."

"No," my new friend laughed, torching the second joint. "No, it's not in the history books."

21

Sea Lane to Paradise

They always say it's an eighteen-hour ride from Havana to Oriente, and then twenty-eight hours later, the train finally stops at some swampy little depot in the middle of nowhere because the tracks are being repaired or a bridge has been destroyed by a hurricane. Riding the rails in Cuba's old Russian trains is always an adventure. They bounce around so much that you constantly think the cars are going to derail. Most of the Cuban passengers like to pull a sheet over their bodies and faces when they sleep. In the more expensive air-conditioned cars, dollar-holding Cubans use sheets because it's always freezing; in the non-air-conditioned peso cars, the sheets create a muslin shield between the body and the cockroaches.

At night the cars are always dim. Over the intercom, the tick-tock of Radio Reloj floats softly into the Cuban night while the unseen fields and small towns drift past windows browned with a film of soot and smoke. Occasionally the train stops at a tiny sugar village in the middle of nowhere and peasants board to sell *caramelos*, homemade hardtack, and cold bottled cane juice for a few pesos. Later, dinner is served, a cardboard box with cold rice and a chunk of *jamonada*. In the lid of the rice box is a perforated cardboard spoon that can be torn out and used, but after three bites, it gets flimsy, and you must eat the *jamonada* with your fingers and drink the rice by tipping up the box like everyone else. A cola costs 10 pesos, and those without 10 pesos bring their own water. Later yet, the train stops again in the middle of nowhere and more peasants board with more candies for dessert, and others armed with thermoses walk through the cars pouring peso shots of sweet hot coffee for those who have a container.

The train rides are a great place to meet a variety of Cubans. Except for a backpacker or two, very few tourists take the trains. There are always *campesinos* returning home after a week's visit to Havana. Others are coming back after special operations available only in the capital. In each car there are usually one or two teenage soldiers who are going home to their families in the hills of Oriente on a weeklong pass. It is very quiet in the train cars as the people sleep. A few men always converge toward the front, talking boisterously, passing around a bottle of cheap rum. The younger people with dollars lean against the windows listening to the latest tunes on their Walkmans, eyes threading along with the shadows of passing palms and a stationary moon.

In the morning, the train stops at the swampy little depot, far from the ticketed destination, and the rest of the trip is completed by a fleet of buses, *guaguas*, which are always idling patiently, waiting to disperse to Las Tunas, Santiago, and Bayámo with their human cargo. I spent a total of about two months exploring Cuba's lush countryside, riding around in these buses on various occasions. On this trip, my *guagua* to Las Tunas was a big red open-air truck with a tin canopy. It was 6:00 A.M., a sliver of sun just shimmering over the horizon, as I pulled myself up into the bed. The driver handed me a peso as I boarded, a refund on the train ticket price which I would later hand to the truck driver who completed the last leg of the trip. I sat on one of the metal benches, the strange foreigner surrounded by *campesinos*. Many of these peasants live without electricity, and spend their evenings sitting around the fire and improvising *decimas*, peasant folk songs, on guitar for entertainment. There is a certain comfort that comes with bouncing along these winding country roads, past banana plantations, past fields of pineapple, past palm-thatched shacks, the roof of the truck rattling loudly, up, around, down into a small valley, up and out of another, kilometer after kilometer, everyone sitting quietly, hands clasped between legs.

The *guagua* stopped at a crossroad, and five men paid the peso fare and boarded. They were *macheteros*, their faces and eyes hardened by the sun. Thick knuckles, hands permanently callused, honed blades of machetes swinging like metronomes in the polished leather sheaths hanging from a few hips. Others who couldn't afford the sheaths held their machetes proudly across their laps. They said nothing and sat quietly absorbing the foggy morning as the *guagua* cleared the last valley into the outlying plains of Las Tunas.

In the middle of nowhere, the truck squawked to a stop and the men bailed out, quickly disappearing into the brake. The place, the men, the cane, the hard living of these peasants, everything here is timeless. The peasants are the direct lineage of their grandfathers, and their worlds revolve around family, blood, and soil. And the only distinct difference between now and a hundred years ago is the modern layer of tar on the road, the Soviet truck, and the roving teachers who drop in twice a week for a half day's lessons. Most of the kids living this far out go straight to the brakes after ninth grade, and it's there they'll stay, following the generations before them.

Rural Cuba is the most beautiful place on earth. The people who inhabit it live in another time, one dictated by the seasons, the crowing rooster. Many of the homes have dirt floors, and the roofs are thatched with *guano*, palm fronds. Out back is the open-air kitchen, the fire pit, the big coffee pestle carved out of a stump of cedar or mahogany. Chickens run in and out of the house, and in the thick, pitch-black subalpine night, the mosquitoes and frogs come to life. Perhaps a dog barks in the distance, and the only light is from an occasional truck winding along the main road in a distant valley, perhaps a motorcycle whose rider has taped a flashlight to the handlebars, crawling in second gear because those unexpected potholes are a killer, and you don't want to hit those random peasants sleeping alongside the road, still waiting for the bus that never came that day.

The people of Las Tunas are similar to the people who inhabit the terrain outlying Holguín or Bayámo or Pinar del Rio or Guantánamo, anywhere in the Cuban countryside. Some areas are populated mostly by fishing villages. Others are more suitable for growing tobacco or rice, and yet others sugar. The peasants who live in towns around the *carretera*, the interstate, make goat cheese during the night, perhaps pick a few oranges, and then stand along the highway all day, selling whatever they can. And when you get out into the backstretches, you realize that Cuba really is a paradise and its only flaw is poverty. But still there is a safety in the passive hills and palm forests. It is not war-torn Cuba anymore. Camouflaged men will not jump out with submachine guns and seize your car. Rebels with machetes will not cut you to threads. Just dogs barking in the night. *Decimas* sung by the fire. The swift ping of the machete slicing into a sweating stalk of ripe cane. Barefoot kids with sticks for fishing rods. Occasional licensed hunters with single-shot .22 caliber state-issue rifles out searching for rabbits. Here the horse is still the main form of transportation, and those who can't afford the luxury either ride a mule or walk.

The area surrounding Las Tunas is so off the beaten track that in the two weeks I spent there, I didn't see a single tourist. Other than a dollar electronics store, a disco for the young people, and the dollar hotel, which is always empty, the provincial capital, Victoria de Las Tunas, birthplace of Cuba's national poet Nicolás Guillén, operates entirely in the peso economy. The only dollars that come in are from relatives abroad and family in Havana who have access. Half the city traffic consists of horse carts and mules, and if the Tuneros can stave off the whimsies of the government in bringing tourism to this last city of virgin Cuba, more power to them.

The problem is that as the Cuban tourist industry replaces sugar as the island's new monoculture commodity, the *centrales*, the sugar plants, are slowly being closed for lack of need. Seventy-five percent of the island's sugar crops are harvested by Cuban-made combines and the rest is brought in by hand. During the "Crisis" years of the Special Period, from 1990 to 1993, Cuba was forced to return to the ox and plow due to a lack of petroleum, and more than half the harvest was cut by machete. In the "Recuperation," from 1994 to 2000, foreign investment and tourist earnings rapidly increased and oil shortages decreased. Today, the harvest is once again 75 percent mechanized, but this is partly due to the decrease in sugar production. Between 1981 and 1990, the island harvested an average of 7.7 million tons annually. Between 1990 and 1993, despite the lack of mechanized combines, the harvest averaged 6.8 million tons. In 2000, the island yielded only 3.7 million tons, only 1 million more than the 1945 harvest, when Cuba had only 5 million inhabitants.

In short, as cane production decreases, less money is flowing into rural Cuba. *Campesinos* who have been dependent on the crop for centuries are now becoming unemployed. To deal with this economic imbalance, the government is building tourist attractions in distant provinces; for example, plans are currently in development to open golf courses and theme parks in areas such as Holguín in the east and Pinar del Rio in the west. Las Tunas, however, will likely always be a sugar province due to its flattish rolling landscape. It is one of the narrowest parts of the island, only forty-three miles wide, and the sugar ports in the south at Amancio Rodríguez and directly north at Puerto Padre make it an ideal layout for rail transportation of the raw cane. According to the Cuban Institute of Independent Economists a radical (for Cuba) nongovernment think tank of Cuban economists, in the 1999 *zafra*, only 42 of Cuba's 156 *centrales* were profitable. Two of these are no doubt at the ports of Amancio Rodríguez and Puerto Padre, both of which operate full time during the harvest. The smaller inland *centrales* are slowly being closed as the harvest declines, and in the 2001–2002 *zafra*, only 70 were used to make the harvest. The rest have been permanently closed. The government finds it cheaper to shut down the factory, cut its losses, and pay laid-off workers half their former salaries than to use tourist earnings to subsidize sugar production in remote towns outlying the areas of Las Tunas, Bayámo, Ciego de Ávila, Matánzas, and Camagüey, Cuba's cradle of sugar. This kind of economic strategy is not about sustaining the people, but about sustaining the more profitable tourism, which will prolong the Revolution, and it's creating a new strain of poverty on Cubans dependent on sugar for their livelihoods. In turn, many of these smaller towns are becoming depressed rural slums (each with a dollar store, of course).

The design of the Unidades Básicas de Producción Cooperitivas (Basic Units of Production Cooperatives) was a partial answer to the rising poverty and the domestic migration crisis of the Special Period. This legislative stroke resulted in an almost complete decentralization of the agricultural sector. In Cuba, there are five primary exportable agricultural commodities in production year-round: sugar, tobacco, seafood, citrus, and coffee. Behind them are the minors for domestic consumption: livestock, rice, plantain, *guava*, grapefruit, pineapple, cabbage, tomatoes. There are three means for Cubans to earn a living in food production: on government-run plantations, which provide a fixed salary; on individual *fincas*, land plots (essentially modern *latifundismo*); or for the UBPCs, which are autonomous agricultural cooperatives that sell their products to the state at fluctuating prices based on fixed quotas and supply and demand. The UBPC principle is "The harder you work, the more you'll earn, and pray that droughts don't kill your crops, because you're on your own."

The UBPCs amount to a community that revolves around a specialized crop, be it coffee, sugar, plantain, or rice, and the UBPC managers are voted in democratically by the workers. By organizing the UBPCs in this way, the government gives power to the workers, who know their specific geographic needs and how to run their own land efficiently while minimizing managerial corruption. The managers make around 400 pesos a month, and if they wish to maintain this salary, they must bring in the most money for the workers. If they don't, they're voted out; the pressure is on them to make the fields efficient and productive. The UBPCs have their own budgets and make their own decisions; as a stimulus, with the exception of coffee, if a crop produces more than the government needs, it can be sold on the open market, the profits divided between the workers.

While the state farms and private *fincas* represent 25 percent of Cuba's arable land, the UBPCs now comprise the other 75 percent.

Although this sounds appealing, the UBPCs essentially create the illusion of autonomy while maintaining dependency on the state and the *libreta*. Through price fixing, the government forces UBPC worker salaries down to around 200 pesos a month to fall in with the national average for the majority of crops. Of all Cuba's agriculture, tobacco farmers, both private and on the UBPCs, have the highest earning potential, sometimes bringing in up to 1,500 pesos a month, or $900 a year, during a good harvest. This is mostly because tobacco is a tourist draw as well as Cuba's most valuable dollar export, and it needs extra care so that the highest standards are maintained. If the state tried to pay tobacco farmers 200 pesos a month, it's likely the quality would decline because most would quickly drop their plows and become taxi drivers.

But tobacco is a small crop, and only certain soils, mostly in the valleys of western Cuba, are suitable for its growth. The majority of Cuba is geared for sugar. Sugar is on the decline. And without direct dollar tourist commodities to replace it, pockets of rural depression are beginning to grip the countryside because the government is providing no alternative niches for the *campesinos* to explore. Because there are no niches, and because they are forced by law to remain in their provinces, *campesinos* suffer even greater desperation, look forward to even less of a future, and live in even more dismal circumstances. Because of this poverty, more state control is exercised. More surveillance, more paranoia. These areas are far outside the tourist corral and are unseen by the world at large. The communities are more like big families where the children go without shoes, without running water, without electricity, and wear threadbare pants that barely hold together. Out there, something as simple as a basketball is as out of place as an American journalist.

I saw this kind of rural poverty almost everywhere in Cuba, along the coast of the north and southwest, around Playa Girón, central Cuba inland, to the far east in Guantánamo. If in Havana there is the manufactured "Cuba" of Prado Avenue with the real Cuba sitting two blocks away, in rural areas, it's the same way. There's the Cuba of the *autopista*, with its Beny Moré dollar rest area; Camagüey, with it's hotels and night life; Viñales, with it's lush valleys and spiffy tobacco tours—yet twenty miles away down some rutted dirt path sits the real thing. One day when I sat in the living room of one of these peasant families, the father led me out into his dirt yard and with great delight showed off his most valuable possession, a massive ox. "Look at this," he smiled, tapping the bull's testicles with a stick. "Look at the size of them." He was so proud. His entire self-worth, his entire being, was contained in his ox and in his own children, now ranch hands at a nearby farm. In the evening, we sat around over coffee, admiring the family's only other possession, a handful of photos of the daughter's *quince,* the sweet fifteen birthday, neatly kept in a plastic bag. Fidel Castro and the Revolution are about as relevant to these people—who represent about 20 percent of the population—as the Pittsburgh Penguins.

During my two weeks spent around Las Tunas, I got out into the cane brakes during the *zafra* to try my hand at the blade along with the *macheteros.* I met planters. I rode in one of the harvest trucks across the fields as the combine shot diced stalks into the bin and the driver explained the process. Snow white *garzas* ingeniously followed the machine, picking tiny frogs from the freshly cut earth with their insightful beaks before flying off to take a rest on some cow's back. *Auras tiñosas,* Cuba's vultures, sunning their lazy wings on fence posts, triumphantly waiting to feast on rotting spoils. Generation after generation, the peasants, the *garzas,* the vultures, the rich red soil, cane bending to the wind, machetes swinging in rhythm with the sea.

≈≈≈

IT IS DIFFICULT TO EXPERIENCE this kind of magic when your mind is possessed with hunger. When the *central* in Lázaro's town began cutting production, the commerce stopped, the world turned cold, and Lázaro became one of those rural Cubans who lost his niche. When the factory was running to full capacity, he was at least able to struggle to survive, but now that option had been taken away by some official in the Ministry of Sugar who was forced to down-size by orders of the Central Committee, and Carlos Lage Dávila, Cuba's chief economist, who had decided that sugar was less profitable than tourism. I met Lázaro at a roadside food stand not far from Camagüey while inching my way back to Havana. He was trying to use a broken peso phone on the side of the building and stood there in his straw hat for about five minutes shoving in centavos until he finally gave up.

"It's impossible to find one that works," he said, and asked me whether I would drive him a few miles to the phone at the next small town. I asked him what he did for a living, and he told me he worked at an *agropecuario,* a state livestock farm. Later, he admitted that the *agropecuario* was actually a Cuban prison, and that he had two months left of a six-month sentence for selling lobster in the black market. It was another case of a Cuban's being punished for tapping the state's money pipeline. In Lázaro's case, not only did they eliminate the competition, but, as they did to Juan the *jinetero,* exploited his labor for six months, systematically profiting on his crime.

"In my town," Lázaro explained, "we never get visitors. But one time some tourists came and they wanted a lobster dinner, so I bought some in the *bolsa negra* for $1 a pound and sold it to them for $2 a pound. The tourists could have gone to a state restaurant and paid $25, but what would you do, pay them $25 or buy from me for $2? The police caught me, and now I must work at the state prison raising their animals."

"Do they pay you for the labor?"

"No," said Lázaro, who is now thirty-four years old. "They don't pay anything. This job would normally pay 200 or 300 pesos a month, but in prison, they keep the money. My mother and father rely on me to support the family, but for six months I have no income. It's been very hard for us."

"Doesn't Castro know that it's impossible to live with nothing?" I asked Lázaro. "Doesn't he realize what's going on?"

"Castro doesn't know anything that's going on in Cuba," he said. "Everyone lies to him, so he thinks everything is fine. One time in the 1970s, Fidel was driving in his jeep very close to here, inspecting the *zafra,* and he told his assistants, 'We need a road built that goes straight from Camagüey to Bayámo. This will make the *zafra* easier, and if necessary, it will be better for mobility of the troops.' So he ordered the con-

struction of a two-lane highway. His assistants told him 'Yes, *comandante.*
We will begin construction immediately.' Of course, it was never built.
Ten years later, he was flying in his helicopter over the same area to
inspect the *zafra* again, and he said, 'Where's the road I ordered ten years
ago?' He was very angry about this, and the road was finally built. But
you can see that Castro knows nothing of what happens in Cuba. I could
tell you a hundred examples like this."

We spent the next couple of hours winding around the country
roads, talking about the difficulties of life in rural Cuba. As we wound
on the kilometers, Lázaro began to trust me more, explaining how he
wanted to leave the island so that he could send money back to his family.

"Yes," he said, "every time they hold the lottery, I mail the letter, but
I haven't been fortunate enough to win the *visa.* I think the only way now
is to leave illegally."

"How would you do it?"

"By boat," he said. "Already some friends and I are making plans. It's
very expensive."

It was getting late, and Lázaro had to get back to the prison. The
boss had let him out of work for a short time to call his parents, and he
was already an hour late. I told him I'd be in the area for a few more days
and would like to visit the work farm and maybe meet his friends and
talk more about leaving Cuba by boat.

"You're not permitted to visit the prison," he said. "Only family can
visit. You must tell him you're my sister's fiancé. And bring a pack of cigarettes with you. The boss likes to smoke, and the cigarettes will persuade him to let me leave. I'll tell him we're going to visit my family."

I dropped into the prison the next day, and Lázaro introduced me to
the boss, who gave me a tour of the stockyard. All this was illegal, of
course, but in Cuba, a pack of smokes goes a long way. Especially for a
prison boss who is paid next to nothing. The prisoners, about twenty-five
of them, stopped their work and came out to meet me. These guys
rarely get visitors, so for them I was a curiosity, and I went around the
circle shaking everyone's hand. There was a man doing six months for

selling beef. Another guy was doing a year for his third offense of repairing car and bicycle tires without a license. A burly gay man from Havana was caught with a small quantity of pot and was serving six months. When the boss broke us up and made everyone go back to work, Lázaro introduced me to another guy, Carlos, who spoke perfect English.

"Man, I love America," he said. "I've been there twice. Good people up there. I really want to go back. I miss it more than anything. Why don't you guys take me along today? I'll go tell the boss. Give me a minute. I'll take you to meet my family."

Carlos was once a famous celebrity who was able to visit the United States on a special visa. It was hard for me to believe that this former star was now doing time in a Cuban prison camp, and when I asked him about it, he wouldn't reveal his crime to me. Later in the day, Lázaro confided to me that Carlos was serving a year for his second offense of trying to leave the island illegally. Merely talking about illegal immigration in Cuba is a crime carrying a six-month prison sentence. The next time, Carlos would spend two years behind bars in a regular prison, so he couldn't afford even to whisper the word "immigration."

"He has special privileges around here because of his status," Lázaro said as Carlos ran off, quickly returning and jumping in the back seat.

"It's good to get out of here," said Carlos. "I haven't seen my mother for two months and I have a few hundred pesos for her."

As we drove on the country roads towards Camagüey, we started talking about life in Cuba. About selling illegal lobster and how impossible it is to live in the peso economy. Across the plains, the *zafra* was in full swing, and the car thumped across the small chunks of cane that had fallen from the wagons. Smoke from smoldering piles of *bagaso*, the remains left after the harvest, floated everywhere like a thin fog.

Carlos said nothing. He was already walking on thin ice with the regime, so he kept his comments to himself. Eventually, we came to his small town and drove past the ghostly hulk of the *central*, which had been closed, and pulled up to his home. It was a typical rural Cuban house, the yard wrapped in sparse *matacallo* hedges, which serve as an organic barbed wire fence to contain the pigs. A massive *flamboyán* tree with its vibrant red blossoms cast shade over a tiny yard. Down the street, a few kids were throwing rocks into the almond trees of the quiet neighborhood, trying to knock down enough to make a few quick pesos.

As I sat on the porch talking over a café with the mother and sister, Lázaro disappeared, returning shortly with Carlos' brother José, a lanky guy in his early twenties. Lázaro had told him I was an American journalist interested in their plan of leaving illegally. I felt fortunate. The day before, I had met a stranger wearing a straw hat and a torn work uniform who was trying to use a broken peso telephone; today, I was sitting on a porch listening to two strangers who have been meticulously hatching plans to leave the island illegally by boat.

"We must be very discreet," José explained. "Let's drive into the hills and talk."

"We must be careful," he continued as we cleared the edge of town. "This thing we're talking about is very dangerous. We have already worked out most of the details, and we're saving our money to leave."

"How much does an operation like this cost?" I asked.

"For $2,000, we can have a boat maker fabricate the craft," said José. "This is the most dangerous part of all, because there are very few boat makers, and even fewer who will take these kinds of chances. It's difficult to hide a boat, and the state watches them closely. But we know a boat maker who will do it."

"What kind of boat are we talking about?" I asked.

"A small but strong boat," said Lázaro. "The kind used for fishing, with tar between the seams. They are big enough to hold six people. The $2,000 dollars will pay for everything necessary for six people to make the trip, including the boat, water, and food."

"How long does it take?" I asked. "How is it done?"

"It takes four to six days depending on the current and the wind," said José. "But you don't go straight to Miami or Key West. You must zig-zag from key to key the entire way. We already have everything laid out and know how to do it. All we need is a nautical map and a payment for the boat maker to get started."

After driving about twenty miles and talking about all the variants and possibilities of this illegal boat trip north, we pulled off into a cane brake. I took a map of Cuba from the glove compartment and unfolded it onto the front seat. Lázaro leaned over the divider, and the discussion centered on points of departure.

"There is very little Cuban coast guard anywhere between here . . . and here," said José, running his finger from Puerto Padre in the far northeast of Las Tunas province, along the hundreds of keys, past Cayo Coco and just northwest of us to Cayo Fragoso in the Villa Clara province. "Because of the tourism, there are more patrols near Cayo Coco, but on either side of that it's clear. For the rest, there might be one patrol per day along that whole stretch of coast. The hardest part is getting the boat. The easiest is clearing the twelve-mile national water mark. Then you pray for good weather."

"The other possibility is leaving from the south coast," said Lázaro, tapping the eastern tip of the island on the paper map. "The coast guard doesn't patrol the south at all and they would never suspect *balseros*. It is necessary to sail around the east of the island, because the gulf current runs northwest. If you leave anywhere west of Cayo Coco, you might end up in Texas."

"But this would give two or three extra days to the journey," added José. "It's safer, because there is less chance of the boat maker getting caught, but there would be more time spent on the water. From the north it's four to six days. From the south it's a week to ten days. Everything depends on the current and the weather."

"What about hurricanes," I asked, "or big waves that might break the boat?"

"This is why it's important to leave between February and April," said José. "The sea is calm and there is steady wind to help with the current. After April it is too hot. After October there are too many storms and it is too cold. Under these conditions you could easily die."

As we discussed the plan, I could only imagine how many thousands of similar conversations had occurred in the Cuban night, men lighting cigars from flickering candles in the shadows, the heightened whispers and debate, fingers splashing down here and here on one-dimensional oceans of hand-drawn maps, big talk about the good life in Miami, everyone piecing together rumors and weighing advice from others who made the journey and survived. They have only one thing in mind: acquiring a boat, and then getting into it. These two had obviously thought of every angle. They were from a small town where the universe had centered around the now-defunct sugar *central*. They had been robbed of an identity that the town had built around the plant, on an island where it's illegal to stay and illegal to leave.

❦ 22 ❦

A Legal Escape

"From this day forward, everyone can refer to me as *The American,*" said the man, his eyes glowing like strobes. "I'm not Cuban anymore. From now on, I'm one of you guys. So just call me," and he paused for a microsecond, just to savor the spice of the words on his tongue . . . *"The American."*

The man was Armando's cousin, Luis, just in from Oriente with his family to get their exit papers in order. I was excited for Luis because I understood the significance of this moment. It was his moment, all his, and nobody or nothing could take it away. Today, he was the most powerful man in Cuba. He had beaten Castro. He had beaten the odds and won his own victory. Never having been to the United States, he had formed all his decisions on hearsay and second-hand information. He began firing questions at me.

"Is it true that if you lose your job, the state you live in will give you a little money and help pay your rent?"

"Sure, that's true in some circumstances," I said.

"Then they've been lying to us all this time. They tell us that in the U.S. the conditions are terrible. That if you lose your job, your family will be homeless and no one will help you. They tell us that Cuban Socialism is the best system in the world. I was also wondering, in the United States, will the government help pay for your children to study at the university?"

"Yes, there is money for poorer families to send their kids to college, and there are loans from the banks as well."

"And can you choose whatever you want to learn at the universities?"

"Yes," I said. "And if you received bad marks in secondary school, there are classes at the universities that you can take to qualify you for whatever field of study you'd like to enter. Even you could get a degree if you'd like."

These were important details that Luis wanted to hear firsthand from a native, mostly because his daughter, now fourteen, was beginning to think about the future. What was she planning to study in the United States? She wasn't sure. But she was the top of her class in secondary school, acing all her exams in chemistry, physics, and science, and would likely continue on this route. Luis's younger daughter of four wanted to become a model when she grew up.

"Luis, why is it important to you to move to the United States?" I asked.

"How much does a new television cost in your country, for example, similar to this one here?" he asked me, pointing to Armando's nineteen-inch diagonal set.

"About $150," I said.

"In Cuba, a new television like this costs $350, not in pesos, in *divisa*. Me, I work for the state as an auto mechanic. I make 185 pesos per month." His mind began calculating the figures. "At 185 pesos a month, if I didn't spend anything on food, without buying shoes and clothes, I could have a new television in . . . three years. If I use my money to feed my family, buy their clothes, and save 50 pesos a month after expenses, which is almost impossible to do, I could buy a new television in . . . twelve years. A car in Cuba costs $4,000. Not a new car, but a good, strong Lada that runs well. If I saved my 50 pesos a month, I could buy this car in . . . a hundred and thirty years. In the United States, can you have two jobs?"

"Sure," I said.

"Not in Cuba. Here, you can have only one job. But even if I could have two jobs in Cuba, then it would only take me sixty-five years to buy this car instead of a hundred and thirty, and by then I'd be dead. Someone told me that in the United States, if I worked hard, I could buy a car within one or two months, is this true?"

"It's possible," I said. "It might not be a pretty car . . ."

"But it would be a car," he said. "It would run and it would be mine, not the state's, and that's my point. That's why I'm taking my family to America. I work very hard. I love to work. But why should I be a slave for the Cuban government? In Cuba, I can work and work and work, and everyday, every year, I'm in the same place. No matter how hard you work here, it doesn't get you anywhere. In the United States, I can work as hard as I want, and the harder I work, the more I can provide for my family. I can have a car, a strong house. I want a future for my family. I want for my children to have nice things and eat good food. Everything we do, every decision we make is for them."

Luis beamed with pride and hope as he spoke, as if his life had finally found some definition, some sharp edges and meaning. He was heading to a new world where he believed the politics and contradictions wouldn't inhibit his family's economic mobility, and there was no looking back.

"You don't have any trinkets or keepsakes that you want to take with you?" I asked.

"No, it's all garbage. We're not taking anything with us," he said. "The clothes on our backs and the photo albums. Nothing more. When we get to the U.S., we're going to be reborn."

Luis's family had won the visa lottery, the Special Cuban Migration Program, called *El Bombo* in Cuba. They were one of four Cuban families I was lucky enough to meet who had actually won. The odds of my meeting them were astronomically low, since only 20,000 Cubans are admitted to the United States annually under this system. The visa lottery works like this: Every two or so years, a Cuban who wants to leave for the United States sends a letter to the U.S. Interests Section in Havana with only his name, address, names of family members also applying, years of education, and the postmark, which must fall under the month specified for registration. Any Cuban between eighteen and fifty-five can apply, providing they meet two of the following three requirements: 1) a high school education; 2) three years work experience in any field; and 3) has a relative residing in the United States.

Luis, forty, a tower of a man, his hairline creeping back to his ears, was eligible to apply because he met the first two requirements. In the 1998 lottery, for which he applied, the competition was steep. That year, 541,500 Cubans applied for *El Bombo,* representing one in twenty. Five percent of the population had shown a desire to leave. Countless others wishing to leave didn't apply, either because of economic shortcomings or the inability to meet the qualifications. When the Cuban newspapers posted a national notice for the registration dates, Luis immediately ran out, bought an envelope and a stamp, and dropped his letter in the mail. In February 2000, sixteen months later, he got his official packet in the mail. It informed him that he had won, and included forms to fill out for each family member, and a date and time in December to report to the Interests Section in Havana for the interview with U.S. officials.

If everything checked out, he would then be issued his papers to enter the United States. After this, the only thing keeping him from leaving would be the plane tickets, and he would have six months to get them and depart. After entering the United States, the family then goes through a three-day immigration process in which temporary work permits and resident cards are issued, medical exams are given, forms are filled out. Next, the family is moved through the relocation program to another city, an apartment is found for them to live in for a year, and Medicaid arranged for the children. Within this year, the new immigrants must obtain employment and establish themselves as permanent U.S. residents. After the year is up, if they've committed no felonies involving drugs and they don't have AIDS, they get their permanent resident cards.

The cost for the entire process of *El Bombo* cuts deep for the average Cuban. The biggest expense is the official medical exam required by the Cuban government. This costs $400 for each adult, and for each child an additional $200, paid to Cuban immigration; for a family of four, this economic hurdle would bite them for $1,200. A fortune for a Cuban needing these imperative four slips of paper.

"At $1,200, naturally I thought they were the most important documents in the file," Luis laughed. "But can you believe this? At the interview for the exit visa, when I handed the medical exam results to the U.S. official, he swept them to the side of the desk as if they were toilet paper. The way he acted, I think he probably threw them in the waste basket as soon as we left."

Luis, like other Cubans wishing to leave, felt that the regime purposefully creates economic obstacles to discourage them from entering the lottery, and, if they do win, makes it impossible to afford departure. The absurd medical exam is one example, because the government knows that the receiving country will require its own medical exam.

"Well," Luis admitted with a chuckle, "the medical exam costs $400 only if you're issued the exit parole, in which case you're no longer Cuban. If you don't receive the visa, then it's free because you're still Cuban and the Socialist healthcare is free."

The other big cost—$150—is the *carta blanca*, the letter of exit parole, issued by Cuban immigration to be shown at airport customs. Then there's the $50 cost per family member for the passports, the airport tax at $20 a head, and, most important, the airline tickets, which cost $238 apiece for a direct flight to Florida. In total, this family must pay $2,382 for the process, or 47,640 pesos. Luis would have had to work twenty-two years without spending a single centavo to be able to take his family out of Cuba. Another example of control by out-pricing, and another way illegal immigration is encouraged.

"We get the money one way or another," Luis explained. "Everyone in the extended family gives whatever they have. Friends from abroad send some. The first goal is to win the lottery. We worry about the money afterwards."

Although Cubans are suspicious that they are being forced into staying in "the prison," in reality, it's more likely that the government merely wants to cash in and get its hands on those dollars. If 5,000 families like Luis's exit every year, the total annual income to the Cuban state from immigration alone would fall somewhere around $12 million. A year after departure, these same Cubans are permitted to return to Cuba and bring their newly earned U.S. dollars to spend in the dollar sector, thus adding to that one-fifth of the island's residual gross income earned from the Miami enemy on which the government leans for its survival. By pricing legal immigration out of the average Cuban's reach, the government ironically encourages illegal immigration. Those who can't afford the costs, tired of waiting, may simply steal a boat, risk their lives, and perhaps die. Years ago, wanting to leave Cuba was considered traitorous to the Revolution. Today, the governmental discrimination against those wishing to leave comes in the form of economic hurdles that hopeful immigrants must jump. But the regime profits in countless ways from this activity.

If there isn't enough money to take out the whole family at once after winning *El Bombo,* the father will travel north alone and acquire two or three jobs so that he can quickly put together the necessary money for the remaining family's expenses. As for selling property to help in the migration expense, that is not an option; in Cuba, everything is repossessed upon exit. The house, car, furniture, stereo, television, beds, refrigerator, the works. So the regime profits yet again on material property. Even if a Cuban pays hard cash for a new television, he pays only for the privilege of using it because it is considered property of the state and is forfeited without the possibility of resale. Luis explained that as soon as immigration receives notice of a Cuban's winning the lottery, an inspector is immediately dispatched to take an inventory of all possessions in the house. If anything is missing on the day of departure, the *carta blanca* is revoked and the departure is cancelled by the state. Cubans, clever as they are, have found ways around this rule by selling whatever they can before reporting to immigration, or trading furniture and replacing it with shoddy stuff before the inspector arrives.

"I couldn't sell my television," Luis said, shaking his head. "It was brand new. I worked years for that television. The problem is that when the inspector comes to take the inventory, he first talks to the president of the CDR. It's the responsibility of the CDR president to know every appliance and piece of furniture in the barrio, and mine knew I had a new TV. But he didn't know about my refrigerator, and I was able to sell it and just about everything else before the inventory."

Luis and his family weren't the only people in the room. Armando and Carmen and Armando's brother Francisco and his wife were there, as well as friends from the barrio. Luis's excitement about leaving was contagious, and everybody was thrilled for him because his life had taken a solid direction with a real future. There was no jealousy. No bad feeling that he was some kind of traitor to *la lucha*. Luis and his family were leaving all that behind for a promising new unknown, and the conversation shifted to savoring memories about others who had left the island.

"Remember the *chorizo* maker from our town?" Francisco asked around the room, turning to me. "There was a famous *chorizo* maker in our town. He was known across the entire province. People came from miles around to buy his *chorizos*."

"That's right," said Carmen with a warm laugh. "He later emigrated, and a lot of people in Miami knew him, and they said 'Claudio, you have to make your *chorizos* again. Nobody here can make *chorizos* like yours.' They pestered him and pestered him until finally he went back into business making his *chorizos* in Miami."

Other stories surfaced. Success stories about poor Cubans who started out as wage laborers in Miami and now own empires. Rags-to-riches stories about friends who had somehow managed to steal a boat and float from sand bar to sand bar all the way to Key West and were now car dealers raking in fortunes. None of the stories were about failure, about the struggle to succeed in the cutthroat world of the United States. To admit that failure does exist for Cubans in the north is to admit that the promised land isn't all it's chalked up to be. It would shatter that illusion of a viable option for many Cubans because they hang onto it as a card to be played, a possible escape if things never do change.

Luis is not a "political refugee." He is not an "exile." The decision was one of economics; he was, like the majority of today's Cuban emigrants, heading to the United States to improve his lifestyle. He loves Cuba, but dislikes the system that prevents him from achieving what he considers success. This is an important distinction. Many believe that all immigrants leave Cuba because of political persecution, but this is untrue. Luis could easily stay in Cuba and continue earning his 185 pesos a month, perhaps repairing cars clandestinely at night for an illegal supplemental income in dollars while waiting for *La Victoria*. But he felt he could go farther in the United States, where he can measure his personal success by the fruits of his labor. In Cuba, there is plenty of opportunity within the Revolution, but the material rewards don't satisfy the majority, and this lack of stimulus is tied directly to both Castro's obstinate vision and the U.S. embargo policy on which this vision is hinged.

A week later, the day he received his family's visas from the Interests Section, I met up with Luis. The mother and daughters had already returned by bus to Oriente, and Luis had stayed in Havana alone to wrap up loose ends. When I arrived at Armando's, there stood Luis with his daughter's student-sized backpack slung over a shoulder, all smiles. He pulled out four manila envelopes, stamped and sealed by the U.S. officials, only to be opened, the warning read, by INS officers in the United States. Stapled to the front of each envelope were the parole papers required for each family entering the United States.

Luis ran his thumb, gnarled from years of cranking nuts and bolts, over the ridges of the official U.S. seal, delighting in what the minute roughness of the broken paper symbolized. He could stay only a few minutes because his train back to Oriente was leaving in an hour, and I congratulated him and wished him the best in his new life.

"And what are they going to call me from now on?" he asked. "The Cuban? No. Now I'm," and he paused again, tasting the words as they burned a hole in his tongue. "Now I'm . . . *The American*."

Epilogue: A Post-Castro Cuba?

O ne sweltering day on my way to Old Havana I dropped by
Armando's for a bottle of mango juice to tell him that I was leaving soon for the United States. During our conversation, he invited me
back for supper. The typical supper at Armando's was soup two nights in
a row. The next night it would be eggs over rice with a cabbage-and-
cucumber salad, followed by chicken the next evening, and then three
days of leftovers. All of this with the traditional black beans and rice and
a variety of fried plantain. But this night was special; he'd received his
sardine ration.

Cubans eat late, usually around 8:00 P.M., and I stopped back early to
catch the news. Armando's television set is one of those that you have to
play with for fifteen minutes while tapping and jiggling it around to get it
working. Once he does finally get it fired up in the morning, he simply
leaves it on all day to save himself the hassle. On this night, the news was
a twenty-minute recap of an interview with Castro's younger brother,
Raul, now seventy-one years old, along with several decorated generals of

the Revolutionary Armed Forces. It was a casual interview. Raul leaning back on a sofa with a warm, self-assured glimmer in his eyes, the crook of one knee folded over the other, dozens of medals dripping from his uniform. The interview centered mostly around Cuba's current military strength, but the climax came when the interviewer asked Raul, "What do you have to say about the future of Cuba?" It was a loaded question. She was really asking, "What will happen when Fidel dies?"

Raul paused a moment for reflection, knowing exactly what the interviewer was getting at, and after taking a breath, in that deep-throated warble, said, "I'm no prophet, but I do know this. *La Lucha* will continue."

The living room was silent as we leaned into the television to absorb Raul's words. It was as if everyone really wanted to hear something different for a change, but there it was, the same old disappointing message: "*La Lucha* will continue." In a way, Raul was only half sincere. There was the subtle hint of a chuckle when he uttered the words, no matter how serious he tried to appear. It was as if he, too, knew that it was a farce, but what else could he say? Raul is like that. If Fidel is the father of the Revolution and the people are his children, Raul is the mysterious uncle over in the periphery, chuckling with the wisdom of old age. I asked Armando what he thought of Raul's statement.

"*La lucha, la lucha,* everything is *la lucha,*" he said. "They won't be happy until they have us all living in caves. The people are tired."

After our sardine dinner, we spent the evening playing Cuba's board game, *Deuda Eterna,* "Eternal Debt." This game is Cuba's version of Monopoly. It was designed in the mid-1970s by orders of the comandante because he wanted the people to understand the principles of imperialism and why Cuba would have no part of it. There are very few complete sets of *Dueda Eterna* left in Cuba, but Armando and Carmen took very good care of theirs. All the pieces are still there, even the game's instruction booklet.

The object of *Dueda Eterna* is simple. The players start out with nothing. They must borrow money from the International Monetary Fund (IMF) to launch certain industries. There are the lesser agricultural industries such as banana and sugar, which sit at Balsam Avenue, leading around the board to the energy industries, oil and utilities, which sit at Boardwalk. On the center of the board is a map of the Americas. The players are in the third world, and the IMF is the United States. Whoever gets out of debt, which is next to impossible, wins the game. They must pay taxes and loan interest, and each player gets three small plastic bars of gold, to be forfeited upon passing Go. The IMF banker is a separate entity and doesn't actually play; instead, he sits like a monarch, overseeing the game. On this night, Armando's daughter designated herself the banker, and before we started, she explained the rules. It had been a few years since she'd played, so she flipped through the rulebook to brush up.

"Oh yeah," she said, reading a passage. "Players may make secret deals with the banker."

"Secret deals?" I asked. "How do these work?"

Everyone around the table burst out laughing. "Hah, Benjamín. The *yanqui* capitalist! Only he would ask this question!"

"What I think is even funnier," I said, "is the idea of a Cuban running the IMF."

The game was a lot of fun, but there were certain ironies about the entire evening. First, we watched Raul Castro promising more of *la lucha* on a television that barely works, just before eating a $2 sardine dinner, which in Cuba is almost like a sacred holiday, followed by a game of *Deuda Eterna*. Because of Castro's refusal to play the real-life game of eternal debt, the Cuban people must continue to live in an impoverished society that barely functions. And Raul Castro was only promising more of it.

"They won't be happy until they have us living in caves," Armando had said earlier. "The people are tired."

As it did many times in many living rooms, the conversation drifted toward a post-Castro Cuba. Would more sectors of the domestic economy be privatized? Who would become Castro's successor? What did the people want?

The mystery of Castro's successor has become one of the world's biggest guessing games, and Castro likes to keep it that way. As written into the Cuban constitution, Raul Castro is lawfully slated as Cuba's next president. But this is unlikely. Raul lacks the support and respect of the people. His street nickname is "The Frog." Castro's is *El Caballo,* "The Horse," and many Cubans joke that Raul is the filly. Clearly, Raul is not presidential material. As a career military leader, he doesn't have the economic savvy necessary to administrate Cuba in the new Revolutionary themes, and both he, Fidel, the ministers, and the people know this. Although Raul is the first vice president of the Council of State, a total of five vice presidents have the authority to succeed Castro.

The second name that many have been throwing around as Cuba's next president is Ricardo Alarcón, who was once the minister of Foreign Affairs, making him a prime candidate as Fidel's successor. However, in 1993, he was demoted to the slot of president of the rubber stamp People's National Assembly, a relatively powerless position reserved for once-important leaders whose names outlive their significance to the cause when the Revolutionary themes change.

Now that the government and the economy have somewhat stabilized and the island is under control, the survival of the Cuban Revolution has transformed into absolute economic terms. The next Cuban president must necessarily be an economic guru, someone who will make the right decisions and who will concentrate on transforming Cuba into a Caribbean empire while continuing to build a global support network with other nations. At this time, there are only two minds in Cuba with these abilities. One is thirty-seven-year-old Felipe Pérez Roque, the current minister of Foreign Affairs, and the other is fifty-year-old Carlos Lage Dávila, the first secretary of the Council of Ministers. They are the only leaders now being groomed to succeed Castro. Unless the Revolutionary themes change again, barring war, one or the other will likely become Cuba's next president. Raul Castro's sole function will be to maintain military order during the transition of power. He will also oversee the provisional government and seize control should things go haywire.

As a candidate for the next presidency, Felipe Pérez Roque is important because, as foreign minister, he has all the necessary contacts with the outside world. He is the bridge builder, the diplomat, the man responsible for maintaining Cuba's umbilical cord with the international community. This is the highest position in Cuba today. Pérez Roque is even more powerful than Castro himself, who has essentially become a mere figurehead. Carlos Lage, on the other hand, is essentially the mastermind behind Cuba's economy. He is a brilliant economist, a young, modern thinker, and by making good decisions, he is largely responsible for the island's relative wealth and economic success since the Special Period. Pérez Roque and Lage hold the most imperative positions in the Cuban leadership. Over the past several years, both have been given more and more air time on Cuban television as they have risen in Revolutionary importance. When Castro collapsed during a speech in the summer of 2001, it was Pérez Roque who immediately took the microphone to quell the confusion, an illustration of his importance.

Which of these two the Cuban people want as their next president is a toss-up. While Pérez Roque sometimes seems the more likely successor, the feeling in the street is that Carlos Lage is the people's candidate. He's charming and likeable, more mild-mannered, less like Castro. The Cuban people feel that he'll be more responsive to their needs and will strike a good balance between Cuba's economic strength in the international community while focusing on the domestic welfare, which has been left in neglect by Castro. Pérez Roque, although young and talented, is geared a little more into the path of international *"amistad,"* which has been Castro's principal domain for the past forty-three years. Pérez Roque's experience on the domestic front is inferior to that of Carlos Lage. However, both are economic geniuses, both are presidential material, and as a team, both are and will continue to be the island's most powerful leaders no matter who takes the title of president. Raul Castro's task has been and will be to oversee the government from the periphery and make sure that the system functions properly; if it deviates from the program, he will seize military control and forestall coups.

When I asked Armando about the possibility of Ricardo Alarcón's succeeding Castro, he shot me a cross look and said—like others I had posed the question to—"Nah. Alarcón is just another Castro. The people don't want it. I'm almost certain it will be Carlos Lage. The people like him. He's more amicable. More understanding."

"What about Pérez Roque?" I asked.

"It's possible," said Armando, "but he, too, is like Castro, and he's too young. He hasn't yet earned the respect of the older people. Both the old and young people respect Carlos Lage. He's young enough to under-stand what the young people want, and old enough to know what the older people want."

Besides the question of Castro's successor, many have been asking the question: Will Cuba become capitalist after Castro? Really, Cuba already is capitalist, both in the peso and dollar economies. Cuba is not Communist. Revolutionaries call it a "market Socialism administered by Communists." However, because of the degree of exploitation people have underwent since 1991, the Cuban government has become capital-ist in the classical sense, which is the greatest irony of all. It has turned into what it purports to stand against, and it must continue to be capi-talist so that it can continue to stand against capitalism. This is the gist.

If Cuba reverts back to the old-track Socialism, which might be pos-sible when the regime finds the economic footing, this new capitalism will be short-lived. For now, the ends justify the means. Clearly though, the people want Cuba to become a fully operating market economy. The proper question is: After Castro, will there be less control?

Cuba can move from its current state of survival into a wealthy empire only if the people are permitted to compete freely in the domes-tic and international markets. This is what the world demands, and the government will necessarily have to bend. Cuba must provide creative outlets to people with innovative ideas while educating the masses not just in basic English but also in how to participate in the global market economy. There are thousands of talented young Cubans who, with sup-port, could be earning the island a taxable mint. The government must facilitate more tax incentives for average Cubans, not just the foreign cor-porations, so that Cubans themselves can acquire the ability to develop their ideas and eventually run their own island in a full dollar economy. Currently, Cubans live in a peso mentality, which means they are operating at only a fraction of their potential. Until the entire population thinks in dollars and rejects its enforced dependency on the welfare state, the economy will continue to suffer. After all, Cuba belongs to Cubans, but on the current track, the island is once again becoming the property of foreign investors. The people are in the same old rut of serving foreign enterprises. Cuba cannot withstand another ten years of the current stagnation, and everyone knows this. Reforms are needed, and Castro is only standing in the way of progress. The longer reforms are postponed, the more desperate Cuba grows, and the more sweeping the changes are likely to be after Castro.

On a morning when I was staying with the Ibáñezs, Castro was giving a televised speech: "Up in the United States, the imperialists always talk about this 'post-Castro Cuba,'" he said. "The Revolutionaries will start talking about a post-Castro, post-Communist Cuba when they start talking about a post-capitalist, post-Bush United States."

"Listen to that crazy talk!" Martina exclaimed, twirling her finger around her ear. "He has obviously lost his mind."

"A post-capitalist United States!" huffed Rolando, punctuating his wife's thoughts. "Listen to him. It's unrealistic. It's deranged."

Today, Castro is irrelevant. He's only holding up the show. He refuses to follow through with the reforms he himself designed and instead eliminates them every chance he gets. He still complains about how the world cheated Cuba when it switched from the gold standard to the stock exchange. He lives in the past and cannot seem to move forward. This is not the destiny the Cuban people envision for themselves. There is only one place for Castro to go, and that is to the grave.

Castro knows this, as do half of Cuba's administrators who are under fifty years old. They are young, and they know that if Cuba is to survive, it must join the competitive global economy. The only way this can occur is to break free from the stagnant and slow implosion of a social experiment that is long overdue for change. They, too, are waiting for Castro to die, and deep down he understands this. The ultimate truth for Fidel Castro is very sad. In the depths of his mind he realizes he has lost his people. He realizes that his mission has become a matter of preserving his place as the first successful liberator in what amounts to a forty-year pit stop in Cuba's ongoing search for *Cubanidad.*

Today Cuba is colonized by outdated and meaningless war symbols. The people are ready to move past the war and get on with the independence part of the equation. The conclusion Armando and I arrived at was this: The Castros, indeed, all the old school Communists and their identities are linked directly to *la lucha.* They know of no other way to exist. As revolutionary veterans, to end *la lucha* would be to take away the meaning of their 1959 victory, and in doing so their own significance. The problem is that these men have retained the power and have transferred the significance of the revolutionary war to an "economic war" against the United States. They embody their entire cause against another nation and its policies. Their importance today lies in being soldiers against the U.S. embargo. When a couple divorces, how healthy is it to spend the next forty years hating the ex-spouse and playing the victim? Against any odds, the divorcee must eventually take responsibility and move forward, even in the face of aggression. It is time for Castro to do this and face up to the waning support of his people rather than foster the role of victim merely to remain in power.

Until now, the embargo has been as important to Fidel as to the Miami exile. Both camps profit from it, and both maintain it. For the exile, the Florida version of *Cubanidad* has been built in a private war waged with Castro. Because the Cuban American identity is for the most part emblematic of this struggle, the embargo is a means to sustain a symbolic lock on Castro, who in turn uses the same embargo to sustain a lock on his own people and, in turn, his power. Today, the economic war boils down to a war between Castro and Miami, and the battle is being fought on a field of newsprint. Every time Castro gets a toehold into some economic growth and power, Miami launches a new smear campaign, and Castro reacts. This happened in 1977 with the "Castro Connection," which eventually died in 1999, just days before Elian González washed up in the Florida Straits and became the new crux of the battle. Both Castro and his enemies in *la fundacion* are running out of

Elians, and the media war is losing strength because the rest of the world is wising up to the game.

As Castro approaches his death, it is imperative that he get the embargo lifted so that he can say to his people, "It was I, Fidel Castro, who gave the Cuban people their victory. We have won." He needs to go down in history as the liberator. Across the gulf, Miami's principal goal is to keep the embargo intact until Castro dies, cheating him of this victory. As trivial as it may seem, this is the bottom line, this is what *la lucha* has devolved into.

As Fidel's hour approaches, his desperation to get the embargo lifted grows. In October 2000, the U.S. Congress voted to allow direct food and medicine sales to Cuba, using third-country banks to finance the transactions. In reaction, Castro proclaimed Cuba wouldn't buy "a single grain" of U.S. agricultural products unless it was a two-way trade, meaning, "You give us your tourists, we'll buy your food." Cuba imports most of its food products from Europe, paying 10 to 20 percent more for shipping than it would if it imported the same products from U.S. markets. On the surface, Castro's refusal to buy from the United States seemed to be a Revolutionary principle. In reality, he merely wanted to wiggle a carrot before the noses of U.S. agriculture firms then as now drooling over the estimated $2 to $5 billion a year market that Cuba represents. A two-way trade ultimatum would force the agricultural lobbies to get the travel ban lifted, which would appease the Communists and enable the new Cuban market to be tapped. If the travel ban were lifted, Cuba's tourist income would likely double overnight, thus empowering the regime and adding to Castro's prestige for the books; at the same time, it would pave the way for a full lifting of the embargo. No doubt the idea frightens the European suppliers and shippers, who currently profit considerably from trade with Cuba.

July 2001 was a pivotal month for the warming of the embargo. On July 15, the new law to sell food and medicine to Cuba was ironed out, and the list of now-saleable commodities was enormous. Not only grain, poultry, and beef were permitted, but also items manufactured from them, including such products as canned ravioli, and even beer. The U.S. agricultural corporations, the manufacturers, the shippers, everyone was excited. A week before the list was released, George W. Bush, under pressure from the old-school exile, gave new orders to reinforce the travel ban on Cuba and increase the fine for illegal travel to Cuba from its former $1,500 to $7,000. Yet a week later, Bush waived a provision in the Helms-Burton bill that gives foreign enterprises who suffered losses from the 1961 nationalizations the right to sue Cuba in U.S. courts for damages. If signed, the provision would essentially lock the embargo into law until these damages are paid. Bill Clinton regularly waived this provision for six-month periods during his tenure. Bush's doing so marked his own tone toward the outlawed island. Waiving this provision is a means of keeping the door open with Cuba, no matter what Bush was saying on television. Although the Senate shot it down, a week later (coincidentally, a day before Castro's national Revolutionary holiday), the House of Representatives, under pressure from the agriculture lobbies, voted by a large margin to stop enforcing the travel ban.

The travel ban is what Castro needs lifted most urgently. Castro knew he was getting close, especially in November 2001, when Hurricane Michelle devastated the Matánzas province east of Havana, and the U.S. government immediately offered humanitarian aid to the island. Instead of accepting the aid, Castro offered to buy a one-time $30 million shipment of U.S. food products to help alleviate Cuba from the hurricane's impact. The catch? Castro offered cash. He could easily have taken his money to England or France for the foodstuffs. Instead, he wanted to scrape another crumb off the plate and let the U.S. agriculture sector drool a little more, thus turning up even more pressure on Congress and Bush to lift the travel ban; this would inevitably have led to the embargo's lifting, which would result in "The Victory," timed perfectly to precede Castro's death. Since the 1970s, this is how the dialogue with Washington has functioned, up and down, up and down. The actions taken on each side are weighed more in tone, not in impact, and the tone since Clinton opened the door on January 5, 1999, was to begin taking steps toward lifting the age-old embargo.

In 2000, after tourism had grown at an annual rate of 19 percent, 1.8 million tourists visited Cuba. Forecasts for future years were looking hopeful; however, in 2001, only 1.8 million tourists came again. It then became apparent to the regime that, despite the world economic recession, perhaps the numbers were tapering off. There are only so many Buena Vista Social Club fans in the world, and although the trend of the world media is now more liberal, many tourists, because of the high cost of Cuba's tourism and its many deficiencies, aren't returning. Because of the tapering numbers, it is now imperative that the regime take steps to get the U.S. travel ban lifted so that it can tap the forbidden, lucrative, nearby U.S. tourist market. Castro is desperate. When the U.S. military began shipping al-Qaida prisoners to Guantánamo in the winter of 2001, not only did Castro button his lip, but he even went so far as to offer any assistance Cuba could offer in containing the prisoners. Cuba's recent invitation to former president Jimmy Carter and his May 2002 visit to Cuba was also geared towards getting the travel ban lifted. Why Carter? Because Carter had lifted the travel ban once so perhaps he could pull some strings to get it lifted again. Even if Carter had taken bad reports back to the United States, it was still good press for Cuba. It showed other Americans that Cuba is a safe country to travel to, not a dangerous pariah state with all the old cold war stigmas that still resonate in the minds of most Americans.

When six barges full of corn and other U.S. agricultural products left from Louisiana for Havana in December 2001, it was the first U.S. shipment of food sold directly to Cuba in thirty-eight years. It wasn't publicized on the island, and most Cubans don't understand the implications of Castro's master plan. Few knew that the shipment was powder in Castro's economic cannon and that it would help him realize his much-needed victory. In October 2000, when the U.S. Congress voted to allow food and medicine sales, there was little news of the law's passing in Cuba. When I talked to friends about what it meant to them, they were severe and pessimistic. "So what. Even if Castro buys the food and medicine, we'll never see any of it. It will all be sold to the tourists for dollars." The people are equally skeptical about rumors of the embargo's being lifted. For years upon years they've believed the rumors, only to have their hopes dashed once again. But one thing is certain; after forty-two years of waging a war against the embargo, most Cubans expect sweeping miracles when it is indeed lifted. They believe their world will turn upside-down. And to provide the illusion that it isn't just the end of another small battle, like that of Elian González, but the true end of the war, the victory will have to be carefully orchestrated. Perhaps rations will have to be doubled, rum given away in the streets, and, of course, a national holiday declared, *El Dia de la Victoria,* the Day of the Victory, when over four decades of Cuban suffering will be remembered in perpetuity. It is Castro's private war. One he is determined to win, even if it means standing against the desires of the people while the generations are tilled under the Revolutionary plow.

One day I was walking through the Colón cemetery in Vedado with a twenty-five-year-old artist friend. Colón is a classic Latin American cemetery, and apparently there are a million graves there, equal to half the population of Havana. The *flamboyán* trees and bougainvillea, when in full bloom, lend a certain vibrancy to the texture of the place with their small explosions of orange, red, and purple flowers. From the dead and the past springs new life, new seasons, change. The lovely old architecture has been poorly maintained. The lids on many of the crypts are caving in, and gold and jewelry has been cleaned out by grave robbers. Here and there around some of the tombs loose bones are scattered. "The *brujas* steal the bones," my friend said, "for their religion."

The Colón cemetery is so big that it takes a day to see it all. Cuba's celebrities are buried here. Some of the graves are those of dissident students shot in cold blood by the police between the 1920s and 1950s. Many are revolutionaries from centuries past. Some even belong to U.S. citizens who loved Cuba so much they made it their home. However, most of the graves belong to Cubans from the wealthier classes, whose families, generation after generation, are buried in the family tombs. At the back of the cemetery is a shady little park with benches, where we sat down to rest. This part of the cemetery is called the Tomb for the Martyrs of the Revolution.

"This is where all Cubans should be buried," I said. "Everyone who died since Castro is a martyr for the Revolution. All the hunger and the suffering. All Cubans are martyrs. However, the park is too small to contain so many Cubans. Why is it so important for Castro to win this war?"

"Castro has always wanted to be the new Simón Bolívar," said the artist. "He's wanted to liberate all of Latin America from neocolonialism. But," he added, holding out his hand, squaring off a sliver of fingernail with his thumb. "This is how much Castro is compared to a man like Bolívar. He's nothing to Bolívar. And besides, Bolívar never did liberate Cuba."

"This was Martí's mission," I said. "To accomplish in Cuba what Bolívar couldn't achieve. Martí failed, and now Castro thinks he's Martí reborn."

"He thinks he's better than Martí!" said the artist.

There's a word that's said a lot in Latin America, *ojala*. You hear it everyday in Cuba. *Ojala*. Loosely translated, it means "I hope so," or "I wish," or "With any luck," and in Cuba it always punctuates a thought with a severe gravity. If someone says to a Cuban, "Soon your lover will come and marry you and you'll be living in America, England, Italy," or, "Soon the United States will lift the *bloqueo*," the response will always be *"¡Ojala!"* When Cubans say *ojala*, it holds a meaning that is different from, say, the Mexican, Argentinean, or Venezuelan *ojala*. In Cuba, more pessimism is implied, and a cross look goes along with the word. When the word *ojala* is uttered in Cuba, it really means, "Yeah, tell me another one." Because the Cuban hopes have been dashed so many times, over and over, pessimism is inherent in the collective consciousness. It's as if everything the Cubans believed in during the last four decades failed them and so now they refuse to invest seriously in anything hopeful in case it turns out to be another disappointment. All Castro's promises which have vaporized over time. All the false promises of marriage foreigners have made to Cubans never to return. All the hopeful signs of the embargo's being lifted. Every time Cubans want to believe in something, it fails, so they think the worst, and if it turns out a little better than expected, then and only then is there cause for celebration. It's difficult to imagine living like this, in a world so shaky that you can't bank on anything but what is sitting on the plate in this very moment; a world in which the future is so unpredictable and unpromising that there's no way to plan, or seriously consider dreams and goals. As if this kind of human need, this future, except in the flimsy rhetoric, seemed to have been etched out of the culture as a whole. No one believes in anything anymore.

"Well, the future is looking good for Cuba," I said to the artist, as we passed a bottle of water under the trees at the Tomb of the Martyrs.

"How can you say this?" he said. "The future. The future. That's all everybody talks about is the future. Fuck the future. I want a now. I want my life to be more than just struggling. Castro will never let us proceed."

"Well look," I said. "He's seventy-five years old. He's going to die soon."

My friend looked at me square in the eye and said *"¡Ojala!"*

It was the first time I'd ever heard a Cuban, in Cuba, say that he "hoped" Castro would die, and it took me by surprise. But the shocking thing was that when my friend uttered *ojala*, it didn't have that Cuban pessimism implied in the word. He sincerely meant it.

"And let it happen soon," he added. "We are ready for change."

When Castro fainted during a speech on June 23, 2001, the Miami exile plotted and cheered. My friends on the island had various responses to the collapse. Some believed that the guards ushered a semiconscious Fidel off the stage, only to bring out his double from a nearby ambulance, refreshed and invigorated. Some felt the collapse was merely a staged test to measure Cuba's national reaction. But when Castro fainted, it did not become mob rules. There were no parades of anti-Castroists storming through the streets. It was a humble mixture of mostly sadness mixed with pockets of joy. Cubans themselves aren't quite ready to turn the page. While change is sought, there is also a resistance to it. When Castro turned seventy-five in August 2001, coincidentally close to the date of his fainting spell, Cubans began churning the scenarios in their minds. Most have always felt that he has an illness that is kept secret. Some say Parkinson's, others swear it's cancer. Every Cuban has his pet disease he's sure the comandante is suffering from. Some believe that Castro's inner circle is slowly poisoning him to get him out of the way. But in the street you'll hear a single phrase. Some say it with pride, others disgust: "Forget about it. Fidel will live forever."

Politically, Castro is already dead. Physically, he is dying. What he is dying from is a mystery; but his failing health is obvious. One week he'll seem dapper, animated, and sharp when he gives a speech. A week later, he's pale, gaunt, forgetful, and two or three assistants have to remind him every few minutes why he's even there. And to date, the military has refused to unseat him, which is evidence that he doesn't have long to live. They will not disgrace him and cheat him of *La Victoria* in his final hour, even though his mind is slipping.

Today Fidel Castro lives alone and fights a war that ended many years ago. The machinery that he built, the *Cubanidad* that he first offered and later imposed on the Cuban culture is passing him by as he fights to the last breath for *La Victoria*.

Will there be a post-Castro Cuba? Never. His legacy will outlive him for decades, even centuries. In many ways, today's Cuba is not much different from the way it was before Castro. There are the rich and poor. There is inequality. There is corruption, exploitation, racism. And although Castro's vision may seem like a failure to a growing number of Cubans, the comandante brought one lasting legacy to the culture. Before Castro, people were slaughtered indiscriminately. Political assassinations occurred daily in the power vacuum. Life was cheap. Peasants were abused. Soldiers shot and killed humans as if they were rodents. The dinner conversation revolved around which politicians should be assassinated. The violence before Castro indicates there was a desperate need for Cuba to free itself from its neocolonial chains. The in-fighting and the ego, the splintered political movements, the rights and lefts and radicals prevented the people as a whole from focusing their energies. One leader was needed in Cuba, and Castro became that leader. And when he came, he said "Stop! Let's see what we have here. Let's find the best part of the Cuban character and let it shine. Let us focus our pride."

Because of this belief, human life is now very precious to all Cubans. Over the past four decades, the island has enjoyed enough peace and stability that the culture has been able to focus on slowly defining itself. The price of freedom is sacrifice, and Cuba has spent the past forty-three years paying its dues. No matter how hopeless it sometimes seems—the current hunger for change, the current desperation—the will to survive, to live, to endure, and even to resist, prevails. These are the ingredients of focused human determination. Today, Castro only stands in the way of the people. They are now prepared to define Cuba's destiny. And in this preparedness, perhaps Castro achieved the greatest victory of all.

NOTES

~~~~

Chapter 1

1. Owing to fears of government retribution and because of the unlawful nature of parts of this book, I have taken painstaking care to protect the identity of several characters, at their insistence, by giving them pseudonyms. They trusted me to obscure their true identities. In no way do these slight changes alter the factual basis of what occurred.

Chapter 3

1. Fidel Castro, "Always with Justice," opening speech delivered to the emergency 4th Congress of the PCC, 10 October 1991 (Havana: Editorial José Martí, 1991), 32–33.

2. Robert E. Quirk, *Fidel Castro* (New York: W. W. Norton and Co., 1993), 474–475.

3. Fred Ward, *Inside Cuba Today* (New York: Crown Publishers, 1978), 90.

4. Miguel A. Figueras, "Tourism and Development," *Business Tips on Cuba* 7, no. 5 (May 2000): 32–38. *Tips* is an excellent publication for keeping up with the trends of the future as well as current focuses on the Cuban economy. I also recommend the monthly *Travel Trade Cuba* magazine.

5. Ibid., 36.

Chapter 4

1. Fidel Castro, Main Report Speech at the Closing, 5th Congress of the Communist Party of Cuba in Havana, 8 and 10 October 1997, trans. Granma International (Havana: Editora Politica, 1998): 164–165.

Chapter 7

1. UNAIDS 2001 world report on HIV/AIDS.
2. The full text of Castro's address to the PNR was reprinted in *Granma* 36, no. 5 (8 January 1999), as an eight-page supplement to the regular edition.

Chapter 9

1. José Bella Lara, ed., *Cuba in the 1990s*, trans. Lisa Makarchuk (Havana: Editorial José Martí, 1999), 90.
2. Ibid., 89.

Chapter 11

1. José Bella Lara, ed., *Cuba in the 1990s*, trans. Lisa Makarchuk (Havana: Editorial José Martí, 1999), 150.

Chapter 12

1. José Bella Lara, ed., *Cuba in the 1990s*, trans. Lisa Makarchuk (Havana: Editorial José Martí, 1999), 89.
2. Ibid., 26.
3. Philip Brenner et al., eds., *The Cuba Reader: The Making of a Revolutionary Society* (New York: Grove Press, 1989), 45, 65.
4. Lara, *Cuba*, 26.

Chapter 13

1. Ernesto Rodriguez Chavez, *Cuban Migration Today*, trans. María Luisa Hernández Garcilaso de la Vega (Havana: Editorial José Martí), 23.

Chapter 14

1. Bill Hinchberger, "Cuba's Internet Elite Emerges," CNN online, 11 April 2000. The *CIA World Factbook* claims that 60,000 Cubans had Internet access in 2000. This seems high.

Chapter 16

1. United Nations, *World Fact Sheet* (United Nations, 2000).

Chapter 17

1. José Bella Lara, ed., *Cuba in the 1990s,* trans. Lisa Makarchuk (Havana: Editorial José Martí, 1999), 44; Philip Brenner et al., eds., *The Cuba Reader: The Making of a Revolutionary Society* (New York: Grove Press, 1989), 173; and Castro's Main Report Speech at the Closing, 5th Congress of the Communist Party of Cuba in Havana, 8 and 10 October 1997, trans. *Granma International* (Havana: Editora Politica, 1998): 156.

Chapter 20

1. Castro's address to the PNR, reprinted in *Granma,* vol. 36, no. 5 (8 January 1999).

BIBLIOGRAPHY

Alarcón, Ricardo. *Helms-Burton: Slavery Law.* Havana: Instituto Cubano Del Libro, 1997.

Arboleya, Jesus. *Havana-Miami: The US-Cuba Migration Conflict.* Translated by Mary Todd. Melbourne: Ocean Press, 1996.

August, Arnold. *Democracy in Cuba and the 1997–98 Elections.* Havana: Editorial José Martí, 1999.

Azcarate Rosell, Rafael. *Historia de los Indios de Cuba.* Havana: Editorial Tropico, 1937.

Bethel, Leslie, ed. *Cuba: A Short History.* London: Cambridge University Press, 1993.

Boorstein, Edward. *The Economic Transformation of Cuba.* New York: Monthly Press Review, 1968.

Brenner, Philip, William M. LeoGrande, Donna Rich, and Daniel Siegel, eds. *The Cuba Reader: The Making of a Revolutionary Society.* New York: Grove Press, 1989.

Castro Ruz, Fidel. "Always with Justice." Speech at the opening and closing of the 4th Congress of the Communist Party in Santiago de Cuba, 10–14 October 1991. Havana: Editorial José Martí, 1991.

_____. "Beinvenida y despedida a Juan Pablo II." Welcome speech for the Pope, 21 January 1998.

_____. *Capitalism in Crisis: Globalization and World Politics Today.* Edited by David Deutschmann. Melbourne: Ocean Press, 2000.

Castro Ruz, Fidel, with Osvaldo Martínez. "Elecciones y religion en Cuba." Speeches during the 10th period of sessions of the 4th legislature of the National Assembly of Popular Power, 13 December 1997. Havana: Editora Politica, 1998.

_____. "En las ciencias esta el futuro." Speech of the closing ceremony for the 11th Forum of Science and Technology, 21 December 1996. Havana: Editora Politica, 1997.

_____. "History Will Absolve Me." Self-defense speech in Court of Santiago de Cuba, 16 October 1953.

_____. Main report speech at the closing of the 5th Congress of the Communist Party of Cuba. Havana, 8 and 10 October 1997. Translated by *Granma International.* Havana: Editora Politica, 1998.

_____. "Our Sovereignty Will Not Be Surrendered, Nor Is It Negotiable!" Commemoration speech at the 42nd anniversary of the attack on the Moncada Garrison, Guantánamo, 1995.

Codiga Civil, Republica de Cuba: Ley No. 59. Havana: Editorial de Ciencias Sociales, 1999.

Codigo Pinal, Republica de Cuba: Ley No. 62. Havana: Editorial de Ciencias Sociales, 1996.

Constitucion de la Republica de Cuba. Havana: Instituto Cubano del Libro, 1976.

Constitucion de la Republica de Cuba. Havana: Editora Politica, 1992.

Didion, Joan. *Miami.* New York: Simon and Schuster, 1987.

Draper, Theodore. *Castro's Revolution: Myths and Realities.* New York: Frederick A. Praeger, 1962.

Elizalde, Rosa Miriam. *Jineteros en la Habana.* Havana: Editorial Pablo de la Torriente, 1996.

Franqui, Carlos. *Diary of the Cuban Revolution.* Translated by Georgette Felix, et al. New York: Viking, 1980. (First published in the Spanish by Editions du Seuil, 1976).

_____. *Family Portrait with Fidel: A Memoir.* Translated by Alfred MacAdam. New York: Random House, 1984.

Fursenko, Aleksandr, and Timothy Naftali. *One Hell of a Gamble: The Secret History of the Cuban Missile Crisis.* New York: W. W. Norton & Co., 1997.

Guevara, Ernesto Che. *Che Guevara Speaks.* Edited by George Lavan. New York: Grove Press, 1967.

_____. *El diario del Che en Bolivia.* Havana: Instituto Del Libro, 1968.

_____. *Guerrilla Warfare.* Edited by Brian Loveman and Thomas M. Davies, Jr. Lincoln, Nebr.: University of Nebraska Press, 1985.

_____. *Reminiscences of the Cuban Revolutionary War.* New York: Monthly Review Press, 1961.

Ignacio Taibo II, Paco. *Guevara, Also Known As Che.* Translated by Martín Michael Roberts. New York: St. Martín's Press, 1997.

John Paul II. *Discursos de su Santitad, Juan Pablo II, en su viaje apostólico a Cuba, 21 al 25 de Enero de 1998.* Havana: Dept. of Media and Social Communication, 1998.

Johnson, Haynes. *The Bay of Pigs: The Leaders' Story of Brigade 2506.* New York: W. W. Norton and Co., 1964.

Lara, José Bella, ed. *Cuba in the 1990s.* Translated by Lisa Makarchuk. Havana: Editorial José Martí, 1999.

Legal Information About Foreign Investment in Cuba, the Activities of Free Trade Zones, and Regulations for Commercial Operations. Havana: Tips-Cuba National Office. November 1996–September 1998.

Leiner, Martín, with Robert Ubell. *Children Are the Revolution: Day Care in Cuba.* New York: Viking Press, 1974.

Liss, Sheldon B. *Fidel! Castro's Political and Social Thought.* Latin American Perspective Series, no. 13. Boulder: Westview Press, 1994.

Martí, José. *José Martí Reader: Writings on the Americas.* Edited by Deborah Shnookal and Mirta Muñiz. Melbourne: Ocean Press, 1999.

Matthews, Herbert L. *Revolution in Cuba.* New York: Scribners, 1975.

May, Ernest R. and Philip D. Zelikow, eds. *The Kennedy Tapes: Inside the White House During the Cuban Missile Crisis.* Cambridge, Mass.: Harvard Press, 1997.

Mirando Bravo, Olga. *The U.S.A. Versus Cuba: Nationalizations and Blockade.* Translated by Fernando Nápoles Tapia. Havana: Editorial José Martí, 1996.

Morales Pita, Antonio. *Programación y Economía de la Zafra.* Havana: Editorial de Ciencias Sociales, 1993.

Murphy, Rear Admiral Marion Emerson. *The History of Guantánamo Bay.* 2d ed. Guantánamo, Cuba: District Publications and Printing Office, Tenth Naval District, 1953.

Ortiz, Fernando. *Cuban Counterpoint: Tobacco and Sugar.* Translated by Harriet de Onís. Durham, N.C.: Duke University Press, 1995.

Paterson, Thomas G. *Contesting Castro: The United States and the Triumph of the Cuban Revolution.* New York: Oxford University Press, 1994.

Pozo Fernandez, Alberto. *Cuba y el turismo: Actualidad y perspectivas de nuestra industria turística.* Havana: Editora Politica, 1993.

Quirk, Robert E. *Fidel Castro.* New York: W. W. Norton and Co., 1993.

Rieff, David. *The Exile: Cuba in the Heart of Miami.* New York: Simon & Schuster, 1993.

Rodríguez Chávez, Ernesto. *Cuban Migration Today.* Translated by María Luisa Hernández Garcilaso de la Vega. Havana: Editorial José Martí, 1999.

Salinger, Pierre. *With Kennedy.* New York: Doubleday, 1966.

Sarte, Jean-Paul. *Sartre on Cuba.* New York: Ballantine, 1961.

Schwab, Peter. *Cuba: Confronting the U.S. Embargo.* New York: St. Martin's Press, 1999.

Suárez Salazar, Luis. *Cuba: Isolation or Reinsertion in a Changed World?* Translated by Carmen González. Havana: Editorial José Martí, 1999.

Suchlicki, Jaime. *Cuba: From Columbus to Castro and Beyond.* 4th ed. Washington, D.C.: Brassey's, 1997.

Szulc, Tad. *Fidel: A Critical Portrait.* New York: William Morrow and Co., 1986.

Tejada, Aurelio Alonso. *Church and Politics in Revolutionary Cuba.* Translated by Maria Luisa Hernández Garcilaso de la Vega. Havana: Editorial José Martí, 1999.

Timerman, Jacobo. *Cuba: A Journey.* Translated by Toby Talbot. New York: Alfred A. Knopf, 1990.

Torreira Crespo, Ramon, and José Buajasan Marrawi. *Operación Peter Pan: Un caso de guerra psicologica contra Cuba.* Havana: Editora Politica, 2000.

Valladares, Armando. *Against All Hope: The Prison Memoirs of Armando Valladares.* Translated by Andrew Hurley. New York: Alfred A. Knopf, 1986.

Walker, Reverend Lucius, and Fidel Castro. *Wave After Wave They Went, Crossing the Border.* Speeches, 27 November 1992. Havana: Editora Politica, 1992.

Ward, Fred. *Inside Cuba Today.* New York: Crown Publishers, 1978.

Wyden, Peter. *Bay of Pigs: The Untold Story.* New York: Simon and Schuster, 1979.

INDEX